Lexcel Office Procedures Manual

Related titles from Law Society Publishing

Marketing Legal Services
David Monk and Alastair Moyes

Profitability and Law Firm Management (2nd edn)
Andrew Otterburn

Solicitors' Code of Conduct 2007
Including Solicitors' Recognised Bodies Regulations 2007
Solicitors Regulation Authority

Solicitors and the Accounts Rules
Peter Camp

Solicitors and Money Laundering
Peter Camp

Strategy for Law Firms
Nick Jarrett-Kerr

All books from Law Society Publishing can be ordered through good bookshops or direct from our distributors, Prolog, by telephone 0870 850 1422 or email **lawsociety@prolog.uk.com,** or by visiting our online bookshop at **www.lawsociety.org.uk/bookshop.** Please confirm the price before ordering.

For further information or a catalogue, please contact our editorial and marketing office by email **publishing@lawsociety.org.uk.**

Lexcel Office Procedures Manual

FOURTH EDITION

Edited by:

Matthew Moore

Contributors:

Derek Eccleston
Rupert Kendrick

WEB4LAW

The Law Society

ISBN 978–1–85328–673–5

Published in 2007 by the Law Society
113 Chancery Lane, London WC2A 1PL

Reprinted in 2008, 2010 (twice)

Typeset by Columns Design Ltd, Reading
Printed by TJI Digital, Padstow, Cornwall

Contents

Preface

This fourth edition of the *Lexcel Office Procedures Manual* has been produced to provide guidance on the new version of the Lexcel management standard – Lexcel v.4 – which takes effect in January 2008. The publication also addresses the Solicitors' Code of Conduct, which took effect on 1 July 2007. Both developments necessitated a review of most of the contents of this work and the aim has once again been to develop a cost-effective compliance tool for legal practices of all types and sizes.

As always, it should be stressed that this publication sets out suggested procedures only. A firm's own way of doing things is always what matters most, and it is recommended that this manual is adapted by users as extensively as possible. Nobody should take any of the contents as being necessarily the best or only way to address the issue that is being covered. The main principle of the work has always been 'better a precedent than a blank piece of paper' (or, nowadays, computer screen). Purchasers of the work are welcome to copy and distribute the contents within their own organisation, but not externally. Likewise, the disk supplied with the book is for use within your organisation only.

It is also important to stress that this work is by way of a general publication only and must not be taken to constitute specific advice that can be relied upon.

There are some new features to this edition, most of which are apparent from the appendices. First, the contents have been checked against Lexcel v.4 and this has meant that firms working towards an assessment under that standard, or revising their existing manual, can locate when and where a sample procedure is included. Second, many firms will be anxious to ensure that their manual has addressed the requirements of the Legal Services Commission's Specialist Quality Mark (SQM) in relation to legal aid or publicly funded work. Appendix 2 highlights the requirements of the SQM in general terms and again shows if and where its provisions have been addressed within the book. Finally, the Solicitors' Code of Conduct 2007 increases the need for a range of topics to be addressed in a practice manual, not least under subrule 5.01 and its requirement for a series of 'arrangements' to be in place. The adoption of appropriate procedures in a firm-wide manual is one of the more convincing ways to ensure compliance with these largely new provisions. Appendix 3 highlights the main references in the book to the 2007 Code.

The contents were written in summer 2007 before the Law Society's amended guidance on avoiding money laundering and terrorist financing was made available. This has meant that it has been difficult to address fully the Money Laundering Regulations 2007 which are due to take effect in December 2007. I hope that the amendments added at proof stage will provide a useful first step for firms looking to ensure that they comply with these important new provisions.

I have been pleased to work with two main contributors to this edition. My colleague Rupert Kendrick has again brought his expertise to bear in relation to the developing area of information and communication technology (section 4A). Section 5 on 'People Management' has benefited greatly from the input of Derek Eccleston, an expert on employment law and staff handbook issues. Sincere thanks are due to both.

In addition, I would want to thank the many others who have checked contents and offered advice. These include:

- Janet Baker, conveyancing issues
- Duncan Finlyson, discrimination and diversity
- Vicky Ling, SQM issues and appendix 2
- Nigel McEwen, finance management
- Elizabeth Richards, anti-money laundering
- Vanessa Shenton, client care compliance

I am once again indebted to Tony Girling for his kind permission to include his sample terms of business in the client care section. It has been a great pleasure to share training sessions on the Solicitors' Code of Conduct 2007 with Tony during the course of this year.

This is an extremely complex work to assemble and thanks are due to those involved at Law Society Publishing, especially Posy Gosling for her assiduous checking of the text in general, also sources and references. I would also like to thank Chantal Haynes of the Lexcel Office for her advice on compliance with the Lexcel standard.

Since this publication is a compilation work it is important that I should also acknowledge the contribution of all who have worked on its three previous editions. Much of their work survives into this edition. I hope that it is fair to mention one in particular. My friend and colleague of many years standing, Mike Dodd, retired earlier this year. This is therefore the first edition of this work that we have not worked on together. I wish him and his wife Pam a long and happy retirement.

Matthew Moore
September 2007
matt@web4law.biz

Notes on contributors

Matthew Moore LL.B, MCIPD, CdipAF: Matthew is a director of Web4Law. He is a law teacher and solicitor by background, with over 20 years' experience of law firm management consultancy and training. In recent years most of his work has been concerned with risk compliance and quality management issues. He has been the principal trainer for the Law Society in the Lexcel standard since 1999 and has advised a wide range of firms on applications for recognition under all of the major quality compliance programmes.

Derek Eccleston MA, FCIPD, ACII: Derek is a consultant specialising in the provision of advice and training on employment law and employee relations through his consultancy Employment Law Training Ltd. He spent over 25 years in senior HR roles in a number of industries which include local government, engineering and financial services, and for six years in a law firm. Derek is a personal tutor on the CIPD's Advanced Certificate in Employment Law, and is an author of several employment law publications. His website provides a comprehensive guide for employees and workers on their rights at work (**www.yourjobrights.co.uk**).

Rupert Kendrick LL.M: Rupert was for many years a partner in a medium-sized law firm in the home counties. After a ten-year spell in publishing he was awarded a masters degree in Advanced Legal Practice (Legal Practice Management) which examined the implications of law firms marketing themselves on the internet. He is a director of Web4Law and is the editor of the company's flagship publication, *Managing Risk*, a quarterly magazine on law firm risk and compliance issues.

1 Structures and policies

▓ Section 1 is based on the first section of the Lexcel standard – 'Structures and policies'. The aim of this section is to set out all the essential policies that are required by an increasing range of legal and regulatory provisions. Fundamental issues such as:

- responsibility for the quality system;
- the circulation of the manual; and
- how it is amended and by whom

are also covered. An important starting point for firms is to consider what will be the best structure for the manual or manuals. This book deals with topics on the basis of one general manual, but many firms separate fee earning provisions from office procedures and the other administrative elements of maintaining a quality system. As always, there is no right or wrong on such issues of system design – all depends on what will work best in each individual practice.

1.1 Introduction: use of this manual

1.1.1 The purpose of this manual is twofold. First, it is a clear description of the purpose, values and structures of the practice. Second, it is a source of reference for all aspects of the firm's operations, at all levels. As such, it is equally applicable to all personnel throughout the firm, whatever their post or seniority. It is therefore a document that will feature in the induction of all staff to the firm, and will then be available for everyone to consult whenever necessary. Access to the manual is via the icon on the desktop. [In addition, up-to-date printed copies are available for inspection at *specify*.]

▓ As more firms become increasingly reliant on computer systems it is now more likely that the manual is only available via the firm's intranet. Where this is not the case it will be necessary to show how personnel should consult its provisions. There is no requirement in any quality standard for everyone in the practice to have their own individual copy of the manual, but everyone must have reasonable access to it. One of the advantages of having the manual on the intranet is that it is much easier to control amendments and updates to it, most obviously by granting the quality partner or director exclusive editing rights to the document. Most firms are willing to allow personnel to download sections of the manual, and will almost certainly need to do so in relation to the many forms within the publication, but if this is the case it is wise to remind all personnel of the importance of using the correct, up-to-date procedures as follows:

1.1.2 It is permitted to print off parts of the manual for personal use, but any such hard copy print-outs must not be stored for future use. The manual is subject to frequent change and it follows, therefore, that the latest up-to-date version (i.e. that appearing on the intranet) must always be consulted.

1.1.3 The documentation forming the risk and quality manual is confidential to the firm and must not be copied outside the practice without the permission of the [quality/risk partner/director/manager – see 1.1.4].

1.1.4 The manual will be reviewed not less than annually, and will be kept up to date by [*name or title*]. For ease of reference (s)he is referred to throughout this manual as the [quality/risk partner/director/manager]. Only (s)he has the authority to make any changes to the manual, although consultation will often take place before any final changes are decided upon. Suggestions for alterations are always welcome at any time (see 1.6.1). There must be clear responsibility for all policies and plans referred to in this manual: see also 6.1.2.

1.2 The legal status of the firm/department

Sections 1.2 and 1.3 of the manual are based on section 1.1 of the Lexcel standard, which requires practices to have and keep under regular review documentation setting out the legal framework of the practice and its business structure. Many firms in private practice have converted to LLP status, while the numbers of firms being constituted or converted into limited liability companies continues to grow. It was reported that the numbers of incorporated firms more than trebled between 2001 and 2006, from 286 to 941 ([2007] *Gazette*, 5 April, p. 16). The manual should record that it is an issue that will be kept under consideration.

The 'legal framework' for a firm in private practice will be a partners' agreement. In order to comply with the requirements of Lexcel the firm will need to be able to demonstrate that this document has covered the following points:

- management and voting rights;
- the authorisation of individual partners, etc. to bind the firm by contract;
- rights to share in profits;
- how capital contributions and rights to interest will be dealt with;
- how capital will be repaid;
- entry to and expulsions and retirements from the firm;
- the rights of partners, etc. to elect for part-time working patterns, and provision for parental leave, including maternity provisions;
- the situation in case of long-term illness or incapacity;
- how succession will be achieved if appropriate;
- continuity of the practice in the event of death or incapacity (for sole practitioners or small practices).

1.2.1 The firm is constituted as a [partnership *or* limited liability partnership *or* limited company]. [Its administration is undertaken from *or* Its registered office is at [*insert address*]]. The owners of the firm are the [partners *or* members *or* shareholders]. They have chosen to regulate the governance of the firm by a [partnership *or* shareholders'] agreement, but this document does not form part of this manual.

[*or*: Throughout this manual, the term 'the firm' is used to refer to the department known as [*name*] which forms part of the overall organisation ('the Organisation') which is known as [*name*]. That organisation is a [local authority *or* limited company *or* other]. The way in which the firm is controlled, within the context of the Organisation, is set out in [*specify briefly relevant legislative provisions or internal documentation as appropriate*]. References throughout this manual to 'clients' should accordingly be read as references to the other constituent parts of the Organisation to whom the services of the firm are provided.]

1.3 Reviewing the business structure

1.3.1 As part of the responsibility of the firm's management, the partners will keep under periodic review the question of whether the current legal status of the firm remains the optimum legal structure for its operation. Included within this consideration will be the question of whether it is appropriate, desirable and possible to limit the personal liability of the owners of the firm, through a change in the legal status of the firm. (This may be viewed in the light of the ability of the firm effectively to limit its overall liability by agreement with its clients.) This process of review will be an inherent part of the review of the firm's strategic and business plans as described in section 2.

1.4 The firm's commitment to quality

▨ Sections 1.4–1.6 of the manual address section 1.3 of the Lexcel standard, which provides that practices will have a quality policy, which must include the role that the quality system plays in the overall strategy of the practice. There is a general note at the start of the standard requiring identification of the person responsible for every policy and plan, which would clearly apply to this section. A documented review of the operation of the quality system is also required at least annually and there must be a process for personnel to suggest improvements to the quality system.

1.4.1 The practice exists to provide legal services. Section 2 of the manual, dealing with strategic and business planning, indicates the ways in which particular types or areas of services are to be selected as those which the firm will from time to time offer to clients. Whatever the type of legal service, however, the emphasis should be on the 'service' element, and the requirements of the client should be accorded priority accordingly.

1.4.2 The firm is committed to the concept that all aspects of its operations should be of the highest quality. As part of this commitment, it [is working towards] [has achieved and is committed to retaining] the following externally certified quality mark[s]:

- Lexcel – confirmation of compliance with the Law Society's Practice Management Standards;
- [ISO 9001 (BS EN ISO 9001)];
- [Investors in People];
- [the Legal Services Commission's Specialist Quality Mark].

1.4.3 There needs to be more to the firm's quality programme than simply complying with a standard, however. The expectations of clients have risen considerably over recent years, and poor service is increasingly less likely to be tolerated. It is therefore not only in order to comply with the beliefs of the firm's management that the provision of a quality service is required: it is necessary for the firm's success. It follows that all personnel within the firm must judge their actions from the client's viewpoint, and be aware that in addition to the provision of the highest levels of technical legal expertise, clients have a right to expect that their lawyers will be:

- available;
- approachable;
- comprehensible;
- prompt;
- courteous.

For details of the firm's client care policy and procedures see section 7.

1.4.4 This manual, by setting out the policies and procedures that should be followed by everyone throughout the firm, aims in general terms to provide a framework within which all will be able to work in a way that will offer the best chance of providing a consistently good level of service to all clients.

1.5 Responsibility for maintenance of the quality assurance system

Lexcel requires one person to have overall responsibility for the quality system.

1.5.1 The person with overall responsibility for the quality system is [*name or title*]. (S)he reports regularly to the management of the firm on the performance of the system, and any concerns that arise in respect of it. (S)he is also responsible for ensuring that the overall performance of the system is reviewed by the firm's senior management not less than annually.

1.5.2 Certain aspects of the operational maintenance of the system have been delegated by him/her, with the approval of the firm's management. It is important that everyone is aware of who has which responsibilities in this connection. Details are as follows [*set out devolved responsibilities*]:

Quality partner

- Plan, control and direct quality policies within the firm and maintain relationships with any external accrediting bodies.
- Determine changes to the firm's quality system and manual.
- Liaise with departmental quality representatives.

Heads of department

- Ensure the effective application of the quality system within their department.
- Consult with the quality partner.

[*or*: Details are set out in an organisational chart which [appears as an appendix to this manual *or* will from time to time be distributed to all personnel].]

1.6 The process of review of the quality assurance system

1.6.1 The quality partner will be considerably assisted in his/her role by receiving suggestions as to ways in which the quality system may be improved. Such suggestions may either be made directly to him/her or be channelled through the appropriate line manager. To facilitate such suggestions, a folder has been created within the firm's word processing network entitled 'Suggestions Box', and all personnel are encouraged to enter ideas for improvement in this way. Others may comment on such suggestions, within the same facility. Anyone using this facility is encouraged to indicate their name, and the date upon which the suggestion or comment is made, in order that the quality partner may discuss this further with them, but such disclosure is not essential.

> Alternatively, or in addition, another common way in which suggestions for improvement can be raised is through departmental or staff liaison meetings.

1.7 Risk policy

> Section 1.2 of Lexcel requires practices to have a risk management policy, which must include strategic, operational and regulatory risk. Strategic risk is addressed in section 2 of this manual (Planning) and operational risk at section 6 (Supervision and risk management). The very wide heading of 'regulatory risk' is addressed in various provisions of both the Lexcel standard and this manual, as with the provisions on discrimination and diversity that follow. It would be useful to have a general risk policy, which in many firms might be combined with, or form an element of, the client care policy required by section 7 of Lexcel. Risk management is concerned with identifying factors that might adversely affect the practice, including those that will impact on client service, and then taking effective steps to prevent or, so far as is possible, control them. Client care policies concentrate on the commitment to provide a reliable and consistent level of service to clients. It follows that risk management and client care are different sides of the same coin. This has a bearing on how practices will describe their manual – 'Risk Manual', 'Quality Manual' or 'Client Care Manual', or any combination of the terms, are all likely to cover much the same territory.

1.7.1 [*Name of firm*] is committed to providing a reliable, effective and expert service to all clients. This policy is achieved through the adoption of risk and quality management processes and procedures ('the risk management system') as contained in this manual.

1.8 Avoiding discrimination and achieving diversity

■ The formal adoption of a policy dealing with discrimination, equality and diversity is a requirement for firms in private practice, while those responsible for in-house departments are required by the Solicitors' Code of Conduct 2007 (2007 Code) to use 'all reasonable endeavours to secure the adoption and implementation of an appropriate policy' (subrule 6.04). In relation to the terms that are used in this area discrimination must be avoided to achieve equality of opportunity. Anti-discrimination legislation is designed to promote fairness in relation to employment, promotion and the provision of services. There are provisions relating to:

- race or racial group (including colour, nationality and ethnic or national origins);
- sex (including marital status, gender reassignment, pregnancy, maternity and paternity);
- sexual orientation (including civil partnership status);
- religion or belief;
- age;
- disability.

'Diversity' is a broader term than 'discrimination' and is more aspirational. Whereas discrimination is about the minimum levels of behaviour needed to avoid legal sanctions, diversity is about the development of policies to encourage the development of individuals, regardless of their background. Diversity can therefore encompass anti-discrimination.

The former practice rule, dating from 2004, worked principally through a model policy that applied in private practice firms by default. Practices were required to adopt a policy, but if they failed to do so the model policy would apply in any event. Furthermore, to the extent that a policy had been adopted that was at odds with the model policy, or that omitted any of its key provisions, the model policy would apply nonetheless. The new Rule 6 of the 2007 Code does not contain a sample or model policy, and requires firms instead to take positive steps to consider the issue for themselves. Quite apart from the fact that failure to adopt a suitable policy will be a breach of subrule 6.03, any such omission will leave firms much more open to a discrimination claim at law, the first line of defence to such claims being that a suitable policy had been adopted and implemented. There will be a heavy onus on any organisation to show on the facts that it did not discriminate if there is no policy in place. The unthinking adoption of a model or draft policy is discouraged, so it is important that firms consider amendments to the draft that follows to ensure that it is truly relevant to them.

The policy that follows is a relatively simple version of what might be required and larger firms in particular should consider whether they require more detailed provisions in relation to employment, training, promotion and monitoring. For example, the use of application forms was encouraged by organisations such as the Commission for Racial Equality, perhaps coupled with monitoring of applicants. (See annex 5J.)

The requisite policy should include a duty to make adjustments in relation to third parties (such as counsel and outside experts) that the firm has professional dealings with. Under the 2007 Code, Rule 6 the duty to make adjustments for disabled people is limited to 'clients, employees, partners, members and directors' (see guidance note 4 to Rule 6).

Introduction and scope

1.8.1 All personnel must be aware of the firm's policy in relation to discrimination, equality and diversity. The policy deals with all professional dealings by personnel with clients, other solicitors, barristers and third parties, and so covers:

- accepting instructions from clients;
- using experts and counsel;
- the provision of services to clients;
- dealings with those representing others;
- interaction with everyone involved in or incidental to the provision of services by the firm.

1.8.2 The policy also extends to the recruitment, training and promotion of people within the practice. In connection with both aspects, it is the case that all personnel must comply not only with the professional requirements of the Solicitors Regulation Authority, but also with the law of the land.

Forms of discrimination

> The one area where positive discrimination is permissible is under the Disability Discrimination Act 1995 since non-disabled people do not have like rights under that legislation. Thus, it is permissible to provide that all disabled candidates for a position, for example, will be offered an interview.

1.8.3 The firm's policy covers discrimination on the grounds of:

- race or racial group (including colour, nationality and ethnic or national origins);
- sex (including marital status, gender reassignment, pregnancy, maternity and paternity);
- sexual orientation (including civil partnership status);
- religion or belief;
- age;
- disability.

The types of action that are against the firm's policy are:

- Direct discrimination, where a person is, without lawful cause, less favourably treated on any of the above grounds.
- Indirect discrimination, where a requirement or condition that cannot be justified is applied equally to all groups but has a disproportionately adverse effect on members of one particular group by reason of any of the above grounds.
- Victimisation, where someone is treated less favourably than others because he or she has taken action against the firm for unlawful discrimination on one or more of the above.

- Harassment, which occurs when unwanted conduct on one of the above grounds has the effect of violating another person's dignity or creating an intimidating, hostile, degrading, humiliating or offensive environment for that person.

Disability provisions

1.8.4 In addition to the firm's obligations not to discriminate against, harass or victimise those with a disability the firm is also subject to a duty to make reasonable adjustments to prevent those employees [partners, members, directors] and clients who are disabled from being at a disadvantage in comparison with those who are not disabled.

Policy statement

1.8.5 [*Name of firm*] is therefore committed to avoiding discrimination in its dealings with clients [partners, members, directors], employees and all other third parties that have dealings with the firm. It is committed to promoting diversity in its professional activities.

1.8.6 Everyone at the firm is expected and required to treat all others equally and with the same attention, courtesy and respect regardless of their:

- race or racial group (including colour, nationality and ethnic or national origins);
- sex (including marital status, gender reassignment, pregnancy, maternity and paternity);
- sexual orientation (including civil partnership status);
- religion or belief;
- age;
- disability.

1.8.7 In addition, the firm will ensure that nobody with whom it has dealings will suffer any substantial disadvantage through any disability that they might have. The firm is committed to making reasonable adjustments for those with a disability in relation to job opportunities, promotion and training within the firm and the provision of services to clients.

1.8.8 All the areas of discrimination set out in sections 1.8.3 and 1.8.6 are collectively referred to as 'the above grounds' in the rest of this section.

Enforcement

1.8.9 Everyone should be aware that any breach of the policy is a potential major risk to the practice. The firm does not carry insurance against the consequences of any illegal breach, and any claims in this regard are also likely to involve the firm in significant commitments of managerial time. Further, a breach may be a serious professional offence, and liability may attach not only to the individual(s) concerned, but to also the owners of the firm. For that reason any breach is likely to be regarded as a serious disciplinary offence. If anyone is concerned that a breach of this policy may be occurring, or has a complaint that they have been the victim of a breach, they should immediately report this to any [partner/member/director].

Training

> Guidance note 22(ii) to Rule 6 of the 2007 Code provides that 'you must ensure that all partners, members, directors and employees are aware of, and act in compliance with, the provisions contained in the policy'. It goes on to provide that 'you may wish to give consideration to providing staff with training'. For details of training sessions or a disk for multiple use contact via e-mail **simon@web4law.biz**.

1.8.10 The firm has arranged training sessions for all personnel on this topic and will arrange further training if and when appropriate. This policy forms part of the firm's induction training programme.

Planning

1.8.11 For its part, the management of the firm has considered all aspects of its operations to ensure compliance with the professional rules. Any developments of the firm's strategic and business planning, or changes in this manual, will similarly be examined in order to ensure that no inadvertent breach of the firm's policy occurs.

Clients

1.8.12 The firm is generally free to decide whether to accept instructions from any particular client, but any refusal to act will not be based on any of the above grounds and care must also be taken to avoid there being any perception that they apply. [*Set out details of facilities for those with mobility problems who use wheelchairs and/or policy on home visits to overcome the problems of access that are common in older buildings. It would be advisable to obtain specialist advice on the reasonable adjustments that can and should be made where this is thought to be the case*]

Barristers and other experts

> See introductory note to this section and 1.8.7 above on extent of commitment required on this point under Lexcel and SQM.

1.8.13 Barristers and experts should be instructed on the basis of their skills, experience and ability. The firm will not discriminate in the instruction of barristers and/or experts on any of the above grounds.

1.8.14 A client's request for a named barrister or expert should be complied with, subject to the firm's duty to discuss with the client the suitability of the barrister or expert and to advise appropriately. The firm has a duty to discuss with the client any instruction by the client as to choice of barrister or expert that is based on any of the above grounds. The firm will endeavour to persuade the client to modify instructions that appear to be given on discriminatory grounds. Should the client refuse to modify such instructions, the firm will cease to act unless the preference can be justified under the permitted statutory exceptions referred to as 'genuine occupational requirements' or 'genuine occupational qualifications'.

Employment, training, promotion and partnership opportunities

1.8.15 The practice is committed to providing equal opportunities in employment. This means that all job applicants, employees and [partners/members/directors] will receive equal treatment in relation to the above grounds. It makes good business sense for the firm to ensure that its most important resource – its staff – is used in a fair and effective way.

1.8.16 The practice will also comply with the law and the professional requirements in relation to its [partners, prospective partners, members and directors]. Thus, where appropriate, the existing partners will not discriminate on any of the above grounds in the arrangements they make for the purpose of determining to whom they should offer a partnership, the terms on which any partnership is offered, or by refusing to offer, or deliberately not offering, a partnership to anyone. Nor shall the [partners/members/directors] discriminate in any way in relation to the provision of benefits to any partner, or in relation to any matter relating to the expulsion of any partner or any detriment to be suffered by him/her.

■ Note: for sample monitoring and application forms see annex 5J.

Positive action

■ Sources on discrimination law should be consulted on the feasibility of positive action which could, for example, involve the provision of special training for female candidates for partnership where they are felt to fare less well than males in the process and there is a current gender imbalance.

1.8.17 Although it is unlawful to discriminate in favour of certain groups on the grounds of race or sex, positive action to enable greater representation of under-represented groups is permitted by law and the appropriateness of such action will be kept under review.

Recruitment agencies

1.8.18 The practice will take steps to ensure that applications are attracted from people without regard to the above grounds and will ensure that there are equal opportunities in all stages of the recruitment process. Since recruitment to the firm is mainly achieved through a small number of agencies, steps have been taken to ensure that these agencies support the firm's general approach to the subject.

Monitoring and review

1.8.19 This policy will be monitored periodically by the firm to judge its effectiveness. The firm has appointed [*name or title*] to be responsible for the operation of the policy. In particular, the firm will monitor the ethnic and gender composition of existing staff and of applicants for jobs (including promotion), and the number of people with disabilities within these groups, and will review its equal opportunities policy in accordance with the results shown by the monitoring. If changes are required, the firm will implement them. Any developments of the firm's strategic and business plans, or changes in this manual, will similarly be examined in order to ensure that no inadvertent breach of the policy occurs.

1.9 Money laundering

The provisions in relation to combating money laundering and the funding of terrorist activities have become significant new aspects of law firm risk management in recent years. The penalties for non-compliance are criminal, as well as civil and professional, and a number of convictions of advisers have now been reported. The substantive offences are principally found in the Proceeds of Crime Act 2002 and the Terrorism Act 2000, as amended by the Serious Organised Crime and Police Act 2005 in particular. The more regulatory elements are contained in the money laundering regulations, which themselves contain criminal penalties for non-compliance. A revised set of regulations is due to come into effect in late 2007 in pursuance of the Third EU Directive on Money Laundering, with the principal changes relating to the need to check the identities of those defined as having a sufficient beneficial ownership of a company or trust, and in the area of record keeping. These new provisions are the subject of amended guidance from the Law Society in place of the original 'pilot' guidelines. References in the following procedures are to the 'MLR' without date reference; firms will need to ensure that they appreciate what is involved in complying with the version in force at the time. Given the pace of change and the importance of ensuring compliance, the up-to-date legal position and the latest Law Society guidance should be checked whenever working on or reviewing this element of the manual.

The Lexcel standard concentrates on the regulatory elements of the MLR. It therefore requires at 1.5 practices to have a compliance policy and procedures to cover:

- the appointment of a 'Nominated Officer' usually referred to as a Money Laundering Reporting Officer (MLRO);
- reporting of suspicious circumstances within the practice and by the MLRO to the authorities;

- identification checking;
- training of personnel;
- the proper maintenance of records.

Not all law firms are subject to the MLR. Exceptions are most likely in areas of litigation. There is no blanket exception for stated work areas, however, and all firms that consider that they may be exempt from the MLR (and are not therefore a 'relevant person') should seek specialist advice or consult the Law Society advice on this issue on its website.

1.9.1 The firm must safeguard against becoming involved in the processing of illegal or improper gains for clients. As a professional practice the firm is particularly attractive to criminals wishing to convert gains to a respectable status. It is the policy of the firm not to assist them to do so. To do so could in any event be an unlawful act on the part of anyone concerned and could place the firm and its representatives at risk of criminal and civil proceedings.

1.9.2 The signs to watch for:

- **Unusual settlement requests:** Settlement by cash (or attempts to do so) of any large transaction involving the purchase of property or other investment should give rise to caution. Payment by way of third party cheque or money transfer where there is a variation between the account holder, the signatory and a prospective investor should give rise to additional enquiries.
- **Unusual instructions:** Care should always be taken when dealing with a client who has no discernible reason for using the firm's services, e.g. clients with distant addresses who could find the same service nearer their home base, or clients whose requirements do not fit into the normal pattern of the firm's business and could be more easily serviced elsewhere.
- **Unexpected and confusing changes to instructions:** Particular care is needed in relation to abortive transactions, surprisingly generous payments being made to supposed opponents or instructions that change for no obvious reason.
- **Large sums of client money:** Always be cautious when requested to hold large sums of money in client account, either pending further instructions from the client or for no other purpose than for onward transmission to a third party.
- **The secretive client:** A personal client who is reluctant to provide details of his or her identity. Be particularly cautious about the client you do not meet in person in which case 'enhanced customer due diligence' is required.
- **Suspect territory:** Caution should be exercised whenever a client is introduced by an overseas bank, other investor or third party based in countries where production of drugs or drug trafficking may be prevalent.

The Money Laundering Reporting Officer and disclosures

1.9.3 A disclosure could be necessary for one of two reasons. First, the Proceeds of Crime Act 2002 (POCA 2002), s.330 imposes a duty to make a disclosure if, in the course of practice, a person forms a suspicion (or should reasonably have done so) that money laundering is or could be occurring. The position is complicated by the fact that this is stated to be limited to the 'regulated sector' and is subject to the defence of legal professional privilege. The defence of privilege will mean that in most circumstances there is no need for the practice to make a report to the Serious Organised Crime Agency (SOCA) on the basis of instructions received. This is not always the case, however, and the partners therefore take the view that any knowledge or suspicion that is formed of money laundering in relation to any activities within the firm must be reported under the firm's internal reporting procedure.

1.9.4 Secondly, it should be noted that a disclosure might also be necessary to gain a defence to a charge under the principal offences under POCA 2002, ss.327–329, most probably that of entering into an arrangement whereby money laundering is facilitated under s.328. There are similar offences in Terrorism Act 2000, ss.15–18. Where a suspicion arises the firm may, subject to the complex provisions relating to legal professional privilege, need to make a disclosure and gain permission to continue to act. Since the rules on the need to make a disclosure are complex and, following the leading case of *Bowman* v. *Fels* [2005] EWCA Civ 226, are different as between contentious and non-contentious work, it is the policy of the firm that all concerns and suspicions must be discussed with and then possibly reported to the MLRO [*in some firms the head of department is the first point of contact for queries and such discussions*].

1.9.5 Please also note that:

- The duty to disclose extends to all 'criminal conduct' that results in 'criminal property' (for the statutory definition of these terms and others used for liability see POCA 2002, s.340).
- In general there are no *de minimis* provisions: any criminal activity, however menial the gain, must be reported for a person to be sure that (s)he has discharged their responsibility.
- The law makes no distinction between fee earners, administrators and secretaries.
- This duty is not confined to disclosure in respect of clients – POCA 2002, s.330 sets out a duty to make a disclosure where a person has a knowledge or suspicion of money laundering, or should reasonably have done so, in respect of 'another person'. In practice this will often be the opponent.
- There is no positive duty under POCA 2002, s.330 for anyone to report suspicions that arise in their personal life – merely their professional activities – but the principal offences in POCA 2002, ss.327–329 apply generally and not just to those who work in the regulated sector.

1.9.6 [*Name*] has been appointed Money Laundering Reporting Officer (MLRO). His/her duties in this regard are to:

- ensure that satisfactory internal procedures are maintained;
- arrange for periodic training for all relevant personnel within the firm;
- provide advice when consulted on possible reports and receive reports of suspicious circumstances;

- report such circumstances, if appropriate, to SOCA on behalf of the firm;
- direct colleagues as to what action to take and not take when suspicion arises and a disclosure is made;
- report annually to the partners on the operation of the anti-money laundering policy and procedures.

1.9.7 It is the duty of all personnel within the practice to:

- attend training arranged within the firm if required to do so;
- conduct identity checks and other due diligence enquiries unless the MLRO signifies that this is not necessary in the particular case in hand;
- report without delay all circumstances which could give rise to suspicion that the firm is being involved in some element of the money laundering process for a client;
- be wary of payment arrangements different from those anticipated or deposits of cash into client account;
- follow the directions of the MLRO when a disclosure has been made, bearing in mind the personal risk to the adviser of 'tipping-off' the client in question either expressly or by implication;
- maintain the utmost caution in maintaining confidentiality for the client and the firm when suspicious circumstances arise.

1.9.8 The partners have determined that [all work conducted by the firm/all work other than [*specify*]] should be regarded as being covered by the Money Laundering Regulations with the consequential need to conduct identity checks (see also 1.9.3 on the need to make disclosures in the regulated sector, subject to legal professional privilege).

1.9.9 A report of suspicious circumstances must be made by use of form ML2. On receipt of a duly completed ML2 the MLRO will:

- consider the form and make such further enquiries as are necessary to form a view on whether a report to the authorities is needed;
- ensure that nothing done by the firm could alert the client in question that a report and an investigation could ensue;
- make a disclosure, if appropriate, making full notes of the reasons for doing so;
- make diary notes in the firm's key dates system of when the firm may continue to act (see the provisions on deemed consent to continue after seven working days at POCA 2002, ss.335–336) and direct the adviser further as appropriate;
- consider whether the intended subject of a disclosure, if a client, needs to be consulted about the planned disclosure for permission to use the privileged information that forms the knowledge or suspicion leading to the need for a disclosure;
- co-operate with any production orders made by the proper authorities;
- maintain all records of disclosures and reports for at least five years.

1.9.10 In certain circumstances advisers may or must report to the client that a disclosure will be made. They might also sometimes have the option of informing a client that a disclosure has been made concerning them, notwithstanding the offences of 'tipping-off' (POCA 2002, s.333) and 'prejudicing an investigation' (POCA 2002, s.342) under the defence of legal professional privilege. Generally, informing the subject about a disclosure would amount to the crime of 'tipping-off' under s.333 where a disclosure has already been made (there is a similar offence in s.342 of informing the person before a disclosure is made where an investigation is pending). However, these offences provide for the defence of legal professional privilege. After some dispute the courts have ruled, in effect, that privilege will be valid and excuse a disclosure to the client as long as the adviser is acting in good faith and there is no criminal purpose on their part. The actual position is very much more complex than this and the firm has determined that the consent of the MLRO is needed if any member of staff intimates to any person in any way that a disclosure to the authorities has been or will be made. Clearly, a person who does not disclose when they should do is at risk of prosecution, but a person who discloses when they should not do so could be in breach of their normal professional duties to the client.

1.9.11 Please note that:

- there are two forms of privilege – advice and litigation;
- the Law Society advice also distinguishes common law privilege from the statutory format of privilege referred to in POCA 2002;
- form ML2 invites you to comment whether you think a disclosure should be made – only complete this part of the form if you feel competent to comment.

You must not intimate to the client in any way that a disclosure will be made or has been made to the MLRO or to SOCA unless and until you receive instructions to do so.

1.9.12 Do not store a completed ML2 form on the matter file to which it relates. This would create a risk that the client might see the disclosure report, especially if the file is sent out of the office. To alert all personnel to the fact that a disclosure has been made, however, and that the firm may do no more for the client until it has permission to proceed, you must:

- place a red sticker on the file when you have made a report;
- place a green sticker on the file when the MLRO says that you may continue to act.

Please be aware of the secret code: proceed with great caution if any file has either or both colour stickers on it.

> Although there is a legal requirement to have reporting procedures in place where the MLR apply the format of the procedures is for the practice to decide. The procedure does not necessarily require forms, nor is there any need to adopt the red and green sticker procedure as above. All such draft procedures are simply examples as to how to meet the requirements.

Evidence of identity

1.9.13 Advisers must obtain evidence of identity for all clients as soon as possible after contact is first established between the firm and the potential client. The Law Society guidelines make the distinction between 'identification' (being told or coming to know a client's identifying details) and 'verification' (obtaining some evidence which supports this claim of identity). In general 'customer due diligence' requires both elements to be addressed. Exceptions to these requirements can only be sanctioned by the MLRO. The evidence of identity check must be undertaken by completion of ML1 which must appear on the first matter file of the client in question [*state here any central lists or databases or client IDs and how they should be accessed*]. There are also obligations to check for beneficial ownership and to investigate the control and management arrangements in certain cases.

1.9.14 Please note that every attempt should be made to meet the client in person to verify the evidence provided, but where this is not possible the client should not be asked to send their passport or driving licence through the post. In these circumstances the adviser should query why a client is unwilling to meet him/her. If there is a valid reason (usually geographical) it is better to obtain certification through local solicitors or other professionals: in these circumstances the adviser must make a check of the validity of the referring firm or organisation in a current directory and note that and how this has been done on ML1.

1.9.15 In the case of commercial clients a copy of the certificate of incorporation must be obtained at the outset of the first matter for that client, along with a companies search or evidence of the identity of two directors or officers, if possible, unless the representatives are known to the firm and have had personal ID checks already. Further checks may be needed in the case of non-domiciled companies. It is, in any case, important to check that those who purport to represent an organisation are actually entitled to do so.

1.9.16 The partners recognise that many clients may resist the request for evidence of identity, but clients should be reassured that this is now standard practice for any financial or professional concern and that there is no choice over it, unless the adviser wishes to risk prosecution for non-compliance with the MLR. The firm's client care letter now reflects the need for identity to be checked and this wording may also assist to reassure clients that our actions are not taken because we mistrust them.

1.9.17 In relation to established clients the firm will compile a directory of standing checks of identities. Even then the current address should always be checked in relation to any future instructions.

> The MLR 2007 have added to the responsibilities for identification checking and records keeping and the up-to-date requirements should be taken into account with these provisions.

Records

1.9.18 The firm is obliged to maintain records for at least five years of:

- what has been done for the client;
- any disclosures made (completed ML2).

Please bear this in mind when deciding a destroy date when archiving files. In addition the firm must maintain ID evidence for at least five years from the end of the 'business relationship' or the close of the 'occasional tranaction'.

Cash receipts

1.9.19 The mere fact that a client pays in cash or wishes to do so is not in itself a cause for suspicion. Nonetheless, the larger the intended cash payment, the more likely it is that suspect money laundering will be suspected. Substantial amounts of cash are often the result of failure to declare income to HM Revenue and Customs and, as tax evasion, would amount to criminal conduct under the money laundering regime.

1.9.20 The approach to cash receipts is therefore as follows:

- In the absence of any complicating factors the firm will accept sums of up to £500 in cash (complicating factors could include, most obviously, a capital declaration from a client in receipt of public funding that they have less than this sum in capital).
- Sums of over £500 should not be accepted and can only be considered in extreme circumstances and with the permission (to be noted on file) of the MLRO or, if (s)he is unavailable, the head of department.
- Where a larger payment than you can accept is offered you must complete an ML2 and forward to the MLRO in order that (s)he can consider if a disclosure should be made.

> Many firms will take the view that an offer of cash sums in the region of the common £500 limit will not be sufficiently suspicious to merit a report to the MLRO. At the other extreme, one of the first convictions of a solicitor under the regime was that of David McCarten, who was liable primarily for not reporting that he had been offered over £70,000 cash towards the price of the property in a conveyancing transaction, even though he did not accept it. There is no clear guidance on what might amount to a suspicious figure and practices may wish to state the figure that they think is appropriate for their client base.

1.10 Mortgage fraud prevention

> Section 1.6 of the Lexcel standard requires that firms providing services to clients in relation to property transactions must have documented procedures in relation to the avoidance of involvement in mortgage fraud. It follows that this need not apply to firms

that do not undertake this form of work. As with so many of the provisions of this section of the manual, these provisions are under review at the time of going to press and subject to imminent change, not least as a result of the fundamental changes to conveyancing practice that are now unfolding. The up-to-date requirements should therefore be checked and monitored.

1.10.1 Another aspect of the criminal law that affects the firm is in relation to the prevention of fraud, especially in connection with mortgages. There have, regrettably, been many instances where firms' clients have been involved in such frauds, and the firms have been unwitting participants in the arrangements that have allowed such frauds to succeed. In such instances, the firms can pay a heavy price, since lenders will often be able to make the firms responsible for repayment of monies lost. In order to avoid this, it is essential that all procedures, as determined from time to time by the head of the conveyancing department, are followed. Further, the provisions of the Council of Mortgage Lenders Handbook should be strictly observed at all times to the extent that there is no contradiction with money laundering provisions or Law Society guidance.

Acting for buyer and lender

1.10.2 Close attention needs to be paid to the duty of confidentiality if the firm is acting contemporaneously for a buyer and a lender. The professional position is as set out in the 2007 Code, Rule 3 (Conflict of interests) and Rule 4 (Confidentiality and disclosure). The position must be considered very carefully if there is any change in the purchase price, or if the firm becomes aware of any other information that the lender might reasonably be expected to think important in deciding whether, or on what terms, it would make the mortgage advance available. In such circumstances the duty to act in the best interests of the lender requires the firm to pass on such information to the lender with the consent of the buyer. If the buyer will not agree to the information being given to the lender, then there will be a conflict between the firm's duty of confidentiality to the buyer and the duty to act in the best interests of the lender. The firm will then have to cease acting for the lender, and to consider carefully whether to cease acting for the buyer.

1.10.3 Solicitors must not withhold information relevant to a transaction from any client and are now under a specific duty of disclosure under the 2007 Code, subrule 4.02. Where the client is a lender, this not only includes straightforward price reductions but may also include other allowances (e.g. for repairs, payment of costs, the inclusion of chattels in the price and incentives of the kind offered by builders such as free holidays and part-subsidisation of mortgage payments) that amount to a price reduction and would affect the lender's decision to make the advance. It is not for the firm to attempt to arbitrate on whether the price change is material: the lender should be notified. The firm's standard letter of instruction informs the client that it would be regarded as fraud to misrepresent the purchase price, and that the firm is under a duty to inform the lender of the true price being paid for a property, but the client may need to be reminded of this.

1.10.4 Some of the measures outlined in section 1.9 above on money laundering are applicable to this section as well, e.g. the requirements for the lawyer to establish his or her client's identity properly. Additional guidance has however been issued by the Law Society, and the following are warning signs that have been identified in that guidance:

Verify the identity and bona fides of your client and solicitors' firms you do not know

The requirements for getting to know the client appear in section 1.9 above. Check also that the solicitor's firm and office address appear in the *Directory of Solicitors and Barristers* or Solicitors Online (a part of the Law Society's website). The same applies to any third parties of whom you may be suspicious.

Question unusual instructions

If you receive unusual instructions from your client discuss them with your client fully.

Examples of these might be:

- a client with current mortgages on two or more properties;
- a client buying several properties from the same person or two or more persons using the same solicitor;
- a client reselling property at a substantial profit, for which no explanation has been provided;
- instructions from a seller to remit the proceeds of sale to someone other than himself.

Discuss with your client any aspects of the transaction that worry you

If, for example, you have any suspicion that your client may have submitted a false mortgage application or references, or if the lender's valuation exceeds the actual price paid, discuss this with your client. If you believe that the client intends to proceed with a fraudulent application, you must refuse to continue to act for the buyer and the lender.

Check that the true price is shown in all documentation

Check that the actual price paid is stated in the contract, transfer, mortgage instructions and report on title. Ensure also that you have a satisfactory explanation for any part of the price (e.g. a deposit) being paid direct to the seller. Where you are also acting for a lender, tell your client that you will have to cease acting unless the client permits you to report to the lender all adjustments in the price, and all allowances and incentives.

Do not witness pre-signed documentation

No document should be witnessed by anyone within the firm unless the person signing does so in the presence of the witness. If the document is pre-signed, ensure that it is re-signed in the presence of a witness.

Verify signatures

Consider whether signatures on all documents connected with a transaction should be examined and compared with signatures on any other available documentation.

Make a company search

Where a private company is the seller, or the seller has purchased from a private company in the recent past, and you suspect that the sale may not be on proper arm's length terms, you should make a search in the Companies Register to ascertain the names and addresses of the officers and shareholders, which can then be compared with the names of those connected with the transaction and the seller and buyer.

Reporting and acting upon suspicion of fraud

Where a suspicion of fraud arises, it should immediately be reported in one of two ways. The wide provisions of the money laundering legislation mean that a report should always be made to the MLRO. The apparent fraud should also be reported to the head of conveyancing. The fee earner concerned, acting together with the head of department (and, if appropriate, the MLRO), will then take the action which is advised to him/her as being necessary.

1.11 Health and safety

■ The Lexcel standard provides at 1.7 that practices must have a health and safety policy in relation to the safety of personnel and visitors to the practice. Following an initial explanation, a sample policy follows.
The practice will be responsible for:

- assessing the risk to the health and safety of employees and others who may be affected and identifying what measures are needed to comply with its health and safety obligations;
- providing and maintaining locations, equipment, protective clothing and systems of work that are safe and without risks to health;
- ensuring that all necessary safety devices are installed and maintained on equipment;
- providing information, instruction, training and supervision in safe working methods and procedures;
- providing and maintaining a healthy and safe place of work and providing a means of access/exit;

- promoting the co-operation of employees to ensure safe and healthy conditions and systems of work by discussion and effective joint consultation (and the establishment of a safety committee, safety representatives and accident investigations where applicable);
- establishing emergency procedures as required;
- monitoring and reviewing the management of health and safety at work;
- keeping this safety policy under review and making any revision it deems necessary from time to time. All such revisions should be brought to the attention of employees.

Introduction

1.11.1 The firm is concerned to ensure the safety of all its personnel (whether at the office or working elsewhere) and all visitors to the firm's premises. To that end the firm has appointed [*name*] ('the health and safety manager') to take particular responsibility for health and safety issues. (S)he will report to the firm's management on such matters as and when they arise, and in any event at least [half] yearly, when a review of the firm's health and safety position will be undertaken. In the absence of the health and safety manager, [*name*] will deputise for him/her. Also, (s)he may from time to time delegate certain health and safety matters to others. In that event all potentially affected personnel will be notified in writing of the details of such delegation.

Policy

1.11.2 [*Name of firm*] is committed to providing for the health, safety and welfare of all employees and to maintaining standards at least equal to the best practice in the legal profession. The practice will observe the Health and Safety at Work etc. Act 1974 and all other relevant legislation, regulations and codes of practice made from time to time. The practice will take into account any recommendations made by the Health and Safety Executive with regard to health and safety issues, and where appropriate will liaise with the Health and Safety Executive on health and safety issues that are of particular relevance to the firm.

1.11.3 The allocation of responsibility within the firm for health and safety matters is as follows:

- [*Name or title*] has overall and final responsibility for giving effect to this health and safety policy.
- [*Name or title*] is responsible for ensuring there is consultation on health and safety matters with staff, either through representatives of recognised trade unions or through representatives of other groups of employees, as appropriate, in order to maintain health and safety at work.
- [*Name or title*] is responsible for the implementation and monitoring of health and safety policies.
- Heads of department [*others*] are responsible for the implementation of health and safety policies in the areas under their control.

- All employees have the responsibility to observe all safety rules and to co-operate with the manager charged with responsibility for the implementation of the firm's health and safety policy to achieve a healthy and safe workplace and to take reasonable care of themselves and others.

Procedures

1.11.4 Detailed procedures on health and safety are contained in part D of section 4 of the manual.

Annex 1A

Identification and verification: Form ML1

▪ Within the MLR 2007 'identification' and 'verification' have distinct meanings. Identification is explained by the Law Society advice as 'simply being told or coming to know a client's identifying details, such as their name and address', while verification is seen as 'obtaining some evidence which supports this claim of identity.' The provisions of MLR 2007 do not, unfortunately, lend themselves to the sort of straightforward client ID checklist that appeared in the last edition of this work. The regulations provide, at r.7(3), that a 'relevant person' must 'determine the extent of customer due diligence measures on a risk-sensitive basis' and that the practice ('relevant person') must 'be able to demonstrate to his supervisory authority that the extent of the measures is appropriate in view of the risks of money laundering and terrorist financing'. It follows that some low risk firms might get away with quite simple client ID checklists, but that others will need very much more complex procedures to be in place.

Issues to be addressed include:

- Whether the client base is local or more widely spread: does the practice represent clients that it does not meet in person?
- The volume of repeat business from established clients as opposed to clients that are new to the firm
- The nature of the work: are there issues of beneficial ownership by others and control structures in areas of work such as company commercial or trusts?
- Is the firm likely to deal with 'politically exposed persons' as defined by r.14(4)?
- Are there other instances where 'enhanced customer due diligence' is needed? If so, what format will the additional steps take? (see r.14)
- How much of the firm's work can be covered by the provisions on 'simplified due diligence' at r.13?
- Does the firm rely on external checking of databases as part of its ID responsibilities?
- The usefulness of referral sources in assisting the firm in its responsibilities
- What actions need to be taken to satisfy the requirements on 'ongoing monitoring' (r.8)?

See chapter 4 of the Law Society website advice on compliance with money laundering and terrorist financing issues ('Customer due diligence').

Taking the above into account, a form (one side if at all possible) might address

- Risk profile of the department in question or firm as a whole
- Existing client (on whom ID evidence is already held) or new client?
- Is this likely to be a new business relationship or an occasional transaction?
- Could there be beneficial ownership by others? If so, what responses have been given by the client on this issue? There should be spaces to identify the beneficial owners with any details of any further checking required
- What is the ownership and control structure of any organisation that is involved?
- ID required for individuals
- ID required in other situations
- Evidence of authority of representative to instruct on behalf of the organisation
- On-line checking if undertaken

- ID and verification provided by another organisation: checks undertaken on that organisation
- General concerns of other risk points to refer to head of department or MLRO

The firm will also need to determine its policy in relation to where the form is stored or if the data should be transferred to another source. There is a need to retain the sort of information listed above for at least five years from the end of the business relationship or the end of the occasional transaction. This could mean that a firm destroying the ML1 form in circumstances where there is ongoing work for the client on other files could leave itself open to prosecution under the money laundering regulations if it continues to rely on the first check that is done.

For more advice for MLROs on conducting risk assessments to supplement the staff procedures in 1.9 above, and for training materials for in-house use, see **www.web4law.biz**.

Annex 1B

Report to the MLRO
STRICTLY CONFIDENTIAL

Client/Matter number

Client
- [ ] Mr
- [ ] Mrs
- [ ] Miss
- [ ] Ms
- [ ] Other _____

> Great care must be taken to ensure that this form is not seen by the client at any time. If you keep a copy of this form do not leave it on the matter file. A copy of this form must be sent to the MLRO who will also keep a copy.

Forenames

Surname

Any alias?

Date and place of birth, if known

Source of client

Address

Phone (day)

Phone (evening)

e-mail (if any)

Introducer (if any)

Nature of instructions

Reasons for report (attach confidential memo if necessary)

Professional privilege apply?*

Should client be advised?*

Signed
(Adviser)

Date of signature

To be completed by the MLRO

Date form received

Report to SOCA?

Reasons for not reporting

I consent to client being informed that we will be reporting/have reported to SOCA on grounds of legal professional privilege.
(Only sign if consent is granted)

Date of consent

Date of report to client (attach copy of letter or attendance note)

* Only express a view if you feel competent to do so. Up-to-date guidance on the Money Laundering Regulations can be found on the Law Society website at www.lawsociety.org.uk

Annex 1C

Report form

HIGHLY CONFIDENTIAL

Client name	Matter number and fee earner	Date of receipt of ML2	Report to SOCA? Reasons	Consent to inform client?	Date of report to SOCA	Date permission to proceed received	7 days expiry	Moratorium period expiry date

2 Planning

Introduction

Section 2 in the Lexcel standard requires various key elements of the practice's business strategy to be committed to writing. The main provision appears at section 2.1: 'Practices will develop and maintain a marketing and business plan'. In years gone by law firms and the services that they provided changed little from year to year, with business planning therefore consisting of little more than monitoring the budgets and keeping an eye on the bank balances and profits. How different now! With fundamental changes to the structure of law firms and an opening of the market to non-solicitor organisations pending in the Legal Services Bill, along with radical changes to the way in which areas such as conveyancing are conducted, the whole process of future planning has become an altogether much more important process in law firm management.

It may well be that firms applying for Lexcel accreditation will not need any procedures in their manual to evidence compliance with this section. Assessors will be concerned to know that there is a planning process and that the necessary plans are in place. Some firms include an outline of their plans in their manual, but this is not a requirement. What follows, therefore, is primarily by way of guidance. The format and contents of business plans will vary so much between different firms that it would be of questionable use to set out a model format for one here. A common problem in the development of a plan is that more effort goes into the accuracy of the drafting than into the action required, with long rambling plans addressing little in detail. As a general rule, most firms do not need long narratives setting out the current position of the firm since this will usually be known to the readers and is generally not contentious. Better by far that the plan confines itself to a few pages of the most pertinent considerations, options and targets. The focus should be on action, not description.

Writing a business and marketing plan

Traditionally the business plan and the marketing plan would be separate documents, usually addressing different timescales. The business plan would address the more fundamental issues of how it is hoped the organisation will develop, probably over a three- to five-year span, while the marketing plan would be a more tactical document setting how the developments in the business plan might be achieved. It has become more common in recent years to merge the two documents, with the marketing element being seen as the means by which the plan will be achieved. The Lexcel standard envisages that the two elements could be combined or separate, and that both need to be kept under regular review.

There is no one way to compile business and marketing plans, but it is useful to consider the process in three distinct stages:

- the formation of an overall business plan;
- the selection of the services that are to be offered by the firm in order to achieve the goals set out in the business plan; and

27

- the choice of the marketing techniques that are to be used to promote those services to the firm's existing and prospective clientele.

The remainder of this section has been compiled on the basis that it will be for the managing partner to take responsibility for the conduct of the process whereby these plans are to be formulated, documented, disseminated and reviewed.

Developing and maintaining the business plan

The object of any such plan, whether in its original format or as revised from time to time, is to articulate clearly:

- the key objectives of the firm over the next year at least;
- additional objectives – whether detailed or outline – for at least the two years following the initial year;
- the features that will chart progress towards achievement of those objectives;
- the financial implications of the above.

In broad terms the purpose of the plan is to show where the firm wishes to go, and to allow the management of the firm to assess how successfully it is doing in its quest to get there.

The first task in connection with the preparation of the plan is to assemble the raw data as to the firm's position, which can then be analysed. That data could relate to the internal circumstances of the firm, or to the external market and other forces that may affect the environment in which the firm is to practise. Typical considerations from within the firm might include:

- a profile of the current client base and an analysis of the key clients or work referral sources;
- the geographical spread of the firm's existing client base;
- the levels of capital available for investment;
- the nature of the expertise within the firm;
- the current financial performance.

External factors that are likely to require consideration might include:

- predicted economic trends;
- forthcoming legislation impacting upon the legal profession and the services provided;
- changes in the competitive environment within which the firm operates;
- alterations in the profession's rules and structure.

It is important that there should be consultation on all such issues. This could be achieved through a questionnaire exercise or via departmental or office meetings. Ideally client feedback should also inform the process, either in relation to current satisfaction levels or on how well the firm's current range of services meets the needs of those consulted. A case could be made for instructing external advisers to conduct the staff and client consultation exercise, but many firms will choose to conduct the entire process from within. It is likely that the partners and any senior managers will need to review what is taking shape at an 'away-day'. Most firms have found that there is unlikely to be sufficient time, or energy on the part of the participants, to deal with such issues at a partners' meeting at the end of a working day. An off-site discussion is more likely to produce the focus and clear thinking that is needed.

Although much maligned by many business academics the 'SWOT' analysis is a good way to get some shape on varied and sometimes contradictory discussions. Data is grouped into four categories, namely:

- Strengths
- Weaknesses
- Opportunities
- Threats

The object of SWOT discussions is then to 'join the boxes': how can the strengths be brought to bear on the opportunities; can weaknesses be tolerated or do they need to be confronted? Such deliberations can assist in the process of identifying priorities and evaluating options.

There are no limitations in Lexcel on the format of plans and, again, they will vary among firms. In some firms the overall strategy is the combination of a number of departmental plans, with the away-day perhaps consisting of reporting back by the various heads of department. This can be quite a disjointed way of compiling plans, however, and common themes might be neglected or overlooked.

Whatever the precise steps taken it is important to deal with the financial implications of the matters under discussion. Lexcel refers in its guidance to a 'finance plan' which is explained as being an examination of the 'financial implications of the strategy or strategies to be adopted'. Many firms would benefit from more in the way of profitability analysis which, in turn, would make for very much more relevant objectives in the eventual plan than is often otherwise the case. Whatever the objectives chosen they should be capable of being tested against the SMART criteria, i.e. that they are:

- Specific
- Measurable
- Achievable
- Realistic
- Time-limited

Not all objectives will be purely financial. Some will be targeted at the overall positioning of the firm. Where this is the case some form of measurement should be included as part of the target setting. Examples of different forms of objectives might therefore be:

- Single-issue achievements, e.g. the opening of a new office.
- Absolute financial measures, e.g. a 10% increase in net profits per equity partner.
- Ratios, e.g. a reduction in costs as a percentage of gross fees.
- Growth, e.g. recruitment of a specific number of new lawyers and attraction of the work for them.
- Market share, e.g. an increase of instructions in a specific work area measured as a percentage of the existing level.
- IT development, e.g. a project to put a PC on the desk of every person within the firm, or to create an interactive website.
- Service improvement, e.g. an improvement in telephone response times, as measured by telephonic monitoring equipment; or client satisfaction, as measured by client satisfaction surveys or other appropriate market research techniques.
- Reputational prominence, e.g. as assessed by the number of mentions in local media over a defined period.

Some objectives may relate only to specific departments or other business units within the firm, and naturally this will be so in respect of any sub-plans.

The plan should not be restricted to just the one year and will need to address a three-year period to be valid under Lexcel. Although many of the same points as above will apply to the choice and framing of the longer-term objectives it is accepted that they are likely to be less detailed, and may be more susceptible to change on subsequent review. The purpose of this part of the exercise is to ensure that the management is not merely planning for one year in isolation. As above, these objectives may be firmwide, or related only to specific areas of the firm.

A final consideration is how far the plan will be published and how it might be edited to make it more suitable for general use. Personnel can be supplied with a summary of the plan or, preferably, staff briefings will be arranged. Those who prefer to see the plan as being entirely confidential to the partners do need to consider the extent to which staff need to contribute to its achievement. Staff morale is an important component of the success of any business and sharing the plan with colleagues is likely to have a positive effect in most organisations.

Documenting the services the firm is to offer

Section 2.2 of Lexcel sets out the need for a 'services' plan. This is not quite the same as marketing or business planning, but is probably best seen as an element of both. The aim is to set out details of the services to be offered and the way in which they will be provided. Clearly, the determination of which services the firm wishes to offer – and those that it does not – is an important aspect of its deliberations on the future. The services selected may be those that the firm is offering already, and/or others that it wishes to develop, either by 'lateral hires' or by organic growth.

An inherent part of the choice of services to be offered will, in many instances, be the selection of the groups of clients to whom they are to be offered. Such groupings may differ according to the particular service in question. Many firms have concentrated too much on their internal structures and not enough on client needs. The distinction between commercial and private client work may be obvious enough, but examining clients as different groups as part of a 'market segmentation' analysis can provide invaluable insights into the planning process. In many firms not all conveyancing clients have the same priorities, and it can be helpful to plan on distinct service levels for first time buyers as opposed to the elderly private client with more disposable income and more anxiety about the process. This method of developing the firm's services requires less emphasis on departmental structures and more on client needs – an important component of developing that 'client-centred practice' that many firms claim to be.

In respect of each selected service, and each selected client grouping, the firm will also need to consider whether there are any special needs attaching to the particular choice, in terms of the means by which the service is to be delivered to the client. Such matters may include:

- the provision of out-of-hours or emergency contact details;
- the availability of facilities for disabled clients;
- a willingness to visit clients at their own premises;
- means of electronic communication and data transfer which may be available to clients;

- an ability to deal in languages other than English (either routinely or by arrangement);
- the possibility of assisting with financial concerns, e.g. by funding disbursements during a case, or by fee arrangements.

It will also be important to state whether the firm undertakes legal aid or publicly funded work. If so, the services plan should include details of the contract categories covered and the policy on matter starts might also be set out in an appropriate part of the manual.

Finally, it might also be advisable to set out the firm's policy on the provision of services to staff and their families – in many firms there is a discount on services such as conveyancing after an initial probationary period.

Producing a marketing plan

Either as part of the business planning process referred to above, or as an adjunct to it, the firm will consider its approach to the marketing of its chosen services. That approach will be such as will best serve the overall strategy of the firm. Without limiting the scope of that consideration, the firm will consider the following:

- Whether, in respect of either all or any specific aspects of its services, it wishes to:
  - reduce or maintain its current level of activity, so that active marketing may be inappropriate; or
  - increase its current level of activity, so that active marketing is required.

- What specific promotional methods will be appropriate for either:
  - each specific area where active marketing is required; or
  - the overall profile and market positioning of the firm.

- What it will seek to achieve by each of the chosen marketing methods, and how those aims will tie into the firm's strategy.
- How the effectiveness of any chosen marketing method may be assessed and evaluated.
- What resources will be needed for any marketing activity, and whether they are proportionate to the anticipated benefits which may be derived from them.
- Whether the chosen methods will comply with the provisions of the 2007 Code, Rule 7 (Publicity).

The process of marketing planning can be most simply represented as the following steps:

- Determine some objectives (as shaped by the business or departmental plan).
- Choose the appropriate promotional methods.
- Set a budget.

In this process, the marketing objectives should not be financial since these will appear in the business plan. What are required instead are some targets that will ensure that the financial objectives are achieved, e.g.:

- Gain two new commercial clients generating over £... fees/year.
- Increase the number of wills written from ... to ....

As to the promotional methods to be adopted it is useful to draw a distinction between those that are 'personal', in that they involve the time and direct input of fee earners, and the 'non-personal'.

Personal	Non-personal
Meetings and networking	The supply of brochures and leaflets
Delivering seminars and other presentations	Advertising and mailshots
Client entertaining	Press coverage
Client training	Websites and e-alerts

However the marketing plan is compiled, firms should ensure that it is more than a well-intentioned 'wish list' of things to do or to achieve. It should cover:

- the aim of the activity, in relation to the strategy of the firm or the appropriate unit within it;
- the financial implications, in terms of both the cost of the exercise and the anticipated yield from it;
- the identity of the person(s) who will be responsible for implementing it;
- the means by which the success or failure of the initiative may be measured;
- the timing of the effort;
- any risks attached to the activity.

Furthermore, marketing plan(s) need to be communicated effectively to all those concerned in their implementation, whether at firmwide, office or departmental level. Those formulating the plan(s) should consider what means of conveying this information would be appropriate, e.g. training sessions, written communications, newsletters or meetings.

Reviewing the firm's plans

All business, service and marketing plans will need to kept under regular review; Lexcel requires such reviews at least every six months. It can be advisable for the manual to set out the ways in which each constituent part of the planning documentation is to be reviewed, and in particular:

- who will take responsibility for the review;
- how the results of the review are to be communicated to those responsible for co-ordinating the planning exercise;
- when the review is to occur;
- what criteria are to be applied in the course of the review, to evaluate the success or failure of the initial plan;
- what authority may be delegated to change the plan;
- how any changes are to be communicated and to whom;
- what effects any change in a subordinate plan may have upon a higher-level plan;
- what the financial implications of the review may be;
- for what period (being not less than a year) the review may apply;
- what is the appropriate method of evidencing the fact of the review having occurred, and the outcome of the review (e.g. minutes of appropriate meetings, revised written plans, strategy papers forming part of the review process, etc.).

2.1 Business and marketing planning

2.1.1 The partners give regular consideration to the future of the practice and keep the business plan under constant review (at least every six months). The plan covers such aspects as:

- the range of services provided;
- targets for growth, in terms of fees, personnel and clients;
- the main steps needed to ensure success in such objectives.

2.1.2 Staff may consult a summary of the current business plan, which was formally adopted in [*specify*] at [*link*]. From time to time a major review of the plan is undertaken and you may well be invited to take part in the consultation process that this entails. The firm's plans are, of course, confidential, and we ask you to respect this while you are employed by the firm and after you leave.

2.1.3 The management of the firm will from time to time review its marketing activity, either as part of the general business planning process or as needs arise. A sustained marketing programme is key to the growth and success of the firm and the partners hope that everyone will play a part in it, even if only by ensuring that this firm is recommended to any friends and family that might need legal assistance.

2.2 Business continuity

Business continuity planning has become a mandatory element of supervisory management under the 2007 Code, subrule 5.01(1)(k). The same requirement appears in Lexcel at section 2.4. As with all other plans referred to in this book there is little value in simply adopting an 'off-the-shelf' precedent without adaptation. The following are the main points to bear in mind:

- identification of the likely risks, especially those that relate to the premises in use;
- key information needed when a problem arises: partner/staff lists with home phone numbers/mobiles so that everyone can be notified as to what is expected of them;
- website information updates;
- backup/emergency facilities – IT and premises;
- training/rehearsal in above.

2.2.1 The firm has adopted a business continuity plan to address the emergencies that might disrupt its operation. The sort of event the partners have in mind is [*specify*] and the main provisions are as follows: [*specify*].

3 Financial management

The accounting and time recording systems used by practices can vary considerably in sophistication but are now almost always computerised. The choice of system will influence the precise financial procedures in use. The following procedures must therefore be seen in this context.

For the most part, accounting in a solicitors' practice does not require accountancy skills in depth. What does make financial management more difficult is that the accounting (and time recording) functions are fragmented by being divided across the number of individual fee earners employed and the range of legal work undertaken. Multi-office practices provide another factor. Complexity is often the issue.

What is essential, therefore, is that the accounting procedures are clearly documented, understood and implemented, and are then monitored closely on a continuous basis.

3.1 Responsibility for financial management

3.1.1 The managing partner has the direct responsibility to the partnership for overseeing and managing financial affairs. [*Where there is no managing partner – for example where the firm is managed by a committee or where there are only 2/3 partners, it is best practice to nominate a partner to take on these responsibilities as the finance partner*] The partners, of course, while passing control and supervision to the [practice manager/accountant] and to the accounts department staff must at all times take full responsibility for the operation of the firm's accounts in accordance with the Solicitors' Accounts Rules, which are available for inspection at **www.sra.org.uk**.

3.1.2 Individual fee earners are responsible for the financial management of their client matters especially as required by the Solicitors' Accounts Rules and the detailed instructions that follow.

3.1.3 If anyone has cause to be concerned about any aspect of financial management, especially as related to client monies, they should refer their concern to the managing partner or other partner at once.

3.2 Computer system

3.2.1 The firm has a centralised accounting and time recording system and all personnel have direct access to much of the system and the data through the computer network. The software is provided by [*name*]. Immediate control is exercised by the [practice manager/office manager/accountant/senior cashier] and any difficulties concerning the system should be directed to [him/her].

3.2.2 Generally, all personnel have enquiry access to all client accounting and time recording data together with related print-outs. In addition, partners have access to the nominal ledger and some of the management reporting facilities. Apart from time recording entries (see section 3.21), only the accounts department personnel have password-protected access to the various posting programs.

3.2.3 Fee earners and secretaries are encouraged to make full use of the accounting information available to support their client work but should refer to the accounts personnel if specific help is required.

3.3 Management reports

3.3.1 The accounting system is capable of producing a very large range of management reports both in respect of client matters and on the firm's accounting performance. The following main reports are produced each month by the accounts department:

- profit and loss account;
- balance sheet;
- budget variance report;
- client debtor report;
- work in progress;
- new matters reports;
- fee earner performance report;
- fee income report by work type;
- client ledger balance report;
- cashflow report;
- amount of outstanding bills;
- length of time bills have been outstanding.

Other reports can be produced on request to the accounts department. The managing partner, with the [practice manager/accountant], has specific responsibility for reviewing such reports. [*The distribution of such reports will vary considerably between different firms*]

3.4 Income and expenditure budgets

3.4.1 Annual income and expenditure budgets are prepared at practice and branch office levels and these are used in the monitoring of the firm's financial performance. Each month the managing partner and the [practice manager/accountant] and the branch office partners review budget variance reports.

3.5 Cashflow

3.5.1 Based largely upon the income and expenditure budgets and any known or anticipated cycles in either, a cashflow forecast for the forthcoming year is prepared by the [practice manager/accountant]. The cashflow forecast is kept under continual review and forms part of the [monthly management review].

3.5.2 While cashflow is largely managed at firm level, it is important that all fee earners remain alert to the need for them to manage their own client matters carefully by ensuring that where possible money on account is obtained, chargeable time is fully recorded, that interim bills are raised when a matter allows, that final bills are raised promptly, that disbursements are monitored and where possible paid promptly, that counsel's fees are properly allocated and that the fee earner remains involved in any credit control action [see section 3.18].

3.6 Receipts of cash and cheques

It is strongly recommended that a policy of refusing all cash receipts is implemented. This would reduce the risk of exposure to the most obvious form of money laundering – 'placing' – where criminal proceeds are introduced to the banking system. Some firms are likely to find this unwieldy or inappropriate to the normal financial dealings of their clients, however, and will consider a cash receipt limit. It should be noted that the Proceeds of Crime Act has no *de minimis* provisions on this subject and funds are treated as criminal property if they arise from criminal conduct or represent such a benefit 'in whole or part' (POCA 2002, s.340(3)).

Another difficulty with substantial cash receipts is the arrangements for staff to bank them safely.

Many firms require all cash to be counted by two persons to minimise the danger of later allegations of loss or dishonesty.

It is advisable to include details of the firm's policy on cash handling in any terms of business or client care letter.

3.6.1 Most money is received by cheque through the post but payment of cash is often offered. The firm's policy on cash receipts is influenced by its responsibilities under money laundering legislation (see section 1.9 above).

[Set out policy, stating limit, if any, and responsibility for checking total amount]

Cash is never to be left unattended, for example on a desk.

3.6.2 Cheques received in the morning post must be sent direct to the accounts department without delay in order that the cheques can be safeguarded, identified and banked on the same day. Fee earners are informed immediately about the receipt of cheques and must give instructions to the accounts department as soon as possible for the cheque to be banked. Cheques received later in the day or direct by a fee earner are also to be sent to the accounts department without delay even if they cannot be banked on that day.

3.6.3 Any cash or cheques held by the accounts department overnight are to be secured in the strong-room.

3.7 Receipts for cheques and cash

3.7.1 Only personnel of the accounts department are authorised to issue formal receipts for cheques or cash. [*State any exceptions*]

3.8 Cheque requisitions

3.8.1 If a fee earner requires a cheque to be drawn on Client General Account, Client Trustee Account or Office Account, the fee earner is to complete a cheque requisition form in duplicate as shown below. The client name, matter number, bank account on which the cheque is to be drawn, payee, amount and brief details of the reason for the cheque, are to be fully completed. The top copy of the requisition form is to be sent to the accounts department and the second copy retained on the client matter file. The accounts copy serves also as the posting form.

[*Alternatively, describe the procedure if cheque requisitions can be made to the accounts department direct from a fee earner's personal computer*]

3.8.2 Cheques are printed daily through the accounting system. The printing run will take place at [3 pm] after which the cheques will be distributed to the fee earners in time for the cheques to be sent out in the afternoon post. If a cheque is required urgently, a handwritten cheque can be prepared by the accounts department but this should remain the exception to the rule.

3.8.3 The accounts department will make the assumption that cheques will be issued on that day and will effect the ledger posting accordingly. If the issue of the cheque is to be delayed, then the fee earner must make this clear and liaise with the accounts department.

[*Include here a copy of cheque requisition form*]

■ It is recommended that there should be some safeguards about signing cheques along the following lines (for partnerships of more than two partners). For cheques up to a value of £1,000/2,000, the signature of one partner is required; for cheques of a value in excess of £1,000/2,000, the signature of two partners is required. For cheques drawn on Office Account, the cheque can be signed by the head of accounts.

3.9 Transfers

3.9.1 A transfer form [as shown below] is to be used for authorising transfers of client and office monies. It is also to be used for authorising telegraphic transfers. Two copies of the form should be raised, the top copy to be sent to the accounts department for action and the duplicate retained on the client matter file. On occasions it may be necessary to support the transfer form with a note of explanation.

3.9.2 The proper transferring of monies is directly the responsibility of fee earners and verbal instructions will not be accepted by the accounts department.

[Include here a copy of the transfer form]

3.10 Payment out of client monies

3.10.1 Payment out of client monies by cheque or transfer, irrespective of the amount, can only be authorised by a partner.

3.11 Write-offs

3.11.1 The write-off of any balance in respect of costs or disbursements can only be authorised by a partner and if the amount is [£1,000] or greater, authority is first to be obtained from the managing partner or the head of the appropriate department.

3.11.2 In exceptional circumstances it may be desirable to write off a balance of client monies where, despite all endeavours, it has not been possible to trace the client. In such circumstances and on the authority of the managing partner, the balance may be paid to the Solicitors Benevolent Association (SBA). The SBA will undertake to repay the money to the firm if the client is subsequently traced.

3.12 Petty cash

3.12.1 All petty cash transactions are controlled by the accounts department. If petty cash is required, a petty cash form [as shown below] is to be fully completed and taken to the accounts department for their action. The form must clearly identify whether the expenditure is in respect of a client matter and is therefore recoverable, or is a charge to the firm itself.

[Include here a copy of the petty cash form]

3.13 Issue of bills and cheques

3.13.1 Occasionally there may be a reason for a fee earner not immediately to send out to a client a costs bill or cheque that has been processed through the accounts department. However, the accounts department will not be aware of the delay and will therefore have posted the appropriate accounting transaction. In respect of a costs bill this could lead to debt collection action being taken for the non-payment of the bill when action should not have been taken. In respect of a delayed cheque, this could cause problems when reconciling the bank account.

3.13.2 Whenever there is delay in issuing cost bills or cheques, the accounts department is to be informed at once. [Ideally the letter accompanying the bill should be sent to accounts so that the accounts department is aware for credit control purposes of the date on which the bill was sent.] If a bill or cheque is to be cancelled altogether, then it must be returned to the accounts department for proper cancellation.

3.14 Amendments to cheques

3.14.1 No cheque, whether drawn on Client Account or Office Account, is to be amended in any way or for any reason without reference to a partner and the accounts department. If the amount of a cheque is to be altered, then it must be returned to the accounts department so that the related posting transaction can be altered. Normally the faulty cheque will be cancelled and a new cheque issued.

3.15 Receipts from third parties

3.15.1 The following steps must be taken in respect of receipts from third parties [*specify*].

> ■ Firms should consider their approach to receipts from third parties in the light of the anti-money laundering regime now in place and follow any Law Society guidance on the point. One possible approach is to photocopy any third party cheque and require it to be stored on the matter file. More details on the payer will usually be required.

3.16 Client ledger balances report

3.16.1 On [the 15th day of each month] or nearest working day, the accounts department will issue a client ledger balances report to each fee earner. The report will show:

- client name, matter number, work type;
- balances on client and office accounts;
- balance of unbilled disbursements;

- balance of outstanding debts;
- balance of work in progress;
- lapsed months since last accounting or time recording activity.

3.16.2 Each fee earner is to review the report against their client files within [three] days of receipt of the report, and to update the matter files by:

- updating the client on costs information (including estimates) and matter activity;
- raising any outstanding client to office transfers (partner authority required);
- raising an interim bill where due;
- hastening any client debts in liaison with the accounts department;
- clearing any remaining small balances on completed matters;
- archiving files that are fully completed.

3.16.3 Through taking such action, client matters will be kept up to date which should be seen as a significant part of client care.

3.17 Investigation and clearance of ledger queries

3.17.1 Inevitably from time to time fee earners will have queries on their client matter ledgers such as those that arise from small uncleared balances. While the accounts department will afford all reasonable help, it is the direct responsibility of the fee earner to first carry out the investigation to clear the query. They have the advantage of having the client matter file to help identify transactions and are able to review the ledgers from their own desk computer. If a problem persists, please raise it with the accounts department as soon as possible.

3.18 Credit control

Credit control is a matter of some professional responsibility. The main rules are that:

- bills should be rendered within a reasonable time of concluding the matter;
- the bill should be sufficiently detailed for the client to be able to identify what it relates to;
- under the Solicitors Act 1974, s.69 a solicitor may only commence proceedings for non-payment of an invoice before the expiry of one month from the delivery of the bill with court leave; the same section deals with the need for a signature of a partner or principal on the bill;
- a client may only be sued for recovery of unpaid invoices if they have been served with the requisite notice for either contentious or non-contentious business, as the case may be;
- firms should consider their policy on interim bills: the bill could be driven either by time or by amount of time expended, or both.

3.18.1 The firm's credit control procedures are based upon the following main principles:

- Wherever possible money on account from the client is to be obtained in respect of fees and disbursements.
- Wherever possible interim bills are to be raised at least [monthly/every two months]. Agreement to this must be obtained from the client – such agreement being set out preferably in the firm's client care letter. Smaller regular bills are less likely to be the subject of non-payment and where this does arise, consideration may need to be given as to whether to continue to act for the client.
- Fee earners remain closely involved in the credit control process notwith-standing any action taken by others such as the accounts department staff. A matter is not completed until the bill has been paid. Early intervention by the fee earner is more likely to generate payment than hastening correspondence from the accounts department.
- There will be a hastening process of escalating severity finalising in court proceedings being taken against the client.
- The credit control procedures will automatically be activated for all client debts unless under exceptional circumstances a partner intervenes to prevent some or all of the procedures from taking place.
- Except under exceptional circumstances, court proceedings will be taken if necessary irrespective of the client.
- The credit control procedures will be actioned as a priority task by whoever has the responsibility. [Name] is the credit controller within the accounts department.

The procedure

> Note that some accounting systems now have an automated credit control facility which would inevitably vary the following procedure. However the principles should be the same.

3.18.2   Once private client bills have been posted on to the ledger, they will be filed in the accounts department in date order on a lever arch binder [with a separate binder being used for each branch office]. When a bill has been paid, it will be transferred to a paid binder with the bills filed in alphabetical/bill number order.

3.18.3   This method of filing will greatly assist with the credit control procedures as it will immediately identify those unpaid bills that require hastening action at whatever stage. In particular, as bills are paid and removed, there will be a residue of bills remaining that justify special attention. Any bill that remains unpaid for three months is regarded as being a potential problem.

3.18.4   Any publicly funded bills are filed in the accounts department in separate binders.

3.18.5   Once a bill enters the credit control process, the credit controller records what action has been taken plus any instruction or information about the debt received from the fee earner or other person concerned. It is most important that fee earners liaise closely with the credit controller to ensure that proper action is taken.

3.18.6 The escalating procedure for private client debts is as follows.

- **Step 1.** Bill sent to client with copy retained on the client file, and a copy passed to the accounts department for posting action and for filing in the unpaid bills binder. This copy is the VAT invoice. Details of the client's rights to a certificate under the Solicitors' (Non-Contentious Business) Remuneration Order 1994, SI 1994/2616 are included on the reverse of the bill.
- **Step 2.** After four weeks the credit controller sends a statement to the client.
- **Step 3.** After six weeks the credit controller asks the fee earner to contact the client about the non-payment. There may be understandable reasons from the client's point of view and a process for settlement could be agreed.
- **Step 4.** After eight weeks, following further liaison with the fee earner, the credit controller sends the client a letter threatening court proceedings if payment is not forthcoming. This letter is always to be signed by a partner.
- **Step 5.** After 10 weeks from the date of the issue of the bill, if payment has not been made or alternative payment arrangements have been agreed with the client, a final letter will be sent to the client stating that court proceedings will be taken unless payment is made immediately. This letter will be signed by the credit control partner who first will have necessarily liaised with the appropriate supervising partner.
- **Step 6.** When proceedings are to be taken a new debt matter will be opened but the outstanding debt will remain on the fee earner's print-out records for analysis and records purposes.

The head of accounts and the finance/managing partner will monitor these procedures and will liaise with other partners when necessary.

Debt management report

3.18.7 An aged debt report will be [produced at the end of each month] and will be distributed to the individual fee earners. All fee earners will therefore be fully aware of their personal client debtor position and should liaise as necessary with the credit controller on any action that can be taken.

3.19 Reserving and write-off of debts

3.19.1 At the end of each financial year [date], all debts that have been outstanding for 12 months or more will be automatically reserved in the firm's accounts. This will have the effect of reducing the profits for that year by the amount of the reserved debts but it will enable the firm to recover any output VAT. The reserved debts will remain on the individual client ledger account and can continue to be hastened for payment. If payment or part payment is received then the profit costs will be reinstated as if it was a new bill. Both the credit controller and the fee earner must liaise closely when this occurs.

3.19.2 Any remaining reserved debts from the previous financial year will normally be written off on the authority of the finance/managing partner after discussion with the relevant supervising partners/heads of departments. Such write-offs will have no effect on the profits as the reduction will have taken place at the reserving stage.

3.19.3 There will be times when a bill should be written off without the need to be first reserved, e.g. following bankruptcy. Again write-off can only be authorised by a partner.

3.20 Billing guides or draft bills

[*Billing guides or the preparation of automated draft bills may be part of the accounting and time recording system. If so, the related procedure should be fully described. A copy of the documentation should be included if practicable*]

3.21 Time recording

3.21.1 Time recording is used to support the billing process and also provides essential management information.

3.21.2 The firm's time recording system is directly linked to the accounting system. When a new client matter is entered on to the system, the time ledger is automatically opened. Time recording information on every matter can be obtained direct from individual desk computers, either on screen or by a printed report.

3.21.3 Time is recorded in six-minute units with each unit being costed as follows:

(a) For private client work at the charge-out rate applicable to the fee earner concerned. For private non-contentious work it is not necessary to differentiate between activities such as attendance on client, letters, telephone calls, etc. Simply record as standard time. For litigation matters each activity is to be differentiated to support the billing process.
(b) For publicly funded work, at the appropriate public funding rate allowed for each activity which must be recorded

3.21.4 The computer time record will show individual time postings per fee earner and a running total on unbilled time shown in terms of hours and minutes, value and activity. All time spent on a client matter must be supported by relevant evidence on the client file such as a copy letter or attendance note.

3.21.5 When a bill is posted on to the matter ledger, the amount of unbilled work in progress is either reduced to nil, or it can be reduced by a set amount as indicated by the fee earner. This may often be the case when an interim bill is prepared.

Time postings

3.21.6 Time postings can be made in one of two ways, or a combination. Entries can be made by the fee earner direct from his/her computer keyboard, usually contemporaneously with the activity. Alternatively, fee earners can maintain a daily handwritten time sheet which will then require the time entries to be separately input on to the time ledgers by [*state by whom and how*]. A combination of the two methods may be appropriate.

3.21.7 The objective is to ensure that all genuinely chargeable time is captured for both billing and management purposes. [*Include details here of any daily, weekly or annual targets or guidelines*]

3.21.8 Non-chargeable time must also be recorded and should be differentiated, e.g. holiday, training, sickness, administration, marketing, etc. A particularly useful non-chargeable activity is 'non-chargeable client time' where brief client work is undertaken, e.g. a phone call after the matter has been finished, and the fee earner is clear that the time will not be charged out.

3.22 Interest

3.22.1 Interest will be paid to clients in accordance with the current Solicitors' Accounts Rules (except where clients have specifically agreed to waive their entitlement to interest under those Rules).

3.23 File closing

3.23.1 Where a file is to be closed, written instructions are sent to the accounts department to close the relevant ledger and include comments as to how to deal with any outstanding unbilled time, unpaid disbursements and any monies held in client account. The relevant accounts information is held in accordance with the Solicitors' Accounts Rules for a minimum of six years.

4 ICT and facilities

This is the most general of the sections in the Lexcel standard, covering all the office facilities and services that solicitors need to function effectively. Within this book there is some overlap with section 1, which deals with firmwide policies. The firm's management policy on health and safety, for example, appears in section 1, while the more detailed procedures are set out here. It is a matter of style as to whether policy and procedures should appear together or be separated in this way.

The most significant new provisions in this section are those relating to the use of information communication technology, in section 4A of Lexcel. Computer use is a growing issue and will become critical to the success of most practices in the next few years, particularly with the advent of e-conveyancing and e-litigation. Meanwhile, there is a bewildering array of regulations affecting most aspects of office computer use, coupled with disturbing evidence that most practices are non-compliant in many regards. The risks of fines, convictions, claims and the resultant publicity for firms should be taken seriously by every practice.

For ease of reference the requirements of this section have been set out in groups of procedures.

4A Information management

4A.1 Management of the firm's IT system

The Lexcel standard at 4A.1 requires a policy on the use of IT facilities within the practice and details of the role of information communication technology (ICT) in providing services to clients. Areas to be covered include:

(a) responsibility for IT purchasing, installation, maintenance, support and training;
(b) the current and planned applications within the practice of IT;
(c) a data protection compliance statement in relation to staff, clients and others and registration with the Information Commissioner;
(d) compliance with all appropriate regulations and requirements;
(e) user safety;
(f) appropriate use of e-mail and attachments, both externally and internally, including storage of messages and the implications of not observing such procedure;
(g) computer data and system backup, to the extent not covered in any disaster recovery plan.

The practice's IT policy should be appropriate to that organisation. The responsibility for its development and implementation could be a partner, an IT administrator or a manager. The remit will be to manage the practice's technology to:

- assess application needs and desired uses;
- ensure integration with client technology;
- assess the financial implications;
- introduce systems that are 'user-friendly' for personnel in the practice;
- identify training needs;
- overcome resistance to IT.

Whoever has the role will need a working knowledge of:

- the legal services provided by the practice;
- solutions most appropriate for the practice;
- competing software solutions and costs;
- installation procedures and costs;
- maintenance and support procedures and costs;
- training requirements and costs.

So far as the current and planned IT applications are concerned it is necessary to start with a view of the firm's likely needs. At the outset, the practice should ask three questions of its overall business plan:

- Where is the practice now in terms of the services it is offering?
- Where does the practice want to be in terms of its profile?
- What steps are needed in terms of IT to enable the practice to get there?

Properly analysed answers to these questions will enable the practice to identify practice areas where:

- no IT investment is required;
- some basic IT investment is required; or
- significant IT investment is required.

The IT introduced will then be relevant to its practice areas and investment can be considered by direct reference to the services that are, or are to be, provided. Driven by the business plan, the strategy will represent the shared views of the partnership and its proper planning will enable the practice to forecast its expenditure, assess any risks and draw up an action plan with assigned responsibilities.

Examples of technologies are now available for numerous legal and office functions including accounts, accounting reporting, time recording, legal aid compliance, databases, diary/scheduling and case management systems. Technologies that are becoming more commonplace include voice recognition, speech recognition, digital dictation and internet telephony.

The trend for practices to offer services electronically to clients is likely to develop, especially with the imminent arrival of e-conveyancing and e-litigation. In such cases it is sensible to have a policy governing how services are supplied and any payment methods involved. The policy should specify:

- the key legal, regulatory, professional and codified provisions to be observed;
- the procedures to be observed for online contracting; and
- the method of handling of electronic payments.

More particular considerations include the following.

Compliance

(a) Identifying the services to be delivered electronically
(b) Ensuring compliance with all legal, regulatory and professional provisions
(c) Providing education and training

Notice

(a) The applicable law and jurisdiction for posted information or advice posted
(b) The law and jurisdiction to apply in the event of legal issues arising

Online transactions

(a) Authorities required for:

   (i)   concluded contacts electronically;
   (ii) giving undertakings electronically;
   (iii) serving and receiving proceedings electronically.

(b) Encryption of electronic documents when delivering legal services
(c) Verification of the identity of clients and others involved
(d) Any limitation of liability for ancillary services from a linked site

Electronic payments

(a) Technology employed for the receipt of electronic payments
(b) Provision of suitable education and training
(c) Consultation with clients on how its administration and reassurance on issues of privacy and security

4A.1.1 The firm is increasingly reliant on computer technology for the preparation and delivery of its services to clients. The firm has invested in case management software to improve certain of its services and an increasing proportion of the firm's clients expect to communicate via e-mail as opposed to the more traditional postal system. This increases the significance of effective computer management systems within the practice. There are also important rules and procedures in relation to e-mail protocols and the use of the internet. [*The practice will need to add future details on the uses of ICT and how it relates to client activities here*]

4A.1.2 The person with overall responsibility for the management of the IT system is [*name or function*]. (S)he is assisted in this role by [*name or function, and any others*]. The [IT partner *or* other] has responsibilities to review the firm's IT requirements in the light of the business plan and to advise the firm on purchases and developments that seem to be appropriate. (S)he is also responsible for organising ongoing training on IT use for all personnel in the practice.

4A.1.3 Computer backup is the responsibility of [chief cashier *or* other] who will back up daily and store the disk off site [*expand on arrangements*].

4A.1.4 The practice is required to comply with legislative and regulatory provisions governing the management and storage of electronic documentation – most notably the Data Protection Act 1998; see below – and should maintain an up-to-date record of new legislation that may impact on this aspect.

4A.2 Data protection

4A.2.1 The firm is required to comply in a number of ways with the Data Protection Act 1998 (DPA 1998). The first of these is registration under the DPA 1998. It is the responsibility of [*name or title*] to ensure that:

- the firm is registered with the Information Commissioner for all necessary activities under the Act;
- there is a process of continual review to determine whether any changes in the firm's registration are required as a result of changes in the nature of the business;
- the details of the firm as registered are kept up to date.

4A.2.2 The second aspect of compliance is the observance of the principles that underlie the DPA 1998, namely that all data covered by the Act (which includes not only computer data but also personal data held within a filing system) is:

- fairly and lawfully processed;
- processed for limited purposes;
- adequate, relevant and not excessive;
- accurate;
- not kept longer than necessary;
- processed in accordance with the data subject's rights;
- secure;
- not transferred to countries without adequate protection.

It is the responsibility of [*name or title*] to ensure that all partners and staff are aware of their obligations under data protection law and are provided with any update as to how they are required to support the practice in ensuring compliance.

4A.3 Information management

Mismanagement of electronic data can result in various consequences:

- proceedings under the Data Protection Act 1998;
- inability to offer services;
- reputational and/or financial damage;
- proceedings for negligence;
- breach of confidentiality; and
- breach of the Solicitors' Code of Conduct 2007.

Practices should assess the various types of data held for both the firm and its clients. In order for electronic data to be safeguarded appropriately, an assessment of the risk to such data should be undertaken and suitable measures should be identified to safeguard its integrity. This includes compliance with relevant legislative and regulatory provisions.

It follows that the practice will need to establish suitable training and education procedures for staff at all levels of the practice to raise awareness of responsibilities over information management.

4A.3.1 The practice has a policy for the overall management of all electronic data. The responsibility for its management is with [*name or position*].

4A.3.2 The practice holds various categories of data [employment, health, financial, marketing, *specify others*], etc.

4A.3.3 The practice has identified the following critical risk(s) to the data specified above [*specify identified risks by reference to categories of data*].

4A.3.4 The practice has in place the following processes, procedures and technology to eliminate, minimise or transfer the critical risks identified above [*specify*].

4A.3.5 The practice provides periodical training to all staff as follows [*specify intervals, categories of staff and nature and type of training*].

4A.3.6 The practice has the following technologies for the management and safe storage of electronic documents [*specify technologies – case management and/or document management; and/or storage networks*].

4A.3.7 Management of the practice's electronic document technology is the responsibility of [*name and position*].

4A.3.8 The types of document to be held in the systems for managing documents are: [*typically, these might include*]

- practice documents (leases, etc.);
- client documents (agreements, court orders, etc.);
- staff documents (contracts, etc.);
- others (as required).

4A.3.9 The practice has in place the following procedures, and operates the following technologies, for safeguarding the integrity of electronic documents:

- [*specify the technology above*]; and
- [*specify the procedures for archiving, preserving and arranging access to stored electronic documents*].

  A further layer of compliance is that there are a number of codes of practice provided under the DPA 1998, which the firm will observe. These may be altered or added to by the Information Commissioner, who is responsible for the administration of the Act. At present, applicable codes apply to:

  - use by the firm of CCTV cameras;
  - various aspects of employment practice, including:

    - recruitment and selection;
    - records management;
    - monitoring at work;
    - medical information.

CCTV cameras

4A.3.10 The firm's management has concluded that it is necessary, for the security of the firm's personnel, premises and property, for CCTV cameras to cover all points of entry to the premises and reception areas. No other methods were felt to offer sufficient protection. [*Name or title*] has responsibility for the operation of the system, and for ensuring its compliance with the appropriate code of practice. For that purpose (s)he will check weekly that the system and the information it automatically records are working correctly and accurately. These checks, and all maintenance of the system, will be logged by him/her.

4A.3.11 The cameras and any recordings taken will not be used for any purpose other than as above. Suitably sized warning signs will inform the firm's personnel and visitors when they are entering an area likely to be covered by the cameras, which will state the purpose of the scheme, the person responsible for it, and whom to contact in respect of it. The cameras do not have a sound recording facility. Any recordings will be kept for no longer than [31] days, unless they are required for evidential purposes in any legal proceedings. After that they will be erased.

4A.3.12 Recordings may only be watched in a restricted area, under the supervision of [*name or title*]. Any request for access to or disclosure of recordings should be made to him/her, and will be logged by him/her. Third party access will only be granted in accordance with the code of practice. Subject access requests will also be dealt with as described in the code.

Subject access requests

4A.3.13 Any individual whose data is held by the firm may make what is called a 'subject access request', i.e. a request to see what data is actually held about them. All such requests should be addressed in writing to the [*name or title*] and (s)he will arrange for the firm to comply promptly with the request.

4A.4 E-mail

> In relation to e-mail use the policy should specify: suitable business use; suitable personal use; the legal implications of e-mail (e.g. defamation and harassment); security issues and standards (e.g. viruses and 'spam' communications); criteria for the use of e-mail notices (e.g. disclaimers, etc.); whether the practice will accept service electronically; and procedures for electronic storage of e-mail.
>
> It will be necessary for the firm to establish its policy on the use of its e-mail system in the course of business. Given the sensitivity over issues such as monitoring of personal messages, the e-mail policy should also be regarded as a condition of employment; similar considerations apply to the use of the internet. It will apply to all staff including temporary and contract staff. The objective is to ensure that the firm and employees gain maximum benefit and avoid exposure of the firm and its employees to any legal liability.
>
> The matters below should be considered for inclusion in the policy.

Sending and receiving e-mail

- The use of automatic messaging systems
- The checking of attachments
- Opening other employees' e-mail
- Replying to e-mail
- The use of lengthy attachments
- The forwarding of e-mail
- Practice information to be included in an e-mail

E-mail protocol

- The content of e-mail
- The style of e-mail
- Prohibited uses (e.g. defamatory or obscene e-mail)
- Permitted personal uses of e-mail
- Forbidden personal uses of e-mail

Legal issues

- Avoidance of negligent, misleading or defamatory statements
- The conclusion of contracts by e-mail
- The giving of undertakings by e-mail
- The issue and acceptance of proceedings by e-mail
- Compliance with Law Society requirements on stationery use vis-à-vis e-mail

Security

- The employment of encryption and digital signatures
- The employment of virus scanning software

E-mail notices

- Confidentiality
- Disclaimers
- Copyright
- Virus protection
- Contracting by e-mail

The position on monitoring of both e-mails and internet use is particularly complex. The firm will need to comply with the provisions of the Regulation of Investigatory Powers Act 2000; the Telecommunications (Lawful Business Practice) (Interception of Communications) Regulations 2000, SI 2000/2699; the code of practice of the Information Commissioner (June 2003); and the Human Rights Act 1998 relating to monitoring. This is achieved by determining:

- how monitoring will be undertaken;
- the software installed on the firm's network to track network activity;
- how the results will be treated;
- disciplinary proceedings if appropriate as a result of any breach.

The policy should be read, understood and accepted and the employee should thereby agree to the firm monitoring e-mail messages transmitted and received in the course of work.

4A.4.1 E-mail is routinely available to all personnel through the firm's computer network [or *include what access there is within the firm. For example, there may be a single designated access point for the firm or perhaps access points for each specialist department, both for incoming and outgoing messages*].

4A.4.2 The following guidance is given to ensure that the facility is properly used and not abused. If there is any doubt or concern, reference should be made to [*name or function*]. If a suspicious e-mail message is received, for example from an unidentifiable sender, especially with attachments, it should not be opened. Particular caution is needed where the message is from a familiar source but there is no text in the message. In such circumstances please telephone the sender before opening that attachment to see if they have indeed sent a bona fide message to you. Alternatively, please refer the issue to the IT supervisor or the supervising partner. Where there is still doubt, the message should be deleted without being opened.

4A.4.3 The overriding principle is that e-mail messages are to be controlled and processed to the same standards as for normal correspondence. Because e-mails, both received and sent, are processed on an individual personal computer, in the majority of instances without the knowledge of a supervising partner, there must inevitably be a high degree of trust from everyone in the use of e-mails. [*If all e-mails are processed on a designated computer(s), describe the control procedure*]

4A.4.4 The arrangements in relation to messages are as follows.

Incoming messages

- All incoming messages related to client work must be printed out and a hard copy placed on the appropriate client file.
- As appropriate, the fee earner is to refer any message of substance to the supervising partner, either by direct discussion or by forwarding an additional copy of the message to the partner.
- Any suspicious or offensive messages received are immediately to be referred to the [*supervising partner/system controller*].
- No undertaking may be accepted by e-mail – a signed letter must be received.
- If a fee earner is away from his/her desk for half a day or more, the auto-office message should be set and the relevant secretary is to check for any e-mails received and should refer messages to the supervising partner.

Outgoing messages

- As appropriate, outgoing messages of substance must first be approved by the supervising partner before being transmitted. [*Where the firm operates checking of outgoing post it will need to consider what arrangements apply with e-mails*]
- A printed copy of outgoing messages is to be placed on the relevant client file.

- Undertakings are not to be given by an e-mail message. On approval of undertakings in general see section 8.18.
- No potentially offensive messages are to be sent. Defamation, harassment and breaches of the firm's discrimination policy are all potential risks. Please also be wary of the temptation to send off a hasty message that, on reflection, would seem unwise. A good rule is to place your initial response in your drafts folder or reply later or the next day if annoyed or offended by action taken or a communication received: allowing yourself a 'cooling-off period' can avoid putting yourself in the wrong.
- The following e-mail distribution lists are stored in the address book:

  - all personnel;
  - all partners;
  - all fee earners.

  [Specify others and details of any protocol or limitation on sending out messages to the whole firm: e.g. personal messages to go on a notice board facility, etc.]

- All e-mails are to be restricted to the firm's professional work *[or state arrangements for personal e-mails]*. In particular, e-mail sent for the purpose of publicising the firm and its services, to clients, introducers or stakeholders must conform to legal and regulatory provisions as referred to in the Solicitors Code of Conduct 2007, Rule 7. [See the 2007 Code, subrule 7.07 and guidance notes 18 and 19 to Rule 7. See also the following guidelines on the sending of unsolicited e-mails.]
- Always check the state of attachments to see that you are sending the correct draft. Be particularly wary of drafts that might have been amended without your knowledge by someone outside the firm – client, opponent or other. Where this is a risk you should attach the document as a pdf that cannot be amended (see IT trainer/IT administrator if you do not know how to do this).

Deletion of e-mails

4A.4.5 It is the responsibility of the individual to review regularly all stored messages and delete those that are no longer required. Please be aware that all incoming and outgoing messages on client matters must be regarded as being normal correspondence and are therefore subject to the normal retention periods. Fee earners are in any event asked to ensure that printed copies of messages, including draft documents, have been placed on the client file before deletion of messages [*or, where the firm operates an electronic storage system, elaborate on the technology, procedures and responsibility for management*]. Please remember that deleted e-mails are still actually stored on the system and could be accessed in future: legal actions have been brought on the basis of incriminating, 'deleted' e-mails.

Virus protection

4A.4.6 The firm's e-mail facility is protected by [*name the system*] and regular protection updates will be received and must be actioned on each individual personal computer. The updates will initially be received on the central computer server [*or describe how*] and the IT supervisor [*name*] will then direct a copy of the update to each PC and will advise individuals by an e-mail message that an antivirus update needs to be actioned. This is done by opening the antivirus program on the PC desktop screen [*describe procedure*]. All antivirus updates are to be processed without delay.

4A.4.7 Nobody may introduce to their PC any disk without the permission of the [system controller/other]. Failure to seek his/her permission before doing so will be treated as a disciplinary offence.

4A.5 Website management policy

■ A policy regarding the practice website should specify the practice's policy on: the management of site content (e.g. facilities for disabled users); the use of disclaimers; jurisdiction and applicable law in respect of site content; linking to other sites; copyright issues; and privacy of data collected from site visitors.

4A.5.1 Management of the content of the firm's website is the responsibility of [*name or position*]. This includes:

* ensuring content is up to date;
* ensuring content does not infringe copyright;
* specifying conditions for downloading material;
* ensuring any publicity conforms to the Solicitors Code of Conduct 2007, Rule 7;
* ensuring compliance with the Disability Discrimination Act 1995;
* ensuring posting of a privacy notice explaining how any data collected from visitors will be managed by the practice.

Jurisdiction and applicable law

4A.5.2 The website will specify that the jurisdiction and applicable law to be invoked as that of [England and Wales] [*or specify any other to be invoked and the circumstances*] in the event of any dispute arising as a result of content posted on the firm's website.

Linking

4A.5.3 The decision to link the firm's website with that of any other organisation will be that of the partners. Linking arrangements will be governed by a contract signed on behalf of the practice. Management of any linking arrangements will be the responsibility of [*name or position*].

4A.5.4 The contract will:

- specify sites to which the firm's website is linked;
- address any legal and business implications;
- specify the circumstances of accessing the linked site;
- include relevant disclaimers;
- address copyright issues.

4A.6 Internet use

A policy regarding use of the internet should specify: the general policy of the practice; suitable business use; suitable personal use; the legal implications of using the internet (e.g. downloading copyright or obscene material); and security standards.
Firms should therefore consider setting out their approach on:

- typical permitted uses in the course of the firm's business;
- the need to ensure accuracy of information downloaded;
- acceptable personal use;
- prohibited uses, including copyright issues.

Issues of security also require attention, in particular:

- the need to observe security requirements;
- security procedures in place, e.g. passwords;
- the type of security installed;
- breaches of security requirements and disciplinary proceedings.

4A.6.1 Access to the internet is possible from [*specify*]. Acceptable uses of the internet are as follows:

- legal research [*specify any sites or services that the firm subscribes to*];
- client or practice research;
- [*specify any other acceptable uses*].

4A.6.2 Common uses of the internet within the firm include: [*provide list of sites where formal links are established – e.g. Land Registry, research agencies, etc.*].

4A.6.3 Any other personal or social use of internet facilities must be kept to a minimum and in no circumstances should any individual within the firm peruse sites that could reasonably be regarded as pornographic or offensive, unless it is necessary to do so in pursuance of client instructions.

4A.6.4 Users must also be wary of breach of copyright from inappropriate downloads.

4B Reception and telephone facilities

4B.1 Premises

4B.1.1 The standard of repair and decoration of the firm's premises, both internal and external, will be maintained through a budgeted rolling [five] year programme prepared by the practice manager and approved by the managing partner. The reception area, including the main office door and the adjacent windows, and the interview rooms, may require more frequent attention.

4B.1.2 The extensive window area at street level and the reception area itself provide important opportunities to display marketing materials about the firm. This must be kept up to date and changed regularly. Professional help in the design of materials is provided by [*name of company*].

4B.1.3 An untidy office does not create a good impression. While it is accepted that files being worked upon and paper in general cannot be hidden, every endeavour is to be made to keep the office tidy during the day and in the evening. In particular, fee earners should tidy their own offices before a client appointment if they are not to use one of the designated interview rooms.

4B.2 The client appointment procedure

4B.2.1 For a potential new client, the enquiry for an initial appointment will normally be made by telephone or through visiting the reception in person. If enquiry is by telephone, the first impression the client gains of the firm is by the manner in which the call is answered. Invariably the name of the firm should be clearly given [*state preference: 'Good morning, Bloggs & Co' or 'Bloggs & Co, may I help you?', etc.*]. If the call is taken by anyone other than the telephonist, it is good practice to give a name ('Mrs Bloggs speaking'). The tone should be friendly, interested and professional.

4B.2.2 The telephonist will need to ascertain what the client enquiry is about and then transfer the call to the appropriate department where the enquiry can be dealt with more fully. Please bear in mind that until the telephonist has transferred the call (s)he is prevented from dealing with any other incoming calls.

4B.2.3 It is understood that for many reasons fee earners are not always immediately available to speak to new clients. Therefore each department is required to designate a secretary or a fee earner on a [daily/weekly] rota basis to be available for dealing initially with all new client enquiries. The telephonist and receptionist are to be informed. Outline information about the client's concerns is to be obtained for it to be passed to a designated fee earner. If at all possible an appointment should be agreed then or it may be necessary for the fee earner to agree it later. The objective is to show the client that something is being done without delay and in a professional manner, and to secure a new client matter.

4B.2.4 If a new client has called in person to reception, then similarly the receptionist is to ascertain what the client wants and then pass the enquiry to the relevant department for processing. All personnel should avoid a conversation about possible services occurring in the reception area (see section 7.3).

Conveyancing quotation

4B.2.5 Some enquiries will be specifically for obtaining a conveyancing quotation. These enquiries are to be directed immediately to [name or names] in the property department who [has/have] responsibility for this task. It may be possible to arrange an appointment at once but often the caller will not make a commitment there and then. In either circumstance, the quotation is to be confirmed in writing that day and is to include a copy of the firm's [client services] leaflet.

Confirmation of an appointment

4B.2.6 If time permits, an appointment is to be confirmed in writing supported by the firm's [Client Services] leaflet which includes a location map of the office and details of parking facilities.

Parking

4B.2.7 There are [four parking bays for clients in the car park at [location]]. These are strictly not for use by the firm's personnel. Parking reservations are to be made through the receptionist. [Alternative public parking is nearby at [location].]

Interview rooms

4B.2.8 There are three small interview rooms (one for disabled persons) and a conference room suitable for meetings of up to 12 persons, located on the ground floor adjacent to reception. If these are to be used, a reservation should be made with the receptionist.

Appointment notification to receptionist

4B.2.9 All appointments in the office are to be notified to the receptionist who will maintain an appointments diary for the office. It creates a good impression if it can be seen that a client is expected.

4B.3 Telephone calls

4B.3.1 The firm's objective is to ensure that incoming calls are answered promptly. At peak times, when the volume of incoming calls may be too much for the telephonist to deal with without delays, a proportion of the calls will be cascaded to designated secretaries to act as temporary telephonists.

4B.3.2 The procedures for telephone answering are as follows.

Telephone switchboard

4B.3.3 The telephonist will give the name of the firm and 'good morning' or 'good afternoon'. The telephonist will ascertain the identity of the caller and the person they wish to speak to. (See section 4B2 for appointment/new work enquiries.)

4B.3.4 The call will be put through to the relevant person as required by the caller, and announced. If that person is not at his or her desk then he or she should have redirected the telephone to whoever is delegated to take the calls.

[*or*: The call will be put through to the relevant fee earner's secretary. The switchboard should announce who is calling and the person the caller wishes to speak to. The secretary should greet the caller by name and say who she is and her role.]

4B.3.5 When the caller requires to speak to someone who is not on the firm's premises the caller will be told that the person is 'out of the office' or 'at a meeting'. It is important that the client is not given the impression that someone else's business is more important than theirs. The telephonist should indicate when the person is expected back before being asked if the caller would wish to leave a message with the relevant secretary.

Individuals' extensions

4B.3.6 Any person answering a telephone, whether the call is internal or external, is to answer with his/her name. It may be appropriate on external calls to explain role e.g. 'secretary to X' as well.

4B.3.7 Any fee earner who leaves his or her desk for longer than a few minutes is required to divert his or her telephone to a secretary, or another member of the firm, for message taking purposes. It is not necessary to notify the switchboard, only the person to whom the telephone has been diverted. [*In most firms automatic divert arrangements will have been arranged and these might be explained here*]

4B.3.8 Group 'pick-up' systems apply to teams of secretaries. Answer another phone in the group by picking up your own phone and pressing [*specify*].

4B.3.9 Fee earners should notify their secretary of the period in the day when they will return any calls that come in when the fee earner is unavailable. This:

- gives a client a time when (s)he will call back;
- prevents the client from calling again before the stated times;
- give a business-like and efficient impression to the client.

Personal calls

4B.3.10 Short, local personal telephone calls are allowed. All other calls should be made with partner consent. You may also receive incoming personal calls, whether on the firm's system or your own personal mobile phone, but please be sure to keep these calls to a reasonable period of time.

[*It may be helpful to include here information on the features of the firm's telephone system, e.g. how to transfer calls; how to divert calls; how to 'camp on'; stored telephone numbers; short codes; group-call facilities. Alternatively, cross-refer to a separate telephone instruction list*]

Direct lines

[*If direct telephone lines are provided to fee earners, include guidelines on how they are to be used*]

> A clear benefit of direct lines is that they reduce any volume pressures on the main switchboard, but if a fee earner widely gives out his or her direct line number, this is automatically inviting interruptions for the fee earner. Selective issuing of direct lines numbers is often the more sensible option.

Voicemail

[*If voicemail facilities are in use state whether they will become active before a call transfers from a fee earner's extension to a secretary – i.e. are calls routed first to the voicemail or to a secretary first?*]

4B.3.11 It is the fee earner's responsibility to check incoming voicemail messages and to respond to them promptly or arrange for a message to be given to callers. If you are out of the office for longer periods of time, please record a specific voicemail message 'It is Monday 5th March and I shall be in court all morning. Please leave any message and I will return your call this afternoon.' It is essential that any dated message is brought up to date without delay.

Mobile phones

[If mobile phones are provided to fee earners, include guidelines on how they are to be used]

■ The use of mobile phone is now commonplace and for many solicitors the use is no more than another office facility. However, a firm may well want to issue guidelines on the use of mobiles such as whether the giving out of individual numbers should be restricted in any way, its views on permitted private use and a ban on use while driving unless hands-free.

4B.4 Facsimile (fax)

4B.4.1 Although e-mail correspondence has to a large extent reduced the volume messages by fax, it still remains an important means of communication with the firm's clients and professional contacts. Fax machines are located as follows:

[Location]	*[Number]*
[Location]	*[Number]*
[Location]	*[Number]*

4B.4.2 While there is no restriction on using fax for transmitting correspondence or documents, the facility should be used with common sense and not just because it is available. The general rules are:

- If there is no urgency to get the document to the addressee on the same day, use the DX or normal mail, first or second class.
- Unless essential do not follow up a fax transmission by sending the original copy by mail.
- Remember that while an outgoing message is being transmitted the fax machine cannot receive an incoming message which may be genuinely urgent.
- For outgoing messages, the standard fax transmission sheet is to be used. This is stored as a standard precedent document.
- Secretaries are responsible for sending their own fax messages including the re-transmission of messages that have become corrupted.

[In many firms there may be further departmental fax machines where numbers are not given out to clients. Elaborate here if so]

4C Post and communications

4C.1 Incoming mail

4C.1.1 All incoming post is to be opened in the presence of a partner or, if a partner is not available, in the presence of [*name and appointment*]. This forms an important component of the overall supervision structure of the firm.

Morning post

4C.1.2 The opening of the main morning post is supervised by a partner, organised on a rota basis. The post opening will commence at [*time*] in order to ensure that the post is distributed by [*time*]. Often substantial amounts of monies are received by cheques and these are to be controlled and passed to the accounts department without delay.

Later post

4C.1.3 Other post can be received throughout the day, usually delivered to reception. It is important that such post is processed properly and expeditiously. The receptionist will inform the office assistant of receipt, and(s)he is to take the post for it to be opened in the presence of a partner, or the practice manager if a partner is not available, and for the post then to be distributed to the relevant department. Hand deliveries can often be marked urgent and the receptionist is then to ensure that the delivery is passed direct to the departmental partner or other partner without delay.

4C.1.4 Post is not to be left on reception desks or anywhere else un-actioned.

Unidentifiable mail

4C.1.5 Where it is not possible to identify the intended recipient of an incoming letter, for example, because there is no reference, it should be placed in the [daily folder] and taken to the [*name or title*]. [*Name or position/office manager*] is first to endeavour to identify the recipient through searching the client database and if this fails, the office assistant is to be instructed to take the letter around the firm to identify the recipient. In exceptional circumstances it may be necessary, if possible, to telephone the sender.

4C.2 Outgoing mail

4C.2.1 Secretaries are responsible for delivering outgoing mail to the general office by no later than [*time*] daily. Post Office mail and Document Exchange mail is to be separated. The juniors will frank the post and take it by hand to the Post Office [*or specify other arrangement*]. It is greatly appreciated by all concerned if batches of post can be with the general office as early as possible to avoid the daily last minute rush [*or* All mail is to be placed in the appropriate basket and will be collected throughout the day].

Document Exchange

4C.2.2 The firm is a member of the Document Exchange (DX) system – a privately operated postal system to which most solicitors belong, together with banks, building societies and barristers' chambers. All secretaries have access to the DX Directory of Members. The DX system is cheaper for the firm to use and is often more reliable. It is to be used in preference to the Post Office whenever possible.

Class of mail

4C.2.3 All mail to be sent by the Royal Mail is sent first class unless second class is stipulated by the originator.

Business reply service

4C.2.4 On occasions, clients may be asked to return documents, etc. to the firm. A supply of first class business reply labels is available for this purpose.

Courier service

4C.2.5 Also, there will be occasions when it is necessary to send mail or documents by means of a courier service when normal postal services will be insufficient. When this is required, the fee earner concerned is to make the necessary arrangement though the [general office].

4D Health and safety

◼ A sample health and safety policy is set out in section 1. A number of more detailed procedures are set out in this section of the manual.

The Workplace (Health, Safety and Welfare) Regulations 1992, SI 1992/3004 complete a series of six sets of health and safety regulations implementing EC Directives, and have replaced a number of old and often excessively detailed laws. They cover a wide range of basic health, safety and welfare issues and apply to most workplaces, including offices.

Employers have a general duty to ensure, so far as is reasonably practical, the health, safety and welfare of their employees and others.

Although working in an office is likely to be less risky than working in a factory, nevertheless accidents do happen and need to be safeguarded against. There is a wide range of extremely helpful publications, many of them free, on health and safety topics that affect office working that are available from the Health and Safety Executive (HSE). Further free advice can be obtained from the Health and Safety Inspector at your local council, usually located in the Environmental Health Department, or from the HSE itself. For details of HSE advice and publications see **www.hse.gov.uk** or **www.hsebooks.co.uk**.

4D.1 Health and safety at work

4D.1.1 The firm is required to inform you of its general policy to look after your health and safety while at work in its offices, and the organisation and arrangements for carrying it out.

4D.1.2 The firm's general policy is to make sure, so far as it is able, that everyone in the firm's offices has a safe and comfortable environment in which to work. The firm is not aware of any unusual hazards to your health and safety and provided reasonable care and common sense is used in carrying out your work, there should be nothing more dangerous encountered here than you would encounter in your own home. The policy can be consulted in full at [*specify link*].

4D.1.3 [*Name*] has been appointed health and safety manager for the firm and has responsibility for advising the partners on health and safety issues and for monitoring standards and for carrying out the annual review of health and safety risks. If you have any concerns about possible health and safety issues, please raise them at once with [him/her].

4D.2 Legislative background

4D2.1 In undertaking [his/her] duties the health and safety manager will take all necessary steps to acquaint [him/herself] with relevant legislation and its development. There are many legislative provisions that potentially apply to the firm, but particular attention will need to be paid to:

- the Health and Safety at Work etc. Act 1974;
- the Health and Safety (Display Screen Equipment) Regulations 1992, SI 1992/2792;
- the Workplace (Health, Safety and Welfare) Regulations 1992, SI 1992/3004;
- the Provisions and Use of Work Equipment Regulations 1998, SI 1998/2306;
- the Management of Health and Safety at Work Regulations 1999, SI 1999/3242;
- the Control of Substances Hazardous to Health Regulations 1999, SI 1999/437.

4D.3 External advice

4D.3.1 The health and safety manager (or others to whom [(s)he] may have delegated responsibilities in this field) may from time to time need to seek external expert advice on health and safety matters. In such cases, among the agencies and businesses they may contact are [*list those which the firm may use*].

4D.4 The role of personnel in health and safety issues

4D.4.1 The law provides duties for employees as well as employers. It is your responsibility to take care in relation to your activities both in relation to yourself and in respect of your colleagues and others who might be affected by your actions. A prime source of assistance for the maintenance of proper working conditions is the help of all personnel throughout the firm. This may take any of the following forms:

- Personnel exercising their own judgement in taking suitable precautions to ensure not only their own health and safety, but also that of all those who may be affected by what they do, or leave undone.
- Participation in consultation exercises that may be arranged with regard to health and safety matters [whether through the staff liaison committee or otherwise].
- Actively supporting the firm's health and safety programme by complying with such procedures as may from time to time be laid down.
- Participating in such training as the firm may arrange.
- Reporting to the health and safety manager any relevant concerns they may have.

Risk assessments

4D.4.2 The firm will take all such steps as are reasonably necessary to ensure proper working conditions for everybody. In order to enable that to be done, the health and safety manager will undertake suitable and sufficient risk assessments, whether by [him/her] or by anyone to whom [(s)he] delegates the task. Any such assessor will need to be trained in the task, and have sufficient knowledge of both current health and safety legislation and standards, and the work processes operated by the firm. Assessments will be repeated as often as circumstances (including in particular any changes to the firm's work, premises or equipment) may require. The health and safety manager will retain records of all such assessments.

4D.4.3 The purpose of such assessments is to detect any potential problems before any damage or accidents occur, in order to identify any measures that can be taken to remove or reduce risk. While it is not intended to limit the scope of such assessments, they will at least cover the following matters, which are commonly recognised as potential risk areas within an office environment:

- floors;
- waste disposal facilities;
- furniture;
- electrical equipment, including:
  - VDUs;
  - printers;
  - photocopiers;

- lighting;
- ventilation;
- heating;
- fire precautions;
- water and sanitary facilities.

4D.4.4 When assessments are carried out, account will be taken of any particular vulnerabilities, e.g. for young persons, for those who are pregnant or nursing, or for those who are known to have any illness or disability. All assessments will be reported on by or to the health and safety manager. Such reports must include details of any problems discovered. It is then the responsibility of the health and safety manager to:

- take such steps as may be needed immediately to ensure safety;
- undertake such consultations, e.g. with the assessor and personnel in the affected area, as may be appropriate to identify appropriate remedial measures;
- take such remedial steps, if that lies within [his/her] authority; or
- report the matter to the firm's management, to agree what steps are to be taken, and then implement them;
- monitor subsequently the effectiveness of the steps taken.

> There is increasing focus on employee stress claims and it should be noted that there is a duty under the Management of Health and Safety at Work Regulations 1992, SI 1992/2051 to conduct risk assessments to establish psychological and physical issues that are a risk to health. The employer's duty to safeguard an employee from stress-related illness was set out in *Sutherland* v. *Hatton* [2002] IRLR 263, CA.

4D.5 Circulating information

4D.5.1 The health and safety manager will take all such steps as may be reasonably practical to inform all personnel of health and safety issues which may affect them, by any or all of the following methods.

- training;
- written information;
- warning signs and notices.

In exercising this responsibility the health and safety manager will have particular regard to the matters which concern visitors to the firm's premises, as well as to the firm's own personnel.

4D.6 First aid

4D.6.1 The firm will at all times maintain no fewer than an adequate number of suitably trained first aiders at its premises. Those first aiders will have been trained in accordance with the requirements of the Health and Safety Executive. The firm will consider providing such training, at its cost, to any personnel who may wish to volunteer for it, and they should contact the health and safety manager to discuss this. First aid boxes will be kept at [*location*] and/or such other places as may be notified to personnel. The health and safety manager will be responsible for ensuring that they are replenished as and when needed.

4D.7 Accident book

4D.7.1 A book is kept by the health and safety manager in which are recorded details of all accidents which happen to personnel, whether on the firm's premises or elsewhere when on the firm's business. It is essential that details of such accidents are fully and properly reported.

4D.8 Central heating

4D.8.1 The heating in the offices is by means of [*heating type*]. The system is regularly checked and if necessary overhauled. If anyone has any reason to suppose that any system is not working properly, or if, for instance, there should be a smell of gas, (s)he should inform [*name of health and safety manager*] or a partner immediately.

4D.9 Working on VDUs

4D.9.1 It is important that any user of a VDU helps the firm to ensure their safe working conditions by taking adequate precautions to ensure that they are using the VDU in a safe manner. These include:

- making adjustments to their positioning so that they are comfortable when using the VDU and can look at it with their head in a natural and relaxed manner;
- taking short breaks from the VDU, to do other tasks, at least once an hour;
- avoiding eye strain or glare.

4D.9.2 If any of the above proves difficult, the operator should contact the [health and safety manager/IT partner]. (S)he will investigate whether the firm ought reasonably to make any adjustments and, if so, will arrange for them to be made. If any operator is concerned that the use of a VDU may be affecting their eyesight then the firm will, at its expense, provide an eye test by a qualified optician of its choice.

4D.10 Smoking

▓ Previous editions of this book have tracked the progress towards a smoke-free working environment. At first there were tentative moves to prevent new employees from smoking at work and the suggestion was made to 'politely ask' clients and other visitors not to light up while on the premises. The Health Act 2006 enabled the Smoke-free (Premises and Enforcement) Regulations 2006, SI 2006/3368 to be passed into law, which duly took effect on 1 July 2007. It is now an offence to smoke, or for employers to fail to prevent smoking, in an area that should be 'smoke-free'. Much of the publicity surrounding the introduction of the Regulations concerns what amounts to 'enclosed' or 'substantially enclosed' places that are open to the public in which the ban must apply. The issue of whether any employees are contractually entitled to 'fag breaks' will also need to be considered and whether a facility can be constructed out of doors that will satisfy the Regulations. There have also been arguments that employers should be compelled to assist staff to cease the habit. More clear-cut are the provisions in the Health Act 2006 requiring 'no smoking' signs to be displayed.

4D.10.1 Smoking is not permitted anywhere on the firm's premises and, since the law changed in July 2007, it is an offence to smoke anywhere within the offices. 'No smoking' signs are clearly displayed in the reception area and meeting rooms and clients and other visitors who do ask to 'light up' must be told not to do so. To permit anyone to smoke while on the premises leaves the firm open to criminal prosecution.

[*Specify whether the ban applies while driving in the course of work duties also*]

4D.10.2 Staff are not permitted to take 'smoking breaks' outside the firm's premises, as this is considered to place an unfair burden on non-smoking colleagues and is, in any event, discouraged by the new legal regime [*or state the scope of any such permission*].

4D.11 Control of Substances Hazardous to Health (COSHH)

4D.11.1 There is legislation covering COSHH. Fortunately, in an office environment there are relatively few substances that might be hazardous to health but there are some such as photocopier toner, typing-correction fluids and kitchen cleaning materials. Where appropriate, the firm has endeavoured to store the main supplies of these substances separately and safely.

4D.12 Teleworkers

4D.12.1 Some personnel within the firm may from time to time make arrangements, with the approval of the firm, to work from home or from another remote location. The firm is responsible for their health and safety when undertaking work in such circumstances. The following points arise:

- The worker should discuss any health and safety problems with the health and safety manager.
- The health and safety manager or [his/her] delegatee will need to undertake a risk assessment in respect of the place from which the person is working. If that is the worker's home, then access is subject to the worker's agreement, and should be by prior agreement. The assessment may only be carried out by the worker himself if he has been trained in respect of risk assessments. The assessment will apply to both the workplace itself and the equipment to be used in it.
- A first aid box should be available.
- Accidents while working at home should be reported to the health and safety manager.
- The principles as to manual handling apply to personnel working from home in the same way as to office-based personnel.
- The use of VDUs is subject to the same provisions as in section 4D.9 above.

■ The Smoke-free (Premises and Enforcement) Regulations 2006 apply to offices used by more than one person, so will not generally apply to those working at home for the firm.

4D.13 Personal security arrangements

4D.13.1 The firm is concerned to ensure the personal safety and security of all personnel, whether in the office or elsewhere on the firm's business. All personnel should comply with such security precautions as the firm has provided, such as locking and access control arrangements, and burglar alarms.

4D.13.2 A panic button is installed in the firm's reception area. If used, it emits a [continuous ringing tone]. If that is heard, all available personnel are asked to go to reception to render assistance.

4D.13.3 The safety of personnel going to meetings out of the office is also a concern. If anyone is going to a meeting with someone they have not previously met, and they are not going to be accompanied, they should ensure that reception knows exactly where they are going, who they are meeting, and what time they are expected to return. If there is subsequently any change in those arrangements, they should inform one of their colleagues in the departments by telephone as soon as possible.

4D.14 Security of premises and property

4D.14.1 The firm's premises are protected by a burglar alarm system. Details of the operation of this, and of the access control system, will be given to those who need to know about them.

4D.14.2 When leaving the premises, all personnel should check that all windows in their area are closed, and that all electrical equipment is switched off (unless notices indicate that particular machines should be left on).

4D.14.3 All personnel are responsible for the security of their own property. They should be aware that this might not be covered by the firm's insurance.

4D.15 Electrical equipment

4D.15.1 Everyone uses electrical equipment as part of their daily work. Personnel must use common sense and caution when dealing with electrical equipment in the office as they would in their own homes. If anyone suspects that equipment, plugs or the supply may be faulty (s)he must report it at once to [*name of health and safety manager*] or a partner.

4D.15.2 Maintenance checks will be carried out periodically by [*name or title*].

4D.16 Fire instructions

> There have been major statutory changes to this area. The Fire Precautions Act 1971 and its considerable supporting legislation was replaced in October 2006 by the Regulatory Reform (Fire Safety) Order 2005, SI 2005/1541. The main impact of the new regime is that the safety of premises in relation to fire risks is no longer certified by the Fire Service through the fire certificate procedure. In its place there is now a need for the practice to appoint a 'responsible person' who will be required to undertake a fire risk assessment. A person can only be regarded as 'competent' if they have undergone the requisite training. This person might like to obtain a copy of an HSE publication, *Fire Safety – Risk Assessment: Offices and Shops* (TSO, ISBN 1851128158).
>
> If the practice does expect people to attempt to put out the fire by the use of fire extinguishers as below it should organise training in their use, given the duty under health and safety legislation to provide staff with training in the use of equipment they are expected to use.

Immediate action to be taken

4D.16.1 If you discover a fire:

- Raise the alarm.
- Attempt to put the fire out if possible with the appliances provided but without taking personal risks.

4D.16.2 Once the alarm has been raised:

- Call the Fire Brigade immediately.
- Evacuate the premises.

4D.16.3 All staff are to assemble at [*location*]. Do not stop to collect personal belongings. Do not re-enter the building until told it is safe to do so.

> ■ Detailed fire instructions, which must be individually considered for each office, should then follow. These need to be based on the fire risk assessment that the competent person must arrange. Some sample headings follow by way of illustration only.

Fire alarm

4D.16.4 The office is fitted with a fire alarm system. Glass breakage points are located at each exit.

4D.16.5 As normal procedure, the fire alarm system is tested at about [*day and time*]. Staff will be notified if other tests or maintenance are carried out on the alarm system. From time to time fire drills will be carried out [*specify if warnings will be given*].

Fire protection in the strong-room

4D.16.6 A fire protection system is fitted in the strong-room. The system will automatically be activated if a fire starts in the strong-room.

Fire extinguishers

4D.16.7 Fire extinguishers are provided throughout the office buildings and extinguishers for use on electrical equipment are provided where required. A maintenance inspection of extinguishers is carried out annually.

Fire wardens

4D.16.8 The following persons have been designated as fire wardens with the prime responsibility for ensuring that the building(s) is/are evacuated quickly and safely and for carrying out a roll call at the assembly point.

[*List of names*]

Fire signs

4D.16.9 There are signs throughout the premises showing the exit routes in the event of an alarm.

▨ Note that under the Health and Safety (Safety Signs and Signals) Regulations 1996, SI 1996/341 words-only signs are illegal and should be replaced by those that include a pictogram. A compulsory colour-coding system for notices also applies including red for prohibition (e.g. do not enter lifts) and blue for actions that are mandatory.

4E Office facilities

4E.1 Photocopying

4E.1.1 Each area of the office is supported by modern photocopiers with [automatic feed and double-sided print features]. The copiers are rented from [*name of company*]. In addition to the basic rental charge, a separate copy charge is levied based upon the volume of copies. The cost of the copiers and copy paper is substantial and all personnel should take care to use them responsibly and not waste copies unnecessarily.

4E.1.2 The cost of all but one of the copiers is absorbed as part of the firm's general overheads. The copier that is located in the [general office] is especially designated for large copying tasks undertaken by the office assistant. This copier is connected into the accounting system so that copies required for client work can be costed and charged direct to the related client matter as a disbursement. The present copy charge is [*x*p per copy].

▨ Some firms include provisions on personal photocopying by staff, imposing similar restrictions of reasonable use as for telephones. If this seems appropriate, include here.

4E.2 Office equipment

4E.2.1 The firm has made a substantial investment in office equipment, computers, copiers, scanners, telephones, facsimile, etc., by which we provide support to our clients. It is the firm's policy to have service maintenance contracts for all main equipment. [*Name or title*] is responsible for arranging maintenance contracts and for keeping the supporting documentation.

4E.2.2 Most service contracts include a minimum call-out time in the event of unserviceability and this will vary depending upon the importance of the item of equipment. A call-out should be requested by the person identified below:

- computer equipment (servers, scanners, modems, PCs) – [IT supervisor];
- computer software problems – [practice manager/IT supervisor];
- copiers – [office manager];
- telephones and facsimile – [telephonist].

4E.3 Library and know-how

4E.3.1 The firm maintains a legal reference library which is sufficient to meet most of the needs of fee earners. [*Name*] has been appointed as library partner and [his/her] responsibilities include the following:

- to ensure that the library material is regularly and promptly updated;
- in consultation with other partners and fee earners, to purchase new books, and control directly expenditure within the library budget;
- to ensure that the library index is kept up to date;
- to ensure that potentially dangerous out-of-date material is removed from the library;
- to review law journals and [*The Times*] for changes in the law and other relevant legal information, and for the prompt circulation of such information to all concerned fee earners.

[*Name*] assists the library partner with much of the administrative support work of the library.

4E.3.2 Circulation lists for certain journals are in use. Please ensure that journals are passed on within a reasonable time limit. Daily law reports from [*source*] are placed at [*location*].

4E.3.3 All fee earners are expected to contribute towards the maintenance of the firm's library by advising the library partner when consideration should be given to the acquisition of new books or the removal of out-of-date material.

4E.3.4 Internet searches can be conducted as follows [*specify procedures*].

5 People management

Introduction

Law firms are people organisations first and foremost. The service provided to clients is based on having the right numbers of people throughout the practice with the appropriate skills and abilities to meet the needs and demands of their roles. Partner and staff morale is also key to providing a quality service – something clearly influenced by how well people feel that they are managed. The practice will need to recruit, retain, train, reward and motivate its workforce so as to maintain and develop the service provided.

For the most part the section in Lexcel dealing with the area of people management requires a number of personnel management devices to be in place. There is some overlap with the section on policies and, as elsewhere, it is a matter of choice for firms whether they have all their policies here, in section 1 or elsewhere. A further alternative is to have the main policy in section 1 and the more detailed procedures in this section. Somewhere there will need to be the miscellaneous general provisions that tend to be at a level below contract terms and can be found in many firms in a separate 'staff handbook' document. The illustrative procedures that follow are intended to cover most of the common issues that arise, but are unlikely to be comprehensive.

Personnel plan

There may be little point in a sole practitioner who employs no staff in developing a personnel plan, but the larger the practice the more important this element of planning becomes. In larger firms preparation of the personnel plan will be a substantial exercise in its own right, carried out by the partners or employed personnel professionals in line with the firm's main strategic plan. In smaller firms the personnel plan is likely to be little more than one section of a general business plan or simply one element of the departmental plans. However achieved, it is important that the personnel plan has some form of direct link with the business plan. There needs to be a clear picture of where the firm is now, where it wants to go in the short and longer term and the recruitment and development needs that this will generate. Investment in recruitment and training is likely to represent a significant cost for most practices. It makes sense, therefore, to keep some form of control over this item as part of the planning process. The Lexcel standard requires recruitment and development to be addressed. The former requirement for welfare and entitlements has been removed, but is likely to be addressed in the contract of employment and the general staff procedures.

Resourcing

The usual process of quantifying recruitment needs is to question:

What is the current establishment?

- How many people does the firm have at what level and in what areas of the firm?
- What are their competencies and abilities?
- What changes will be needed as a result of the current business plans for the practice?

Projecting forward

- How many of the current complement are likely still to be in place over the period of the plan allowing for likely retirements, estimated leavers, maternity/paternity leave plans where known, and other changes?

The other elements of the strategy will then need to be addressed:

- If growth or contraction is planned, how will this adjust the likely personnel needs?

Ideally it should then be possible to state a forecast of likely recruitment needs as:

Recruitment needs = (current resources ± adjustments) ± (practice growth or retraction)

From this simple arithmetical calculation it should be possible to review how the firm will identify and fill vacancies and over what timescale (see the Lexcel standard at section 5.3 on recruitment). Alternatively, if the plans dictate a future reduction in headcount, this will also have to be addressed, possibly with the formulation of a redundancy policy or plan. See annex 5A for a pro forma personnel plan outline.

Development

The second part of the exercise is to assess development and training needs. This may well be a separate training plan, but could form part of a personnel plan, again driven from the overall business plan for the firm. Either way, the steps are to:

- assess current skills, using regular (as a minimum, annual) reviews of performance;
- consider developments in the work of the firm, the way that it will be organised and any development of roles;
- consider the needs of those joining the firm; and thus
- draw conclusions on the training programme required and the most appropriate arrangements to achieve it.

Recruitment and selection

One of the most obvious ways to improve the quality of service provided is to ensure that the right decisions are made in relation to partner and staff appointments. Viewed another way, there is considerable risk to the practice in making unsuitable recruitment and promotion decisions. It is useful to break the appointments process into two parts: recruitment (attracting a range of suitable candidates) and selection (choosing the appointee). Job descriptions are a useful tool in clarifying roles and responsibilities and required for all personnel by section 5.2 of Lexcel, though not necessarily in a conventional job descriptions format. They help to establish relationships within a practice and, if used properly, should ensure that everyone understands what is expected of them. They are not a legal requirement as such, and it should be made clear that they are for guidance only and do not form part of the contract of employment, if this is indeed the case. It should be added that various regulatory codes of practice covering discrimination recommend job descriptions as the first step in any recruitment campaign since they are likely to make the process more objective than might otherwise be the case.

It is only fair to add that job descriptions are not without their detractors among human resources professionals. The concern is sometimes expressed that they might be limiting for the organisation. This can be mitigated by making it clear that the job description is general and illustrative rather than contractual (as mentioned above). Another option is a 'sweep-up' clause added to any list of responsibilities along the lines of: 'perform any other duties the partners require'. This could be seen to devalue the more specific clauses that precede it, but in practice the employment tribunals will apply a reasonableness test in any dispute over duties arising from it.

Although most obviously useful in settling the firm's needs of the jobholder and clarifying to the appointee what will be expected of them, job descriptions are also helpful in the subsequent appraisal or review process. The departure of an employee offers a good opportunity to review the current situation. Every vacancy represents an opportunity to reconsider the position and see whether the role has changed, or needs to be changed in some way. The temptation to replace like with like as soon as the vacancy arises may be understandable, but should be avoided.

A job description should include:

- a job title;
- a summary of how the role fits in to the practice – positioning and reporting lines;
- a short description of the major objectives of the role; and
- a list of the major tasks.

Following on from a description of the job itself, the next stage is to create a description of the ideal candidate in the format of a person specification, using the requirements of the job description. A person specification describes the job in terms of the characteristics necessary for successful performance. It should therefore include items such as:

- the standard of experience, skills or education required;
- the standard of training required;
- any special skills or attributes needed;
- particular qualifications that are essential for the job;
- circumstances (i.e. must work away from home);
- previous experience;
- personal disposition (assertive, flexible, confident).

There are obvious risks of discrimination in the person specification exercise which will need to be taken into account by those undertaking it. The risks can be avoided by not making the person specification too restrictive. A clear distinction should be made between those characteristics that are considered to be essential for the successful performance of the job and those which are merely desirable. Any candidate who does not possess all of the essential criteria should be rejected at the shortlist stage, and it can be useful to consider how the firm would feel in discarding an otherwise excellent candidate for that reason. It should also be borne in mind that it is no longer acceptable to insist on a certain level of qualification simply to control the number of applicants. There are also much publicised risks in insisting on a level of post-qualification experience which cannot be justified as this could amount to a breach of the Employment Equality (Age) Regulations 2006, SI 2006/1031.

The Disability Discrimination Act 1995 (DDA 1995) makes it unlawful to specify any physical requirements that are not seen as being essential to the successful performance of the job. The DDA 1995 requires employers to make reasonable adjustments to the job, or the workplace, in order to accommodate any disability. General comments such as 'must be fit and healthy' need careful thought and should be expressed as a specific job requirement if justifiable – must be able to drive or operate a keyboard, for example.

Competency frameworks have become an increasingly popular way to deal with the requirements of a person specification. A competency is a set of skills or behaviours that an individual needs to bring to a job in order to perform that job with competence. Competencies should thus link the behaviours of the individual with the job and explain how the person should apply their knowledge, skill and experience to achieve their objectives.

An example would be:

Duties: To answer the telephone.

Competencies: Answer all telephone calls promptly, professionally and courteously. All callers must be greeted in accordance with firm policy and no caller should be left waiting for more than xx minutes without contact from telephonist.

A well-developed competency framework can form an alternative to a job description and this would be possible under Lexcel, which requires job documentation to be 'usually' in the form of a person specification.

It is important to keep job documentation under regular review, as by referring to it in appraisals and any other personal reviews.

Sample job descriptions can be found in annexes 5B to 5H. Further guidance on a person specification is contained in annex 5I.

▨ Recruitment and selection – the legal background

Discrimination claims have become more common at employment tribunals in recent years. Quite apart from the reputational harm of a claim being brought against the firm compensation awards in discrimination cases are unlimited, since they can include an element of damage to feelings. The Employment Tribunal Service has reported discrimination compensation payments approaching £200,000 in recent years. Little wonder that an increasing number of professional firms require any personnel to be trained in the recruitment process before being allowed to expose the firm to such risks.

Organisations such as the Disability Rights Commission (DRC), the Commission for Racial Equality (CRE) and the Equal Opportunities Commission (EOC) have created codes of practice to assist employers and those involved in the recruitment process will be expected by a tribunal to have an awareness of the content of such codes. The disparate nature of the legal provisions and the accompanying codes is far from ideal and the government has declared its intention to consolidate both the various laws and the responsible bodies. The Commission for Equality and Human Rights (CEHR) replaced the DRC, CRE and EOC in October 2007. The various codes may differ in content, but a consistent theme in recruitment is the importance of fair selection criteria, involving the use of job descriptions, person specifications, trained personnel and good record keeping. It is beyond the remit of this book to set out a detailed summary on discrimination law and there are numerous texts that can be consulted (see e.g. Jenny Mulvaney, *Discrimination in Employment* (Law Society Publishing, 2006)). It is useful to note here, however, some of the most significant practical recruitment risks on discrimination and related topics.

Disability

Initially the DDA 1995 did not apply to smaller businesses, but this is no longer the case. The size and resources of the firm will be taken into account, however, if there is a dispute over what is 'reasonable'. Employers are legally obliged to make reasonable adjustments to their recruitment processes, the work or indeed the workplace in order to ensure that disabilities are accommodated where possible.

Since December 2005 certain illnesses such as most cancers, multiple sclerosis and HIV became classed as disabilities from the point of diagnosis, thus reducing the burden on claimants of having to demonstrate they fall within the Act. As with sex and race discrimination, the legislation applies not only to employees, but also to prospective employees, contract staff and self-employed workers.

It is important to be aware of the requirement to make reasonable adjustments and these need to include interview arrangements. Thought should be given to the location of interviews and it is advisable to check in advance if an individual has (for example) hearing, sight or mobility requirements that will require special arrangements to be made. (See annex 5K.)

Religion and belief

The Employment Equality (Religion or Belief) Regulations 2003, SI 2003/1660 apply to employment and vocational training and cover job seekers too. In the employment context, it is now unlawful to discriminate in relation to recruitment, terms and conditions, promotions, transfers, dismissals and training on the stated grounds. Two limited exceptions will apply to the principle of non-discrimination: first, where being of a particular religion or belief is a genuine occupational requirement or qualification for a particular job and, secondly, where the employer has an ethos based on a particular religion or belief. This should not be taken to mean that a Christian or Muslim firm can insist on appointing members of that faith only, however. If it were to arise as a disciplinary matter the Solicitors Regulation Authority (SRA) would be likely to question whether faith was an integral element of that particular role.

'Religion or belief' is defined in the Regulations as meaning 'any religion, religious belief or … philosophical belief'. This fairly broad definition has been strongly criticised by a number of commentators, who make the point that defining a religion or belief can be a far from straightforward process. ACAS's guidance, however, states that in the event that a dispute goes to a tribunal, it will be obvious in most cases what is and what is not a religion or a belief. While it is clear that people who belong to established religious traditions – such as Jews, Methodists, Catholics and Muslims – are covered, the Explanatory Notes to the Regulations (which admittedly have no legal force) from the Department of Trade and Industry (recently renamed the Department for Business, Enterprise and Regulatory Reform (DBERR)) suggest that tribunals may consider a number of factors when deciding what is a 'religion or belief' including whether there is collective worship, a clear belief system, or a profound belief affecting way of life or view of the world. In April 2007 the protection was extended to those who have no religious belief.

Sex and sexual orientation

The Employment Equality (Sexual Orientation) Regulations 2003, SI 2003/1661 were also introduced in 2003 to deal with discrimination or harassment on the ground of sexual orientation, which is defined as meaning 'a sexual orientation towards (a) persons of the same sex; (b) persons of the opposite sex; or (c) persons of the same sex and of the opposite sex'. The law therefore protects people from discrimination whatever their orientation.

It should also be borne in mind that any decision not to appoint a woman on the ground of her pregnancy alone is liable to be discriminatory on the ground of sex.

Age

From October 2006 the Employment Equality (Age) Regulations 2006, SI 2006/1031 added age discrimination to the list of unlawful practices in the UK and the area also therefore became an element of the professional regulations on the topic. Age discrimination legislation now:

- covers all types of worker, including employees, self-employed, agency staff, partners and those undertaking vocational training;
- applies to all stages of employment from recruitment, training, pay, benefits, promotion and dismissal to post-employment discrimination (covering references, for example);
- prohibits direct discrimination, indirect discrimination, harassment and victimisation;
- extends to individuals of all ages and outlaws discrimination against the young as well as the old; and
- enables complaints to be made in employment tribunals for unlimited compensation.

In exceptional cases, age might be a 'genuine occupational requirement' (GOR) for a particular job, for example as an actor or possibly a model. It remains to be seen whether a firm could impose an upper age limit for trainee solicitors or legal executives on the ground that they should be able to recoup their investment over a number of years. Much clearer is that age limits in job advertisements are no longer permitted unless an age limit is a genuine requirement of the job, which will be unlikely in most law firms. Terms such as 'dynamic', 'energetic', 'senior' or 'mature' should obviously be used with caution, however well intentioned they may be.

Trade unions

It is unlawful for an employer to refuse employment on the grounds that an individual is a member or is not a member of a trade union. If an applicant feels that he or she has been denied a job, or the opportunity of a job, because of trade union membership, he or she has the right to complain to an employment tribunal.

The Rehabilitation of Offenders Act 1974

This Act makes it unlawful for employers, or prospective employers, to take into account offences that are deemed under the legislation to be 'spent'. After a certain period of time, which depends on the seriousness of their offence, the person concerned should be treated as if the conviction had never taken place. Candidates may legitimately omit to give details to employers and such offences must not be considered in the selection process. If an employer discovers that an employee has a spent conviction, and takes action against the employee, this will be unfair. Solicitors and barristers, however, are within the range of exceptions, meaning that all previous offences should be disclosed, and questions can be asked about any previous offences.

The Criminal Records Bureau (CRB) is an agency of the Home Office which enables employers to investigate the criminal records of job applicants (or indeed existing staff) if they choose to do so and where relevant for the job in question.

Part-time workers

The Part-time Workers (Prevention of Less Favourable Treatment) Regulations 2000, SI 2000/1551 make it illegal to treat part-time workers less favourably than a full-time worker carrying out similar work at the same establishment. Although not directly covered by the 2007 Code, Rule 6, part-time workers do feature in guidance note 5(b) to Rule 6. The law also applies to recruitment and selection, so part-time workers should not be offered terms and conditions of employment that are inferior to those of a full-time person doing similar work. Since this legislation applies to all 'workers' – not just employees – casual members of staff, agency personnel and homeworkers are also protected. The provisions also need to be borne in mind when planning training and at internal selection procedures. Part-timers who are women will also often be able to claim indirect sex discrimination over many part-time issues, as the majority of part-time workers are female (see, for example, *Sinclair Roche & Temperley* v. *Heard (No.1)* [2004] IRLR 763, EAT).

Fixed-term contracts

The Fixed-term Employees (Prevention of Less Favourable Treatment) Regulations 2002, SI 2002/2034 give fixed-term employees the right in principle not to be treated less favourably than permanent employees of the same employer doing similar work. Although less favourable terms may be justified on individual items in the contract, the overall package must not be less favourable than that of a comparable permanent employee. The Regulations give fixed-term employees the right to ask for a statement of reasons for less favourable treatment and require employers to provide such a statement in 21 days. Failure to renew a fixed-term contract on termination amounts to dismissal for the purposes of unfair dismissal.

Asylum and Immigration Acts

The government has introduced changes to the types of documents employers are required to check in order to avoid employing illegal workers. It is a criminal offence for an employer to employ someone, aged 16 or over, who has no right to work in the UK, or no right to do the work offered. Checking and copying certain specified original documents provides the employer with a statutory defence against conviction for employing an illegal worker. The checks must be carried out before the person begins employment with the firm, so candidates for interview should be asked to bring the documents with them. There are risks in assuming that certain candidates are British and requiring only those who are assumed to be foreign nationals to produce documentation – to do so may result in the employment of an illegal immigrant or alternatively might be regarded as discrimination. If employees are recruited through an agency the checking and copying of documentation is still the employer's responsibility.

Access to Medical Reports Act 1988

This Act allows a person to have access to a medical report about him or her where it is prepared by that person's own doctor. During the recruitment process, some employers require medical reports. Applications to a candidate's medical practitioner require the candidate's permission and the candidate has the right to see the report before it is released to the employer and to request amendments to the content. Ultimately the person has the right to stop the report from being sent to the employer. Reports that are prepared by a specialist, however, are not covered where these are the result of a medical examination.

Recruitment and selection – best practice guidelines

The following best practice guidelines might be helpful when embarking on any recruitment exercise:

- Ensure that all interviewers are adequately trained.
- Use proper selection techniques including structured interviews based around identified competencies, appropriate selection tests, job descriptions, person specifications, etc.
- Keep an accurate record of each interview, any test results and any references obtained. Be aware of the Data Protection Act and guidelines covering the recruitment process.
- Follow the codes of practice produced by the EOC and the CRE, the code of practice on the employment of disabled people produced by the DRC and the recruitment code issued by the Chartered Institute of Personnel and Development.
- Consider paying reasonable travelling expenses even if they are not asked for, particularly where individuals have travelled some distance and especially if they are unemployed.
- Clarify at the interview stage, if you have not done so previously, when references will be obtained and whether medicals will be required.
- Notify unsuccessful candidates as soon as possible. No reason has to be given to candidates at this time, but it is recommended that you keep a clear note of why a candidate was turned down and then provide feedback if requested.
- Apprise recruiters of the implications of the Data Protection Act and Human Rights Act covering the right to protection of confidential information and the right to privacy.
- There is no one authoritative view on the use of application forms, though organisations such as the Commission for Racial Equality were in favour of them. The SRA does not currently insist on the use of forms or monitoring the profile of applicants, but this position could be subject to change at a future date. A sample form appears at annex 5J.

Recruitment and selection – the process

There are four main phases of a recruitment campaign:

- identifying and describing vacancies;
- attracting candidates;
- shortlisting and final selection process;
- pre-joining checks and contact.

Identification of vacancies

Responsibility for recruitment may rest with a number of individuals within the firm. Increasingly, human resources professionals are playing an important role in the process.

There may well be different partners or managers in charge of fee earner recruitment and trainees as opposed to secretarial and administrative appointments. If planning is in place (see 'Personnel plan' above) a practice's recruitment requirements will be defined in advance as far as is possible and the case for taking on new staff will be evident. When a resignation is tendered the following questions should be asked:

- Is the job still valid? What is the volume of work this person is doing at present and could it be done any other way, e.g. has IT taken some of the administrative burden from the job or would outsourcing be a better option? Have the job boundaries changed? Could the work be done elsewhere by other means?
- Is the role a 'whole' or 'part' workload?
- Is this a development opportunity for anyone else in the practice offering some promotion potential?

If it is evident from such analysis that the job still exists then the recruitment process can proceed, in which case the job description should be reviewed, taking into account any changes to do with the position and how it fits into the overall situation. This is more likely to lead to a more appropriate advertisement and will provide better details on the role for candidates. Various other codes and the Specialist Quality Mark of the Legal Services Commission require an 'open' recruitment process. In practice this will mean avoiding the exclusive use of word of mouth recruitment and the 'old boys' network.

If the practice decides to advertise, it is important to use words that are gender neutral and photographs or illustrations should not lend support to the idea that only one particular group of applicants is invited to apply. There is no requirement for law firms to carry an equal opportunities statement, and if a firm does do so it must be prepared to back this up. If the placing of a sentence in advertising is in fact the sole commitment to an equal opportunities policy, this will not influence courts or tribunals in the event of a discrimination claim and may even count against the firm.

Selection methods

It is easy to overlook the fact that selection is a two-way process: the firm will wish to select the right candidate, but the candidate will also be assessing whether they will wish to accept a job offer. This suggests that the greater the professionalism of conducting the selection process, the greater the prospect of the firm appointing the desired candidate. Clarity as to the selection process should help to identify a suitable candidate as efficiently as possible.

An increasing number of firms seem willing now to employ different techniques beyond interviewing, such as psychometric or ability tests, and to make assessments based on activities such as delivering a short presentation. Where personality testing is used it is essential that it is professionally administered. The interview continues to hold sway, however. For guidance notes see annex 5L.

Induction

The induction process should ensure that the individual feels comfortable in his/her new role and is also therefore productive for the firm as soon as possible. Risk management is also a consideration – the firm is clearly exposed to greater risk of errors while the process of adjustment continues. An effective induction process will shorten this adjustment period. Lexcel requires that the induction process should occur within a reasonable time, while the SQM stipulates within a period of no more than two months (see D2.1). Both standards require or suggest that the induction process should extend to those transferring roles within the firm (in SQM see Guidance to D2.1; in Lexcel section 5.4). An induction training form can be found at annex 5Q.

Contracts of employment

The contract of employment should be seen as the cornerstone of the relationship between employer and employee. Superimposed upon this are a large number of statutory rights and restrictions, along with terms and conditions reached through collective agreements if there is a recognised trade union at the firm. The contract also gives rise to enormous potential uncertainty since it does not have to in writing to be valid (despite the statutory obligations to provide written particulars) and can include terms implied by custom and practice, which can be difficult to define.

Employment legislation requires all employers to provide a written statement of terms of employment. This is not the contract as such but contains most of the relevant information about the employee's terms. This must be issued within eight weeks of the employee starting work and is best issued as part of the recruitment process rather than separately at a later date. If all of the information is provided as part of an employment offer there is no obligation to issue it again. (Guidance on statement of terms of employment is contained at annex M; a sample precedent contract of employment is at annex N.)

The statutory statement must contain the following particulars:

- the names of the employer and employee;
- the date on which employment began;
- the date on which the employee's period of continuous employment began (taking into account any employment with a previous employer that is to be included);
- the rate of remuneration and the intervals at which it is paid;
- terms relating to hours of work;
- terms relating to holidays;
- terms relating to sickness absence and sick pay;
- any terms relating to pensions;
- the notice period;
- job title;
- the length of time employment is to continue, if not permanent;
- the place of work;
- any collective agreements that affect the terms of employment;
- details of any work outside the UK;
- details of any disciplinary procedure, including how to appeal and details of a grievance procedure;
- a statement as to whether a pensions contracting-out certificate is in force.

During employment – personnel policies

Employment-related policies covering a range of issues are likely to be in place at most firms already. The range and content of the policies will largely be determined by the size and prevailing culture of the business. Larger firms may well wish to provide an employee handbook, either in hard copy or, more commonly, via their intranet.

Where the firm does not enhance or improve on the rights and benefits provided by employment legislation, it is sufficient to refer to the statutory position. This will probably be the case in most smaller firms. Here it is appropriate to have the following type of statement:

The firm does not have any sick pay scheme other than statutory sick pay.

or

The firm complies with the statutory maternity leave and pay rights conferred by relevant legislation. If you have any questions regarding maternity rights and pay, see the office manager. If you are pregnant you should inform the office manager at the earliest opportunity so that appropriate health and safety action is taken.

and

There is no disciplinary policy other than the statutory disciplinary and grievance procedures, details of which can be found [*specify*].

Some other employment policies might be classed as essential while others are considered worthwhile but not essential.
It is recommended that firms (particularly larger firms) have policies that cover:

- absence rules and sick pay entitlements;
- whistleblowing;
- maternity, paternity, adoption, parental leave and pay;
- flexible and part-time working;
- stress management policy;
- smoking, alcohol and use of drugs;
- home working rules (where appropriate).

Some of these matters are covered in annexes 5M, 5ZA, 5ZB and 5ZC, but for more information or a policy designed for your firm, see **www.eltraining.co.uk.**

Objective setting and performance appraisal

The performance appraisal or review is essentially an opportunity for the individual and those concerned with the individual's performance – usually their line manager – to get together to engage in a dialogue about the individual's performance and development, also the support required from the manager. It should be a genuinely two-way process with a constructive conversation in which a range of views is exchanged.

Performance appraisals usually review past contributions and so provide an opportunity to reflect on past performance, but the emphasis should be more on the future. There should ideally be no surprise comments, with past issues having been dealt with at the time. The interviews should mainly be a basis for making development and improvement plans and reaching agreement about what should be done in the future. There will need to be a process of setting performance objectives for all personnel within the practice – partners included – ideally followed by some form of affirming review at a later stage. This is not to say that the review process needs to be the same process for all personnel and it may well be in smaller firms that very much less detailed paperwork is appropriate for partner reviews than would be the case for employees.

The underlying philosophy of this system of performance management is that all personnel are likely to do better when they have a clear idea of how their contribution to the firm is viewed and also how it should be improved or developed. The objectives should be informed by the overall strategy of the firm and the appraisal meeting should shape the individual's contribution to its achievement.

Performance appraisals work well where:

- the appraiser has prepared well for the meeting and has raised difficult issues in advance;
- there is an opportunity for genuine two-way discussion;
- there is time to explore views;
- the atmosphere is not intimidating or oppressive, but the appraiser is in control of the process nonetheless;
- any criticism is specific and fair examples can be provided;
- both appraiser and appraisee are looking to concentrate on future improvements, not allocate blame for what might have gone wrong in the past;
- clear, specific objectives can be agreed for the (year) ahead;
- a clear action plan, be it training activity or other, is agreed;
- there is monitoring during the year, if the firm operates an annual process, so that the discussion is not simply forgotten until appraisal time next year.

The five key elements of the performance appraisal are:

- **Measurement** – assessing performance against agreed targets and objectives.
- **Feedback** – providing information to the individual on their performance and progress.
- **Positive reinforcement** – emphasising what has been done well and making only constructive criticism about what might be improved.
- **Exchange of views** – a frank exchange of views about what has happened, how appraisees can improve their performance, the support they need from their managers to achieve this and their aspirations for their future career.
- **Agreement** – jointly coming to an understanding by all parties about what needs to be done to improve performance generally and overcome any issues raised in the course of the discussion.

There is no one right way to conduct an appraisal. Some firms develop an appraisal form with space for appraisers to rate appraisees on aspects of their work such as their contribution to the team, role development, effectiveness, etc. The approach will depend on the nature of the business and the people involved. It is helpful, however, to have a form to collect consistent information on the appraisal. Annexes 5R to 5Y contain review forms and guidelines.

As a general rule it is helpful to have some information on the following:

- **Objectives** – whether they were achieved and if not the reasons why.
- **Competence** – whether individuals are performing below, within or above the requirements of the role.
- **Training** – what training the individual has received in the review period and what training or development they would like to receive in the future.
- **Actions** – a note of any actions that need to be carried out by the individual or the appraiser.

There is a view that the content of appraisal discussions should be confidential to the individual and the appraiser, but this may well be unrealistic or inappropriate in many firms. Other people might legitimately need to access the information and others again might be involved in storing the records. Some thought needs to be given to who will see the documentation and why, and this should be set out in the paperwork to comply with data protection principles.

Most firms prefer to conduct all appraisals in a set timeframe. This enables the firm to plan its training for the period ahead with a better overall view of training needs. Some firms do prefer, however, to conduct the review on the anniversary of the individual joining the firm.

The first appraisal schemes in law firms date from the 1980s when individual performance-related pay was at its height. Most early systems were therefore ratings based, with scores of A–E or 1–10 for each assessment. Most firms have since abandoned ratings in preference for a comments-only form and this is reflected in the sample forms that follow. The advantages of requiring a comment instead of a mark are:

- It can be too easy to apply a mark and discussion may not be encouraged.
- Middle banding often occurs in ratings-based systems – as long as the shape of marks looks acceptable the process seems to have been properly conducted.
- Inconsistencies between different appraisers can lead to appraisee resentment.

The objectives which come out of the meeting should conform to the oft-quoted mnemonic of being 'SMART':

Specific
Measurable
Achievable
Realistic
Time-limited.

This can be more straightforward for financial targets than others: e.g. to bill £100,000 with a recovery rate of no less than 95%. The value of appraisals is generally seen as being more to do with the 'soft' elements of performance, however, in areas such as:

- personal efficiency;
- motivation;
- client manner;
- internal working relationships;
- new skills and responsibilities.

There are different considerations in relation to partner appraisal schemes. In larger firms differential profit-sharing arrangements are becoming more commonplace, but these can be divisive and their implementation needs great care. A well-functioning partner review scheme will certainly help with any such developments.

The conventional advice on linking pay and rewards into the review scheme is that to do so can result in the employee seeing the meeting as little more than pay bargaining, which is then likely to fail to provide the quality of discussions that should be hoped for. The focus should be more on development and target setting for the performance review to be really beneficial to the employee and the firm. For this reason the general advice is to conduct salary reviews and performance reviews separately, preferably at different times of the year.

■ Training

Training should ideally be more than simply collecting continuing professional development (CPD) hours. Important though compliance may be, training should be a more important consideration for everyone in the practice, regardless of role or status. Training needs for each employee should be identified through the performance appraisal process. Other training needs might stem from the business plan for the firm, which will indicate the business aims and objectives for the next few years. The Lexcel standard requires all personnel to have their training needs assessed at least annually. The firm should be concerned to ensure that all training is relevant, appropriate and effective. Many firms have found in recent years that better management of training can lead to substantial savings on budgets. The most likely way to achieve this is to evaluate training requests more carefully than might have been the case in the past and explore the prospects of conducting more training in-house or closer to the office.

For details of how to obtain an in-house CPD authorisation agreement allowing the firm to apply CPD hours to its own training meetings, or for up-to-date information on the training requirements, contact the Training Department of the SRA at Redditch.

5.1 General policy

5.1.1 The firm recognises that the quality of its service to clients depends directly on its partners and staff and strives to provide the sort of working environment that will enable you to do your best in all your duties for the firm. As part of this commitment the partners urge you to raise problems with us without delay. The firm will address all problems that may arise with consideration and a resolve to help where possible.

5.1.2 All offices open at 9 am and close at 5.15 pm. Generally, employees have one hour for lunch, taken between 12.00 noon and 2.30 pm and finish work at 5.15 pm. Reception remains open the whole working day.

5.2 Holidays

5.2.1 The holiday year runs from [*month* to *month*]. The partners attach considerable importance to all staff taking their full holiday entitlement. Unused holiday entitlement may only be carried forward in exceptional circumstances, by special arrangement with [*name or title*].

5.2.2 It is the responsibility of all staff, and particularly of fee earners, to ensure that arrangements are made for their work to be covered while they are away. Holiday dates must therefore be agreed in advance with [*name or title*] who also has responsibility for ensuring that clashes of holiday dates do not deprive the departments of adequate supervision. The firm reserves the right to refuse permission for staff to take a holiday at any specific date but may only do so if this refusal is notified to the staff member within one week of receipt of their request.

5.2.3 Over Christmas and the New Year, it is important that departments are adequately staffed. Accordingly, holiday entitlement can only be taken over the Christmas and New Year period by prior arrangement with [*name or title*].

5.2.4 Employees have the following holiday entitlement [*specify*].

> ▨ Note that the granting of additional reward days for long service may now be subject to challenge under age discrimination provisions.

5.3 Absences

5.3.1 Any absence from the office through sickness, or any reason other than holidays, must be notified to [*name or title*], if possible, on the morning of the first day of absence. The details of the firm's sickness policy are outlined in employees' contracts of employment.

5.3.2 If a member of staff is absent in order to care for another family member, this does not count as absence through sickness. Any agreed period of absence to cover family sickness will count as unpaid leave, unless taken as annual leave.

> ▨ Under the Employment Relations Act 1999, employees have the right to take a 'reasonable' amount of unpaid time off to care for a 'dependant' who has become ill and in certain other emergencies, such as where the dependant has died or care arrangements have suddenly been interrupted. An emergency concerning a child's schooling is also covered. 'Dependant' includes a parent, spouse, child and anyone resident in the same house (except tenants or lodgers). Notice of intention to take the leave must be given to the employer as soon as is reasonably practicable.

5.3.3 There is no statutory requirement for the firm to grant paid compassionate leave. However, partners will determine applications for compassionate leave in special circumstances. Such leave is totally at the discretion of the firm and will be dealt with on an individual basis. It is recognised that compassionate leave is often requested on an immediate and emergency basis and that this is often not the best time to establish detail. Accordingly, the following are guidelines concerning paid leave:

- Domestic emergency: up to one day's paid compassionate leave would normally be granted where it is essential to sort out a domestic emergency, such as burst pipes or the aftermath of a burglary.
- Family illness/care of dependants: up to one day's compassionate leave would normally be granted in order to stabilise a problem and make alternative care arrangements for any dependant, e.g. partner, child, elderly relative, etc. This would normally be unpaid leave except in special circumstances.
- Serious illness: if there is a serious illness in an employee's immediate family, up to five days' paid leave of absence may be granted. Any further time off may be taken either as part of holiday entitlement or as unpaid leave.
- Bereavement: if there is a death in an employee's immediate family, paid leave of absence will be given to attend the funeral. Up to one week paid time off may be granted. Any further time off may be taken either as part of holiday entitlement or as unpaid leave.

- Employees who wish to apply for paid compassionate leave should contact [*name or title*]. Otherwise, the time off will be viewed as part of holiday entitlement.

5.4 Jury service

5.4.1 There is now no prohibition against solicitors and their staff being called upon to perform jury service, but staff would, of course, be prohibited from acting in any case in which the firm is participating or has an interest. The principles are:

- All requests for jury service should be made to [*name or title*].
- The Jury Summons document from the court must be produced when making a request.
- Employees should claim from the court the maximum amount to which they are entitled in respect of loss of earnings under the Juror's Allowances Regulations.
- If employees report for jury service and are not called upon to serve, they will be expected to attend work on that day if reasonably practicable.
- [*Name or title*] will make arrangements for pay adjustments if necessary.

5.5 Recruitment

5.5.1 The firm considers its recruitment and training needs as part of the annual business planning process. This forms part of [the main strategic review/office plans/the departmental plans/other]. [*Name of firm*] recognises the vital role that all personnel play in the development of the practice and is committed to providing rewarding careers for partners and staff alike. It is the responsibility of [*name or title*] to maintain and update the plan.

5.5.2 It is the policy of the firm that all personnel have agreed job descriptions. These are based on [one of the job descriptions shown in annexes 5B to 5H, if possible]. Other more individual roles are specifically agreed with the partners. Members of staff will be invited to comment on the appropriateness of their job description at every appraisal/career development review and to suggest any amendments. Such discussions will be considered by the partners and, if appropriate, an amended job description will be agreed and then placed on the individual's personal file.

5.5.3 An opening for a fee earner, whether through the departure of an existing member of any department or through growth of the firm, requires partnership approval. [It is the responsibility of the [managing partner/other] to draft the job description and a person specification.] [The job description and person specification is in the format contained at annex 5C.]

5.5.4 It is for the [managing partner/other] to determine the appropriate strategy for developing a suitable field of candidates. Methods employed include personal contacts from within the firm, the firm's own advertisement and recruitment agents. Consideration is always given to internal promotion once the job description and person specification have been determined.

5.5.5 Selection methods are confined to interviews. A first interview will be conducted by [name or title]. A second interview is normally held and will involve two interviewers, including a representative of the department in question. Fee earners will be asked about their disciplinary record. Following a decision to employ an individual, and with their consent, telephone references are taken. An interview assessment form (see annex 5O) will be completed in respect of each interviewee. Along with the accompanying interview notes this will be retained by [name or title] for no longer than 12 months. [Include details of any medical examinations]

5.5.6 Appointments of support staff are in line with the above procedures save that:

- first interviews are generally held by the administrative manager alone;
- keyboard skills are subject to appropriate testing as part of the selection procedures;
- a second interview is less likely, but if it does occur a fee earner will probably be required to assist.

5.5.7 The firm will often be asked to provide references on personnel who are leaving the firm or who have previously worked for it. References must be made or copied to [name or title] and must be accompanied by the following disclaimer: 'This reference should not be relied upon in any decision which the recipient is considering. We accept no liability for any decisions taken or not taken as a consequence of information provided in this reference, whether direct or indirect.'

[Set out here any separate arrangements for trainee appointments]

5.6 Induction

5.6.1 When people join the firm, it is important that they learn its practices and procedures as quickly as possible, so that they integrate within the firm in the shortest possible time. Induction is the responsibility of [state who is responsible for all inductions, or the different arrangements for different roles within the firm]. The induction process will cover the issues contained in the induction training form (see annex 5Q). Induction training commences on the first day of any appointment with a meeting with [name or title] on fundamental aspects of the firm and its main policies. The full process may continue later. Certain aspects may be relevant when existing personnel transfer roles within the firm. The full induction programme for staff (other than trainee solicitors) is carried out at least monthly and is the responsibility of [specify].

5.7 Objective setting and performance review

5.7.1 The firm operates a performance review system (appraisals) for all members of staff. There is a similar procedure at partner level. The system involves an annual discussion which includes the setting of objectives for the year ahead. The appraisal scheme is an opportunity to discuss the following:

- **Potential:** the appraisal provides feedback for the firm and individuals to ensure that each individual is meeting his or her potential.
- **Motivation:** appraisal allows each individual to know where he or she stands and to suggest what the firm can do to improve working conditions.
- **Development:** a means of assessing individual development. The appraisal will provide the opportunity for the firm and the individual together to assess skills, how those skills may be developed, how new skills may be acquired and what training and assistance from the firm is needed and can be given.
- **Views:** the appraisal provides an opportunity for individuals to air their views on the firm and its procedures, particularly if they feel that improvements can be made.

5.7.2 The characteristics of the appraisal scheme are that it should be:

- **Open:** the appraiser and the appraisee can be frank and open in the interview. Nothing recorded by the appraiser will be kept secret from the appraisee. Both parties will sign the appraisal form.
- **Confidential:** only the appraisee, the appraiser, the [departmental head and the managing partner] will see the completed appraisal report form.
- **Consistent:** the main procedures will apply to all staff (although there will be different appraisal forms for fee earners and for support staff). The managing partner will also review and monitor all appraisal reports to ensure fairness and consistency of treatment.
- **Objective:** the appraisal will focus on actual conduct, performance and personal attributes, and not on generalisations or personalities.
- **Self-assessed:** appraisees will be encouraged to contribute fully to the comments, problem solving, objective setting and conclusions that will come from the appraisal.
- **Forward looking:** a major value of reviewing past performance is to identify successes that can be built upon, problems that can be tackled by both the firm and the individual, training needs and new opportunities. Objectives for future action can be agreed.

5.7.3 With two exceptions, all staff will be appraised annually as follows:

- fee-earners: October;
- support staff: November.

The two exceptions are that trainee solicitors will be appraised six-monthly to coincide with their change of work area disciplines and assistant solicitors who have been admitted for less than three years will be appraised six-monthly.

5.7.4 [*Name or title*] will be the appraiser. Administrative support staff will be appraised by [*specify*].

5.7.5 [*Name or title*] will have responsibility for administering the appraisal procedures. (S)he will be assisted by [*name or title*] in the preparation and co-ordination of the appraisal documentation. The appraisal documentation will comprise:

- the appraisee's job description (individuals will already have their own copy but a copy will also be provided to the appraiser);
- a copy of the previous year's appraisal, which will be provided to both the appraisee and appraiser;
- a pre-appraisal questionnaire for completion by the appraisee, which will be discussed with the appraiser;
- an appraisal form.

5.7.6 The written objectives, pre-appraisal questionnaire and the appraisal form will be prepared and issued to the relevant appraiser at least two weeks before the date of the appraisal. The appraiser will then arrange an interview time with the appraisee making sure that sufficient time is given for the appraisee to consider and prepare for the appraisal interview and for completion of the pre-appraisal questionnaire which the individual will keep.

5.7.7 The appraiser will ensure that sufficient time is reserved for the appraisal interview to be carried out thoroughly. The appraisee will keep the pre-appraisal questionnaire and will be given a copy of the agreed objectives. At least an hour should be allowed for the appraisal. Avoid setting appointments immediately following the time allocated for the appraisal.

5.7.8 Following the interview the appraiser must ensure that the appraisal report is fully completed and signed by both parties so that the report can be forwarded to [*name or title*] within two weeks of the appraisal date. Although the form should be completed during the meeting, the appraisee should have the opportunity to read the appraisal form and sign it subsequently if (s)he wishes. The appraisal report will be put in the appraisee's confidential personal file and a copy will be provided to the appraisee.

5.7.9 An important part of the appraisal procedure is to agree objectives with the appraisee that will provide the framework for the coming year's work, including the continued development of the individual. Objectives will set a higher standard for performance than before, perhaps designate additional responsibility, or assign a new project.

5.7.10 It will be the immediate responsibility of the appraiser to follow up any action that was agreed as part of the appraisal. This may necessitate discussion with, for example, the departmental partner or the training partner. The appraisee should be kept informed of action being taken. It is also possible that the appraisee will be required to take some form of agreed action. In such circumstances, responsibility will rest with the appraisee as well as with the appraiser to ensure that action is taken. Where necessary the appraiser should arrange an interim follow-up interview and not leave matters until the next annual appraisal.

5.8 Training

5.8.1 It is the policy of the firm to maximise the job satisfaction and performance levels of all personnel through the provision of appropriate training, whether legal, management, ICT or other. Training needs are identified in appraisal interviews. All partners and staff should discuss any training needs that arise at any other time of the year with [name or title], who also maintains details of external training courses.

5.8.2 The firm regards the training and development of all members of staff as being vital to its future and to achieving its overall objectives. It is the policy of the firm to ensure that all personnel are competent to perform all tasks for which they are responsible and are developed in a manner that is appropriate for a forward-looking professional practice.

5.8.3 [Name] has been appointed as training partner for the firm with the responsibility for planning, co-ordinating and overseeing the firm's training needs and implementation. All staff share responsibility for the planning, implementing and evaluating of their own training needs. Training will, therefore, be a particularly important subject for discussion at each person's annual appraisal.

5.8.4 The practice subscribes to the [training organisation] subscription scheme and therefore qualifies for [percentage] discount on all training courses. External courses should generally be [training organisation] courses unless there is a course of particular significance organised by another provider.

5.8.5 There are now a substantial number of providers of legal training and frequently they market their course details direct to individual solicitors or other staff as well as to the firm itself. All staff are therefore encouraged to look out for appropriate courses to develop their professional skills and knowledge, especially if such courses relate to the training needs identified at the time of the annual appraisal.

5.8.6 A training record for all personnel, partners and staff will be maintained as part of the individual personnel records. In order to maintain the central records, individuals must evaluate all external courses attended using a training evaluation form. This also confirms attendance.

5.8.7 The partners are prepared to consider day or part-day release courses on merit from any member of staff. Applications should be made [specify]. The current policy on legal executive training is available from the training partner.

5.8.8 In order to review the effectiveness of training a feedback form (annex 5Z) must be completed by anyone from the firm attending an outside training course.

Similar forms will be distributed at any in-house sessions arranged by the firm.

5.8.9 Any fee earner attending an external course will be required to offer a lunchtime talk to explain the contents of the course.

5.8.10 Computer training for all personnel is conducted by [*name or title*].

5.8.11 Any further training needs should be raised with [*name or title*].

5.8.12 The training plan is determined each year by [*name or title*].

[*Describe here any special training methods, e.g. video updating services and arrangements for viewings*]

Annex 5A

Personnel plan outline

	YEAR 1	YEAR 2	YEAR 3
1. Current resource			
Partners Fee earners Trainees Secretaries Administrators			
2. Changes during the year ahead, e.g. planned growth, successful tender, etc.			
Partners Fee earners Trainees Secretaries Administrators			
3. Total needs (1 + 2)			
Partners Fee earners Trainees Secretaries Administrators			
4. Gains, e.g. trainee qualifiers, intake from merger, promotions			
Partners Fee earners Trainees Secretaries Administrators			
5. Losses: (a) Retirements (b) Turnover* (c) Promotions out of category			
Partners Fee earners Trainees Secretaries Administrators			
6. Total available (1 + 4 − 5)			
Partners Fee earners Trainees Secretaries Administrators			

	YEAR 1	YEAR 2	YEAR 3
7. Requirement (3 – 6)			
Partners Fee earners Trainees Secretaries Administrators			

* Turnover calculation:

$$\frac{\text{Number of leavers in a specified period (usually one year)}}{\text{Average number of employees during the same period}} \times 100 = \text{Turnover}$$

Annex 5B

Job description: partner

Job title:	Partner
Reports to:	The partnership/managing partner
Reported to by:	[Names]

Main purposes of role

1. Undertake and supervise fee earning work in [category] and supervise/deputise in the [work area].
2. Ensure the successful development of the firm in line with the strategy identified in the business plan.

Key tasks (not an exhaustive list)

3. In their personal fee earning work billings of at least £[amount] will be expected, other than where exceptional circumstances apply. These could include illness and/or absence, high profitability of team or substantial management contribution.
4. Perform fee earning work accurately, reliably and in accordance with the firm's quality and risk management procedures [Lexcel].
5. Ensure proper control of work in progress, billing and cash collection. As a guide [give details of targets].
6. Attendance at most or all partnership and other office or departmental meetings, leading by example with contributions made at and subsequent to such events.
7. Acceptance of need for collective responsibility and confidentiality: partner disagreements should not be disclosed to staff and confidential practice matters must be safeguarded.
8. Provide leadership and supervision to all staff that they oversee or supervise, whether on an office or departmental basis. All partners should provide direction and encouragement to staff and should be careful to support the practice line on issues. Cabinet responsibility should apply.
9. Be effective in developing new work from existing clients and seek new clients for themselves and others. Will develop and support marketing initiatives.
10. Maintain and nurture an appropriate network of contacts and referrers and endeavour to promote the firm in their professional and personal lives.
11. Gain or maintain IT skills appropriate to modern legal practice, such as ability to send, forward and respond to e-mails with or without attachments, conduct research on internet and ensure proper filing of all data.
12. Understand the main uses and applications of the office telephone system – e.g. be able to re-route calls, set up conference calls, etc.

Annex 5C

Job description: fee earner

Job title:	Fee earner
Reports to:	Head of department
Reported to by:	Secretary

Main purposes of role

1. Undertake fee earning work and provide a profitable contribution to the work of the department.
2. Ensure the successful development of the firm in line with the business plan.

Key tasks (not an exhaustive list)

3. Conduct of matters on behalf of clients.
4. Supervision of fee earning work undertaken by colleagues.
5. Management of support services for which (s)he is responsible, including supervision of own secretary.
6. Participation in marketing activities whether on a firmwide, departmental or office basis.
7. Financial control with particular regard to cashflow control through collection of monies on account and billing procedures.

Annex 5D

Job description: paralegal

Job title:	Paralegal
Reports to:	[*Name or title*]
Reported to by:	[*Name or title*]

Main purpose of job

1. To provide cost effective administrative and secretarial support to the partner and other senior fee earners in the team in the work of the department.

Key tasks

2. Undertake certain elements of fee earning work under supervision. In particular:

    - file creation;
    - generation of suitable client care correspondence;
    - completion of client questionnaires;
    - drafting of petition/court documentation;
    - attendance at routine directions/interlocutory hearings.

3. The jobholder is not designated as a matter handler for file review purposes and does not therefore have her/his own file caseload.
4. Deal wherever possible with routine client enquiries and communications.
5. Manage the collation of matter start and matter completion data and prepare all claims for costs, referring major matters to costs clerk by agreement with [*specify*].
6. Deputise for [*specify*] in their absence, passing urgent issues to another senior fee earner for guidance (if a small team).
7. Co-ordination of the key dates reminder system as outlined in the office manual.

Annex 5E

Job description: legal secretary

Job title:	Legal secretary
Reports to:	[*Name or title*]
Reported to by:	[*Name or title*]

Main purpose of job

1. The prime role of the legal secretary is to provide direct support to his/her principal to enable them to operate at optimum efficiency. This will include but will not be limited to the main responsibilities given below. The legal secretary is expected to use a high degree of self-management and initiative.

Key tasks

2. Prepare correspondence and documents through audio-typing and word processing.
3. Administer filing which will include daily filing and the opening, closing, storage and retrieval of client files in accordance with the detailed procedures contained in the office manual.
4. Prepare mail and enclosures for dispatch.
5. Arrange for all copying to be done, in person if the office assistant is not available to undertake the task.
6. Make appointments, arrange meetings and to maintain an up to date diary for his/her principal.
7. Prepare the conference room for meetings as necessary and for the tidying and clearance of the room at the end of the meeting.
8. Provide refreshments when asked to do so.
9. Provide support to other secretaries as required.
10. Provide guidance to junior and temporary secretaries when required to do so.
11. Attend clients both in person and on the telephone and to provide such support in a professional and friendly manner in keeping with the firm's standards for client care.
12. Undertake any specific training when required to do so and overall to have a responsibility towards self-development.
13. Ensure the confidentiality of all the firm's and clients documentation and information.

Annex 5F

Job description: receptionist/telephonist

Job title:	Receptionist/telephonist
Reports to:	Office manager
Reported to by:	[*Name or title*]

Main purpose of job

1. Process all incoming telephone calls without delay.
2. Receive and process all clients and other visitors to the firm in a helpful, friendly and professional manner.
3. In both of the above respects, there is a high degree of responsibility to project the image and ethos of the firm at all times.

Key tasks

4. The effective processing of all incoming telephone call including the logging of calls and the conveying of messages.
5. The provision of telephone support to partners and other staff members as required.
6. Deal with all visitors to the reception area especially new clients.
7. Administration of the facsimile machine.
8. Ensure the tidiness of the reception area.
9. Undertake other clerical and administrative duties as may reasonably be required from time to time.

Annex 5G

Job description: legal cashier

Job title:	Legal cashier
Reports to:	Office manager
Reported to by:	[*Name or title*]

Main purpose of job

1. Assist in the smooth running of the practice by attending to the various financial transactions arising from the work of the firm and its internal operation.

Key tasks

2. To undertake daily banking functions including bank reconciliations.
3. The administration and reconciliation of petty cash.
4. The processing of client and office accounting transactions including postings.
5. The preparation of cheques.
6. The processing of bank transfers.
7. The control of designated client deposit accounts.
8. The preparation of credit control advice.
9. The administration of the purchase ledger.
10. Financial management reporting as required.
11. The preparatory work for the annual accounts.
12. PAYE.
13. VAT administration and returns.
14. Administration of the partnership cars, office insurance, practising certificates, professional indemnity insurance, etc.

Annex 5H

Job description: office assistant

Job title:	Office assistant
Reports to:	Office manager
Reported to by:	[*Name or title*]

Main purpose of job

1. Assist in the smooth running of the practice by providing a range of support services within the general office function.

Key tasks

2. Deliver messages to the courts.
3. Undertake photocopying tasks.
4. Collect and distribute Document Exchange mail.
5. Deliver Document Exchange mail to [*scheme*].
6. Prepare post for dispatch.
7. Take special deliveries to the Post Office.
8. Return library books to [*local law library*].
9. Act as relief telephonist/receptionist.
10. Provide refreshments when asked to do so.

Annex 5I

Person specification guidance notes

Introduction

The job descriptions at annexes 5A–5H do not include person specifications. This will certainly be important when the job description is used as the basis for a recruitment exercise. Beware the risks of imposing conditions that are either discriminatory or likely to exclude good candidates. The following notes should assist.

Do you know what you're looking for?

In order to attract the right applicants, to be able to make a sound recruitment decision and to protect against claims of unfair treatment or discrimination, you need to establish at an early stage just what skills and qualities you are looking for in your ideal candidate.

Rather than basing your specification on the previous jobholder, for example, you might ask yourself the following questions:

- What skills must a person have to be capable of doing this job?
- What qualities will make them particularly successful in the role?
- What other abilities would be useful to them, either now or in the future?
- What sort of characteristics or behaviours would prevent them performing satisfactorily?

By answering these questions, you will have identified a number of skills and qualities, which fall into one of the following three categories: essential, desirable or contra-indicators.

Essential

Essential attributes are those that are vital to successful performance of the role. They should be clearly communicated to any prospective candidates. If a candidate does not possess essential skills, consider whether it will be possible to train them. If not, you must conclude that the candidate will never be able to perform the role satisfactorily and must therefore be rejected.

Desirable

Desirable attributes distinguish excellent performers from those who are just satisfactory. If you have several candidates who all possess the essential skills, your decision will be based on the level of additional, desirable skills.

Contra-indicators

These are the qualities, or behaviours, that would make a person unsuitable for the role. For example, a candidate with poor eyesight would not be suitable for a pilot's job.

Use this category with care – if your contra-indicators are not directly related to the job specification, they could be regarded as discriminatory.

Annex 5J
Application form and separable monitoring form

The information on this sheet will be separated from your application as soon as it is received. It will not be passed on to anyone involved in shortlisting or appointment to this post.

Post applied for:

Job reference no.:

Equality monitoring information

The firm operates an equality and diversity policy. To help us monitor its effectiveness, it would be appreciated if you could complete this section. Please tick the appropriate boxes below. (Note that providing this information is not compulsory.)

What is your gender?	☐ Male	☐ Female
Do you or have you ever considered yourself to be transgender?	☐ Yes	☐ No
Do you consider yourself to have a disability?	☐ Prefer not to answer	
	☐ Yes If yes please complete relevant section	☐ No

Please choose ONE section from A to E below, to indicate your ethnic group.

Then complete boxes F to I for age range, sexual orientation, religion and belief.

A. White

☐ British
☐ English
☐ Scottish
☐ Welsh
☐ Irish
☐ Any other white background – please write below

B. Mixed

☐ White and Black Caribbean
☐ White and Black African
☐ White and Asian
☐ Any other mixed background – please write below

B. Asian, Asian British, Asian English, Asian Scottish or Asian Welsh

☐ Indian
☐ Pakistani
☐ Bangladeshi
☐ Any other Asian background – please write below

D. Black, Black British, Black English, Black Scottish or Black Welsh

☐ Caribbean
☐ African
☐ Any other Black background – please write below

E. Chinese, Chinese British, Chinese English, Chinese Scottish, Chinese Welsh or other ethnic group

☐ Caribbean
☐ African
☐ Any other ethnic background – please write below

F. Age

☐ 19 and under
☐ 20–24
☐ 25–29
☐ 30–34
☐ 35–39
☐ 40–44
☐ 50–54
☐ 55–59
☐ 60+

G. Sexual orientation

☐ Lesbian
☐ Gay
☐ Bisexual
☐ Heterosexual
☐ Prefer not to answer

H. Religion

☐ Christian
☐ Buddhist
☐ Hindu
☐ Jewish
☐ Muslim
☐ Sikh
☐ None
☐ Prefer not to answer
☐ Any other religion – please write below

I. Belief

☐ Agnostic
☐ Atheist
☐ Humanist
☐ None
☐ Prefer not to answer
☐ Any other belief – please write below

The information on this sheet will be separated from your application as soon as it is received. It will not be passed on to anyone involved in shortlisting or appointment to this post.

Post applied for:

Job reference no.:

Disabilities

Please complete this section if you have a disability or impairment.

These forms can be made available in accessible formats such as Braille, e-mail, audiotape or large print. As a disabled person you can complete the form in your preferred format. The firm and its staff and agents will not discriminate against disabled people in the way they deal with their applications.

The purpose of this section is to demonstrate the firm's commitment to eliminating unfair discrimination from all aspects of its work.

[*Optional:*- All applicants with a disability who meet the minimum criteria for shortlisting will be guaranteed an interview.]

If you wish to be considered for employment, please give details of any impairments below. Please indicate whether you have any special requirements, should you be invited for an interview, as we will make all reasonable necessary adjustments.

Nature of disability/impairment:
Special requirements for interview:

Signature .... Date ....

The information on this sheet will be separated from your application as soon as it is received. It will not be passed on to anyone involved in shortlisting or appointment to this post.

Post applied for:

Job reference no.:

Personal details

Surname	
First names	Title (Mr/Mrs/Ms/Dr/other)
Known as	
Date of birth	Marital/civil partnership status
Address	Home tel. no.
	Work tel. no.
	Mobile no.
Preferred contact telephone number	☐ Home ☐ Work ☐ Mobile
Nationality	National insurance number
Do you require a permit to work in the UK?	☐ Yes ☐ No
Type of permit	Date of expiry
Place of issue	
Current or most recent salary/benefits (*evidence of this may be requested*)	

Annex 5K
Sample letter: invitation to interview

Dear

Further to your recent application for the position of [*specify*], I am pleased to invite you to attend an interview on [*date*] at [*time*]. The interview will take place at our [*give location address and directions*] and, on arrival at reception, you should ask for [*name*]. The interview will be conducted by a panel consisting of [*specify names/positions*].

As part of the recruitment process, you will be required to complete a [keyboard [*or other*]] test, which will take 40 minutes, and an interview which should last approximately one hour.

The above process is designed to ensure that our recruitment decisions are based on selecting the best person for the job. The firm's selection decisions are based on ability and competence for the job regardless of sex, orientation, age, race, religion, creed, marital status, disability or any other unfair or discriminatory factor.

If you have any impairment that requires an adjustment to these arrangements to enable you to attend the interview or to complete the occupational tests, please let me know in advance so that your needs can be accommodated.

I hope that these arrangements will be convenient for you and I would ask you to confirm that you will be able to attend as requested. I look forward to meeting you.

Yours sincerely

Annex 5L
Interview checklist

- Organise appropriate training for all those involved in selection interviewing.
- Ensure that all questions asked are relevant to the job in question. Lexcel requires that fee earners be asked about their disciplinary record, or it will need to be checked in some other way.
- Concentrate on those requirements that are essential to do the job.
- Do not ask questions about membership or non-membership of a trade union – it may indicate an intention to discriminate on grounds of union membership. This is illegal and risks a tribunal claim. Awards of compensation for this are significant.
- Never allow the pregnancy of an applicant to influence the interview. If a woman is rejected for being pregnant, she has the right to claim sex discrimination. Compensation is unlimited.
- Questions regarding criminal offences should be handled carefully. The Rehabilitation of Offenders Act 1974 permits applicants for certain jobs to treat previous convictions as 'spent', i.e. they do not have to disclose them. Avoid questions unless relevant.
- Deal with questions regarding health issues sensitively. The Disability Discrimination Act 1995 does not prohibit questions regarding disability.
- Do not make assumptions or comments about age, that someone is either too young or too old for the post.
- To avoid suggestions of sex discrimination, consider whether a question could be put to a member of the opposite sex. A line manager is less likely, for example, to ask a man questions about childcare arrangements. Never ask a woman questions regarding her intentions to have a family. Do not question applicants about marital status/relationships, unless this is an occupational requirement of the job.
- Prepare interview questions in advance and have a series of questions that are put to all the candidates. It is often the spontaneous type of question that leads to problems.
- Make a record of the candidate's responses. Immediately after the interview, produce interview notes (remember – interview notes become evidence at tribunal and a line manager may be asked to read them out).
- Use positive body language and actively listen to the candidates.
- Have a colleague present during interviews. Interviewing alone can prove difficult, particularly for the inexperienced trying to simultaneously handle all the skills required. Having someone else present enables the interview to be broken up and provides time during the meeting for essential issues such as note taking.
- Remember to provide some information on the job and the organisation.
- Provide opportunities for the candidate to ask questions that they might have.

Suggested structure for a recruitment interview

- Open the interview with an icebreaker, e.g. discuss the candidate's journey, the weather, offer a coffee, etc.

- Introduce yourself and any others involved.
- Summarise the agenda for the interview. Tell the candidate what is going to happen, approximately how long the interview will last, whether any other people are going to be involved in the interview and what their role will be.
- Carry out any tests that may be required. It is important to include these early in the interview to avoid putting additional pressure on the candidates. Candidates should have been made aware before the day that testing would be involved.
- Conduct the main body of interview:

  (a) find out the information you want to know about the candidate;
  (b) check the information you already know about them from the application form or CV – probing any areas that need further investigation.

- Close the interview. Tell the candidate about the firm, the position and the role of the successful applicant. You should also cover any conditions of employment, benefits and promotional prospects. Give them the opportunity to ask questions.
- The interviewer should, in closing, ensure that the candidate has a clear idea of what the next steps are, and of the likely timescale. Will there be a second interview? How long before a decision is made?
- Make notes. The interviewer should make notes about each candidate straightaway. This will help to ensure that the decision-making process is as effective as possible and also ensure that all relevant information has been recorded in the event of any queries regarding equal opportunities. Interview notes should be kept for at least six months, possibly for up to 12 months, but no longer.

Managing the post-interview discussion

It may be helpful to identify answers to the following questions to aid clarity in the decision-making process:

- Did the applicant demonstrate the skills level required for the position?
- Did the candidate have the required qualifications?
- Did the candidate give actual examples that were directly demonstrative of the job requirements?
- Is the candidate's experience commensurate with the levels expected for the position?

Feedback

Any candidate may request feedback from an interview process. The requirement for the provision of feedback to unsuccessful candidates that did exist at 5.3(f) in Lexcel does not appear in Lexcel (4th edition), but remains a requirement for legal aid firms (see D1.4 in the SQM). It is an established and recommended way of individuals being satisfied that the decision was fair. It also helps them as part of their personal development to learn and prepare for future interview processes. Those involved in recruitment must identify and record clear reasons for selection at each stage of the process. A designated person should be appointed to give feedback when requested and therefore post-interview or post-shortlisting notes must be clear and demonstrate links between the individual and the post. The individual should be aware of the need to be factual in communicating the decision-making process and observations at interview. A written post-interview record is helpful to guide this process.

Pre-selection/appointment information

It is good practice to ask for references in support of the candidate's application and, increasingly, references a requirement of insurers. Any information provided must be actual and true – judgements and opinions are dangerous. As a result references are now primarily to confirm dates of appointment in a job and such factual information as job titles, sickness records, records of 'unspent' disciplinary records and so on. Sight of academic certificates, permissions to work in the UK, national insurance details and other relevant documentation – even including photographs – may be necessary to contribute to the verification of the individual's identity. If a medical examination is a part of the required process, notification and detail of the process must be provided in advance.

Job offer

The next stage in the selection process normally involves making an offer of employment to the preferred first choice of candidate. While offers of employment can be made verbally, it is recommended that they be put in writing. Note that verbal promises can be contractual, so do not make promises that the organisation cannot honour, such as holidays or bonuses. (If there is a good second candidate, do not reject them at this stage, as your first choice may decide not to accept, or there may be problems with references, etc.)

Do be aware that a formal job offer eventually forms part of the employment contract with the individual. Once the job offer has been made and accepted, it is in effect a contractual agreement between the two parties. This agreement is therefore binding and neither party can unilaterally withdraw from it without agreement. It is therefore very important that the most significant terms and conditions of the job are spelt out in the offer letter or in affirming documents.

Pre-joining communication

Where some time elapses between appointment and start date (as, most obviously, with trainee solicitors) keeping in touch with the future employee will start to develop an effective relationship and will reassure the individual about their choice of employer.

Annex 5M

Statement of the terms and conditions of employment

All employees whose employment will last for one month or more are entitled by law to a written statement of their terms and conditions of employment. This must be given to them within eight weeks of the start of employment (Employment Rights Act 1996). The Act also lays down the headings that must appear in the written statement, although much of the detail will depend on the terms that the employer is offering, e.g. holidays and sick pay.

The written statement is not in itself a contract of employment but is taken as illustrative of the arrangements between the parties. Employers should therefore take care not to include in the written statement rights which they may not later wish to honour, as employees should be able to rely on the terms. In practical terms the difference between a statement and contract is negligible.

This checklist covers the headings required by law and, where there are minimum statutory terms, what those terms are. It also outlines some of the issues that employers should consider in arriving at the terms and conditions. Employers are free to be more generous if they wish, but cannot offer less generous terms than the statutory minimum. Where terms are not contractual, the written statement or any supporting policies, e.g. on sick leave, should make this clear.

While there is no legal obligation to have the written terms signed, to do so makes good sense. A signed copy on employees' files indicates that they have received (and hopefully read) the basis on which they are employed. The induction process can also be used to emphasise the main points and to clarify anything which has not been understood.

Suggested written terms and conditions

Legal requirement	Considerations for the employer
Name and address of employer	[*Name and address of employer*]
Place of work	[*Where this is static, the address alone will be enough. If the employee is expected to work from different locations, the terms and conditions should reflect this, e.g.:* You may be required to work at any of the organisation's other offices/premises in the UK on a temporary or permanent basis. Or, for service engineers, etc.: Your place of work will vary depending on the needs of our staff. The office to which you should report on a daily basis is [*address*]. *However, even where a mobility clause exists, the employer must also be reasonable in exercising their right to call upon this clause*]
Name of employee	[*Name of employee*]
Date employment started under this contract	[*This will normally be the first day of employment, but take care to be clear if the person has worked through an agency in the same location or if the person has been employed before*]
Date continuous employment started (if different)	[*This clause is needed where the written statement is being issued because of changes in the terms of employment or where it is being issued because of a transfer or merger. In both cases, the employee has continuity of service and the first date on which they were employed by the organisation should be entered here. If there is no previous service, the clause can be omitted*]
Additional clause if the contract is for a fixed term	Date on which employment will end. [*The main distinction between an open contract and a fixed-term contract is that the latter has its end determined from the start. This may be a date, e.g.:*]

This contract is for a period of two years, starting on [*start date*] and ending on [*last day of contract*].

Or it may be the ending of a project, e.g.:

You are employed to complete the integration of the HR and payroll records which we estimate will take six months. Your employment will cease when the project is satisfactorily completed.]

Rate of pay and intervals of pay	Hourly rate (£[*amount*] per hour)/Weekly rate (£[amount] per week)/Monthly rate (£[amount] per month)/Annual rate (£[amount] per year)

[*Employers may not pay less than the national minimum wage (NMW) per hour in force at the time*]

Method of payment   [*Payment may be in cash, cheque or bank credit transfer. Employers may not pay their employees in kind, e.g. goods*]

Hours of work   [*In most instances, hours of work are expressed by the week, e.g.:*

Your hours of work are 39 per week, 09.00 to 17.30 Monday to Friday with one hour's unpaid lunch break.

Employees cannot be required to work more than 48 hours per week, averaged out over 17 weeks, unless they have signed an opt-out agreement (the future of the opt-out is still uncertain).

If the employer wishes to make overtime a compulsory element of the working week, this should be clearly expressed in the written statement. Where overtime is not stated, or is said to be voluntary, the employer cannot insist that the employee work it. A clause might read:

You will be expected to work a minimum of three hours' overtime per week and your supervisor will inform you of the days and hours one week in advance.

Where overtime is compulsory it is usually paid, but there is no legal requirement to offer a premium for overtime working (though many employers do so). A suitable clause might read:

Overtime working is paid at time on Mondays to Fridays, time and one quarter on Saturday, and time and one half on Sundays and public holidays.

If the employer does not make a payment for compulsory overtime working, the hours will count towards the calculation of the NMW, so the employer needs to ensure that the total gross pay for the period, divided by the total number of hours worked, still leaves the employee with at least the NMW per hour.

Earnings for compulsory overtime count as part of a week's wages for the calculation of some payments, e.g. redundancy pay]

Holiday entitlement

[From October 2007 the minimum entitlement has been 20 days plus four public days.

The terms and conditions must set out the holiday entitlement, the holiday year and the way in which holiday is calculated in the years of joining and leaving, e.g.:

Your holiday entitlement is 20 days in a full holiday (calendar) year, plus public holidays. This will be calculated on a pro rata basis in the years of joining and leaving. Entitlement accumulates at the rate of 1.66 days per full calendar month worked.

The terms also need to give the employer explicit permission to recover any overpayment of holiday pay in the year of leaving, e.g.:

If you leave having taken more paid holiday than you were entitled to by virtue of your service in the relevant holiday year, the organisation reserves the right to make a deduction of the amount of overpayment from your final salary.

Employers must give leavers pay in lieu of any statutory holiday earned but not taken at the date of leaving, and this right can also be set out in the written terms, e.g.:

If you have not taken holiday to which you were entitled, you will receive pay in lieu of your final salary payment. Pay in lieu of holiday will not be given in any other circumstances.]

Job title

[This should be straightforward but the employer might wish to include an element of flexibility, e.g.:

We do require our employees to be flexible and during the course of your employment you may therefore be asked to undertake a variety of duties as required by the needs of the business. Any such additional tasks will be discussed with you beforehand, will be reasonable and within your capabilities.]

Notice

[The notice given here is the statutory minimum. Employers are free to be more generous if they so wish. There is no statutory right to notice in the first month of employment. Employers should also note that while the notice from the employer to the employee increases with service, the notice the employee is required to give does not, unless this is changed by other contractual terms.

If you wish to terminate your employment, you must give the organisation one week's notice in writing. If the organisation wishes to terminate your employment, after the first month's employment, you will be given one week's notice for each complete year of service up to a maximum of 12 weeks' notice after 12 years' service.]

Sickness absence

[Employees need to know how and when they should contact the firm, e.g.:

Should you be ill, you must notify *[name or title]* as early as possible on the first missed day of work, saying why you are unable to attend and how long you think you will be absent. On your return, you must report to *[name and title]* who will ask you to complete a self-certification form. If you are sick for more than seven days, you must produce a doctor's certificate from the eighth day and weekly thereafter.

Employers are not obliged to pay more than statutory sick pay (SSP) if employees are off sick. Even for the payment of SSP, however, it is necessary to have proof of illness, e.g. a self-certificate for the first seven days of sickness and a doctor's certificate thereafter. A clause in the written terms might therefore say:

The firm does not have a sick pay scheme. Your entitlement is to statutory sick pay (SSP) only, if you are eligible for this payment. The personnel department will give you the current levels of SSP if you ask.]

Pension

[*There is no obligation to have an occupational pension scheme and even where there is one, the level of contribution from the employer and employee is for the employer to determine. Employees cannot be required to join an occupational pension scheme. Where there is no organisational pension scheme, the employers must offer access to a stakeholder scheme where there are five or more employees but need not contribute themselves. A typical clause might be:*

The firm does not offer an occupational pension scheme but provides access to a stakeholder pension. Details can be obtained from the personnel department. Employees remain contracted into the State Second Pension (S2P).

Where there is an occupational scheme, the written terms and conditions can refer the employee to the details, which can be in a separate document. However, the written terms should still make it clear whether or not employees are contracted in or out of the S2P, e.g.:

Employees who do not join the pension scheme will remain contracted into the S2P, but pension scheme members will be contracted out.]

Collective agreements

[*If the employer does not recognise trade unions and the terms and conditions of employment are not determined by a third party agreement, then the statement should say:*

The firm does not recognise any trade unions for collective bargaining purposes and the terms and conditions of employment are not dependent on any other negotiated settlement.

If the firm does recognise a trade union(s) for collective bargaining purposes, the terms should say:

The firm recognises the [*name of union or unions*] for the purposes of collective bargaining. Certain terms and conditions of your employment are contained in agreements negotiated and agreed with the [*name of trade union*]. These terms and conditions form part of your contract of employment with this firm, whether you are a member of the union or not. The relevant collective agreements are accessible to you at your place of work on notice boards or from the personnel department. From time to time, variations in your terms and conditions resulting from negotiations and agreement with the union and this organisation, will be notified to you separately or otherwise incorporated in the documents to which you have access. Management undertake to ensure that future changes resulting from these agreements will be entered into these documents or otherwise recorded for you to refer to, within one month of the change.

It is important to include this clause in the terms and conditions of each affected employee because collective agreements themselves are not usually legally binding. The clauses of the collective agreement become legally binding on the employee through the individual terms and conditions of employment]

Disciplinary procedure

[*The Employment Act 2002 (Disputes Resolution) Regulations 2004 require all employers to set out the disciplinary procedure in the written terms and conditions of employment or to indicate to the employee where these can be found, e.g.:*

The firm has a formal disciplinary procedure which is attached to this document. You have the right to appeal any disciplinary action taken against you and to be accompanied at any disciplinary hearing by your trade union representative or another employee of your choice.]

Grievance procedure

[*The Employment Act 2002 (Disputes Resolution) Regulations 2004 require all employers to set out the grievance procedure which employees should follow if they have a grievance to raise with their employer, e.g.:*

Should you have any grievance about your employment, and cannot resolve it by informal means, you should first raise it in writing with your line manager or supervisor. If they cannot resolve the matter, you have the right to take it to [*name or title*].]

Additional clause if the employee will work abroad for more than one month

[*If the employee will have to work outside the UK for a period or periods of one month or more, details of this period(s), any additional remuneration or benefits to which they will be entitled while abroad and any terms and conditions relating to their return to the UK should be included*]

Signature

[*This may say:*

I have received a copy of my written terms and conditions of employment and understand that they constitute the basis of my employment rights and duties with the firm.]

Signed (employees)..

Date..

Annex 5N

Contract of employment precedent

To:

From:

The following particulars are the terms on which you are employed and are given to you pursuant to relevant employment legislation. There are no collective agreements in place within the firm.

1. Parties

Employer

The partners collectively at any particular time practising as [*name*] of [*address*] or their successors (hereinafter called 'the partners')

Employee

Surname:

Forenames:

2. Date of employment

The date when your employment began was [*date*]. Any employment with a previous employer does not count as part of your period of continuous employment with this firm.

3. Appointment

Your appointment is as an assistant solicitor. It is a condition of employment that you remain on the roll of solicitors.

4. Hours of work

The normal office hours are [*specify*] Monday to Friday inclusive with a lunch period from [*specify*], subject to any variation required in the normal course of business or as otherwise agreed with the partners.

5. Salary

Your current salary is [*amount*] per annum payable monthly in arrears on the [25th day] of each calendar month direct into your private bank account. [Your salary will be reviewed annually as at [1 November] in each year of employment.] [(*for newly admitted solicitors*) Your salary will be reviewed as at [1 November] and [1 May] in each year of your employment or until you have been admitted for three years. Thereafter your salary will be reviewed annually as at 1 November.]

6. Pension

The firm has contracted into the state pension scheme.

7. Motor insurance and motoring expenses

7.1. You are required to have a motor vehicle for your own use on the firm's business and you are to ensure that it is fully insured for such purpose. The cover must include a situation when another member of staff may be carried as a passenger in your private vehicle when being used on the firm's business and that the passenger may be travelling on different firm's business to that of yourself.

7.2. A mileage allowance at a rate to be determined from time to time by the partners will be paid to you for any mileage that you may make on the firm's business.

7.3. [You will be provided with a local authority car park season ticket.]

8. Other expenses

The firm will pay for your [practising certificate, membership of the Law Society, local Law Society, Solicitors Benevolent Association and other professional organisations] as the partners may approve.

9. BUPA

From [*date*] the firm will pay for membership of BUPA on an individual basis.

10. Holidays

10.1.   During the first five years of employment you are entitled to 20 working days per year.

10.2.   Upon completion of five years of employment excluding any time under articles, you are entitled to 25 working days per year.

10.3.   In addition to public holidays you will be entitled to additional days holidays at the discretion of the partners.

10.4.   The holiday year commences on [1 May] and subject to agreement by the partners there is no restriction on when holidays may be taken or the number of days taken at any one time.

11. Retirement

The normal retirement age will be 65.

12. Sickness

The provisions of the Social Security Contribution and Benefits Act 1992 relating to the payment of statutory sick pay will apply. In order to maintain the statutory sickness records, you are required to report all periods of sickness to the partners, and for periods of sickness of seven consecutive days or more, a doctor's medical certificate is to be provided. You are required to make application for sickness benefit when eligible in accordance with the statutory provisions for the time being in force. Your full salary, abated in full by any sickness benefit, will be paid to you for the following maximum cumulative periods in any 12-month period terminating on the day to which entitlement to remuneration is being calculated at any time.

12.1.   During the first 12 months of employment, [one month].

12.2.   Between 12 and 24 months' employment, [two months].

12.3.   After 24 months' employment, [six months].

13. Recovery of damages

If at any time whether during or after the termination of your employment with the firm, you recover damages from any other person or in personal injury resulting in absence from work with the firm, you shall, whether it is demanded of you or not, repay to the partners an amount equivalent to the total of all remuneration paid to you by the firm in respect of the period or periods of any such absence (save that you will not be required to pay under this provision a sum greater than the sum recovered by way of damages which is attributable to the loss of remuneration).

14. Notice of termination of employment by the employee

The following periods of notice of termination of employment are to be given by the employee:

14.1.   The minimum period to be given is four weeks.

14.2.   After 12 months' completed service, two calendar months.

14.3.   After 12 years' completed service, 12 weeks.

15. Notice of termination of employment by employer

The following periods of notice of termination of employment will be given by the employer:

15.1.   The minimum period to be given will be four weeks.

15.2.   After 12 months' completed service, two calendar months.

15.3.   After 12 years' completed service, 12 weeks.

16. Waiver

Employers or employees can waive their rights to notice or to payment in lieu of notice. Either party can terminate the contract of employment without notice if the conduct of the other justifies it.

17. Pay on termination of employment

On termination of your employment, you will be entitled to pay calculated as a proportion of one month's salary equivalent to the same proportion which the number of days worked bear to the number of days for the month in which the employment terminates plus payment for any days holiday accrued but not taken.

18. Discipline and grievance procedure

18.1.   A breach of the following rules may result in instant dismissal without warning by any two partners:

- improper use of or disclosure of information concerning the partners' practice or the clients of the firm which may come to your knowledge by reason of your employment;
- any conduct which in the opinion of the partners may have the effect of bringing the integrity and reputation of the firm into disrepute.

18.2.   In the event that any one of the partners is dissatisfied with your work, conduct, time keeping or any other aspect of your employment, any such one or more partners may give you a verbal warning as to the matter causing dissatisfaction. If after a reasonable period the partners remain dissatisfied with the matter complained of, you may be given a final written warning and if the partners continue to be dissatisfied with the matter complained of, you may be given the minimum notice of dismissal to which you are entitled by virtue of the length of your employment with the firm.

18.3.   If during the course of your employment you receive more than one verbal warning under sub-paragraph 18.2 of this clause for any one or number of matters, then you may be given a final written warning that if any matter subsequently warrants a further verbal warning, you may be dismissed.

18.4.   No disciplinary action will be taken until your case has been investigated by at least two partners. If any disciplinary action is taken, you will be given a full explanation by the partners.

18.5.   If you are dissatisfied with any disciplinary decision relating to you or have any grievance relating to your employment, you may apply in writing within 14 days of such decision or the occasion of such grievance, to the branch partner or any other partner who is acting branch partner in his or her absence, or to another branch partner. You will be given the opportunity to state your case to him or her before any decision is reached and you may be accompanied by any one employee of your choice from the firm.

18.6.   If you wish to appeal against any decision taken by the branch partner relating to your employment this should be made in writing within 14 days to the senior partner present at the time. An appeal will be heard by three partners (including the branch partner when possible) and you may be accompanied by any one employee of your choice from the firm.

18.7.   If you wish to raise any issue by way of grievance please do so initially by talking to your head of department. If this does not resolve matters to your satisfaction please address your concerns in writing to the managing partner. In all cases we will take all steps that we are reasonably able to do to address any problem brought to our attention.

19. Restrictive covenant

Save with the written consent of the partners you will not:

19.1.   during the period of one year after the termination of your employment with the firm canvass, solicit or approach any client of the firm for the purpose of providing or giving legal advice or services to that client;

19.2.   during the period of one year after the termination of your employment with the firm either alone or in partnership or as an agent, consultant or employee of any other person or firm practise as a solicitor within a range of [one/two/three] miles from any office from which the partnership practises at the date hereof. The foregoing restrictions are considered reasonable by the partners and shall be treated as separate obligations and shall be severally enforceable as such.

20. Unions

The partners confirm your right to join a union of your choice and to take part in its activities.

21. Pregnancy

In the event of your becoming pregnant, the maternity provisions set out in the Employment Rights Act 1996 as amended will apply. These regulations will be explained in detail should the need arise.

22. Money laundering

The firm has a responsibility to ensure anti-money laundering training for all personnel and it is a condition of your employment that you undertake such training as instructed.

23. Compliance with quality system

The firm is committed to the Lexcel scheme of the Law Society and you must follow the firm's policies and procedures as set out in our quality system.

Signed ....

A partner for and on behalf of [*name*]

Signed .... Dated ....

Employee

Annex 5O

Interview assessment form

[Bear in mind that this form, when completed, will be disclosable under data protection principles to the candidate that it relates to. Also ensure that all criteria are objective and necessary for the position in question.]

Vacancy:

Candidate:

FACTOR	COMMENTS	RATING A = Excellent B = Good C = Average D =Poor E = Very poor				
		A	B	C	D	E
Qualification and training						
Experience						
Knowledge and skills						
Personality						
Recommendation						
Comments and actions						

Interviewer/head of panel .... Date ....

Annex 5P
Competency based interview paperwork

1. Competency definition example

JOB TITLE	SOLICITOR
Client contact	Demonstrates client management skills
Legal advice	Applies technical know-how in a practical and commercial way
Time recording and billing	Completes and provides time records
	Meets targets
File management	Presents high quality of work
	Demonstrates good personal work
	Management skill and is able to handle high workload
Management and supervision	Uses internal resources effectively

2. Interview assessment form example

Name of applicant:
Date of interview:
Interviewers:

COMPETENCE 1	PROBLEM SOLVING	NOTES OF EXAMPLE
Question 1	Describe the most complex client issue you have dealt with recently	Competence demonstrated: Y/N
Competence definition	• Finds new ways of solving problems • Identifies clear goals and proceeds logically through the decision-making process to achieve the goal • Gathers information from range of sources	

	• Analyses information to identify issues • Considers risk and has alternative strategy for action • Takes a systematic approach • Identifies inconsistencies in information • Considers views of others	
Total score		
COMPETENCE 2	**INFLUENCING**	**NOTES OF EXAMPLE**
Question 2	**Give an example of an occasion where you have had to advise a client or a partner or a colleague to make a difficult or controversial decision**	Competence demonstrated: Y/N
Competence definition	• Delivers powerful argument • Sells benefits • Negotiates to find solutions • Challenges others when it is in the client's or firm's best interests to do so • Supports arguments with facts, logic and reason • Handles objections with skill • Understands others' position • Involves others appropriately	
Total score		
Total overall score on measured competences		

Annex 5Q

Induction training form

Name: **Job title:** **Supervising partner:** **Start date:**

Pre-start date	
Check work area Appoint a supportive colleague Brief other staff Book any introductory training – IT, telephone? Book appointments to meet 'key' colleagues/partners First day lunch arrangements	
First day	
Welcome Show the individual their personal working area/desk/office Introduction to key staff Tour of the building – key areas Cover key staff/legislative issues – fire drill, security, accident, smoking, breaks, staff exits/entrances outside hours – door codes etc Check receipt of key documents – Staff Handbook/ contracts, etc. Explain structure of team/firm – key names and job holders Explain quality procedures Allow for questions Book follow -up meeting Short--form money laundering package provided and explained?	
Within 3 weeks	
Check health/welfare – risk assessment Ensure policies and procedures understood Allow for questions	
After 12 weeks	
Training needs Check knowledge and understanding of role and firm	
Within 6 months	
Initial performance review Set objectives for period up to formal annual review	

Annex 5R

Guidelines for appraisers

Communication

Before starting the individual review meetings, make sure that everyone is clear about the purpose of the meetings, and the overall aims of the scheme. For example, a team meeting might be used to discuss the following points:

- why the firm has an appraisal scheme;
- how you as a manager will use the review process to achieve your goals;
- when and where the review meetings will be held;
- how staff members should prepare for their review meeting;
- how you make your assessment of their performance;
- what happens to the review forms afterwards.

Information gathering

Gather the information that you will need in order to assess performance and give constructive feedback. This might include the following:

- if there is one, the job description (make sure it is correct and up to date);
- last year's review record, or other facts on individual performance;
- performance statistics from work carried out during the year (output, targets, error rate, etc.);
- specific details of achievements and/or problem areas to be discussed;
- specific details of any new knowledge and skills acquired during the year;
- feedback from clients (specific, not vague or hearsay evidence);
- feedback from team members and/or other departments.

Suggested preparation

It is important that this review process is not seen as just a form filling exercise. While the form is important (as both a record and a working document), it is the quality of the discussion that is crucial.

- Issue a copy of the performance review form to the staff member, with a copy of the employee guidelines, and agree the date and time of the meeting. The staff member should prepare his/her views and make some notes for each section in preparation for the discussion.
- Review your staff member's performance towards meeting their current objectives and make some notes to aid you in the discussion.

   Give an indication of the level of performance that has been achieved in each area, adding comments to support your view. Try to make the comments as specific as possible, with examples of the particular behaviours you have observed and based your assessment on.

Remember that satisfactory performance means that the individual is meeting the standards that you have set for the job – this may already indicate a high level of achievement, and should not be interpreted as just average or adequate.

If performance is less than satisfactory, some remedial action is required (which may already be under way) and this action must be recorded.

- Consider what objectives you intend to set for the member of staff, any changes you would like to see in their behaviour at work, and any training and development needs you have already identified. When setting individual objectives, look at the firm's objectives for the year and reflect these in the process. These are issues that will be discussed at the meeting, so that training and development documentation can be completed afterwards.
- Statements should be as clear as possible in terms of setting priorities and timing. Both the manager and the employee should try to ensure that all items listed pass the SMART test:

  - **Specific** – are both of you clear about what is to be achieved?
  - **Measurable** – can success be recognised in quantitative or qualitative terms?
  - **Agreed** – are you in agreement about and committed to the objective?
  - **Realistic** – sufficiently stretching but also realistic given other priorities.
  - **Time-limited** – a clear timeframe so that success can be planned for.

  Once agreed, it is recommended that the frequency of ongoing review be decided, e.g. three-monthly, six-monthly.

- Arrange a suitable venue for the meeting, free from distractions and interruptions.

Performance review meeting

It is not essential that the items on the forms are discussed in a particular order – you will probably find it more natural to take each issue as it arises in the course of the discussions. However, you should make sure that feedback has been given on all relevant aspects of performance, including the specific examples identified, and that all the relevant items have been covered in depth.

It is also important to give the employee the opportunity to give you some feedback on your performance as a manager, and any changes they would like to see in your working relationship. At the end of the meeting, make sure that you have agreed the objectives for the coming year, including both business objectives and personal development goals. These should be both specific and measurable in all cases. This section of the documentation can be completed at the meeting, or filled in after the meeting by either the manager or the staff member.

Never criticise the person – focus on the facts regarding poor performance, poor attendance or poor conduct. You will not change the employee's personality, but you can attempt to modify their behaviour at work.

The review meeting is not the opportunity to apportion blame or commence disciplinary proceedings. Everyone makes mistakes, it is how people learn from the mistakes that is important. Avoid a blame culture as this creates a negative atmosphere. Remember to praise for good work, good results and even good effort where the results were not outstanding!

Follow up

After the meeting, pass all sections of the appraisal documentation to the staff member, for their comments and signature. The staff member is not obliged to add comments, but should sign the form to confirm that the appraisal meeting has taken place – even where agreement has not been reached on specific issues!

If a member of staff is unhappy with the performance review process, or outcome, they should be offered the opportunity to use the firm's grievance procedure. Remember, they can also complain if they do not receive regular performance reviews!

Retain one copy of the completed documentation for your own use, and give one copy to the member of staff. These should be used for review and reference throughout the year, and in preparing for next year's review meeting.

Make sure that all action points agreed at the meeting are incorporated into your on-going plans. For example, if training needs are identified, ensure that the appropriate training is requested, and follow up afterwards. Use your diary to ensure you keep your promises.

Finally, remember that, as a manager, one of the ways in which your own performance will be assessed is how effectively you use the appraisal process to motivate and develop your team.

Suggested questions for manager's feedback

- Is there anything more I could be doing to help you to be successful in your job?
- Are you happy with the amount of time I spend with you on a day to day basis?
- Do you think I spend enough time in communicating with the team as a whole?
- How well do you think I have been able to share my own and the company=s objectives with the members of our team?
- Do you and the other team members feel okay about discussing problems with me, or asking for my help?
- Is there anything I have done in the past year that has caused you to feel upset, or annoyed?
- How well do you think that you and I work together?
- If you were managing this team instead of me, what would you do differently?
- Any thoughts on how working practices could be improved?

Annex 5S

Guidelines for appraisees (employee)

Guidelines for employees

The annual performance review meeting is an opportunity for you to review with your manager your progress and achievements over the past year, to agree objectives and goals for the coming year, to give and receive feedback on performance, and to agree any changes needed. To get the most out of this opportunity, both you and your manager need to spend some time preparing for the meeting and thinking about the things you would like to say – about your job and your hopes for the future, your training and development.

Information gathering

What thoughts do you have on your last year's performance?

Gather the information that you will need in order to review your own performance over the past year and set goals for the future. This might include the following:

- If you have a job description – is it accurate and up to date? If not, what changes are needed? Are you clear about your main tasks and responsibilities? If there is not a job description, set out what you think your main duties are.
- Your most recent performance review records, where appropriate.
- Any performance statistics from work you have carried out during the year – what were they?
- Specific details of achievements and/or problem areas you would like to discuss (volume of work; relationships; organisation structure). What were your main achievements over the last year?
- Specific details of any new knowledge and skills you have acquired during the year.
- What training or development needs do you have? What skills or abilities do you have which you are not using at work?
- Feedback from clients.
- Feedback from your colleagues.
- What are your objectives for the coming year? Do you have any longer-term career plans?
- What parts of your job do you enjoy most/least? Why?

Preparation

Review the goals and objectives that were set at your last meeting, and consider what has happened since then. Have you attained those goals? If not, is this because something happened to prevent you? Did these goals change during the course of the year? Were any new goals set? Did you receive the necessary support?

Consider what actions and behaviours of yours either helped or hindered you in achieving your goals. If you had the chance to attempt those goals again, what would you do differently? What actions and initiatives of yours were particularly successful?

Identify all of the new things that you learnt in the course of the last year. Did you acquire any new skills, or attend any training courses or seminars? Remember that we often learn from our own mistakes, or from things that go wrong, as well as from our successes and from more formal training events. What skills and abilities do you have now that were not so strong before?

Establish some goals and aspirations of your own for the coming year. What changes would you like to see in your job? Do you have any plans for developing your career? What would you like the company to do for you, and what personal goals have you set?

Make some notes as a reminder during the interview itself – take them in with you, do not be afraid to refer to them in the meeting.

Do you have any comments or observations on departmental issues – workloads, organisation, skills, relationships? This is your opportunity to formally put your views across.

Performance review meeting

At the review meeting, which will probably last between half an hour and one and a half hours, you will have the opportunity to discuss all of the topics you have prepared, and will be given feedback by your manager on the various aspects of your performance which have been monitored through the year. If your performance in any area has been less than satisfactory, you and your manager will need to discuss and agree the ways in which this can be rectified.

Your manager should also be looking for some feedback on his or her own performance, and this is your opportunity to raise any issues that you feel will help to improve your working relationship or work results. You should feel free to discuss any dissatisfaction you might feel about the way your manager works, as well as highlighting those aspects of your relationship which you find particularly helpful or motivational. Focus on the future and keep the discussion as positive as possible.

You and your manager will also discuss the objectives to be agreed for the coming year. These may include the following:

- **Business objectives**: these are the work-related targets and goals on which your performance will be measured. They must fit in with the overall business goals of your team or workgroup, and they must be very specific, so that success can be easily measured by you and your manager.
- **Personal development objectives**: these are the individual goals that you will set, and that reflect the changes you want to make in the way you do your job or behave at work. For example, you might set an objective to make more

proactive contributions at team meetings, or to build your confidence in dealing with customers, or to be less critical of colleagues in other departments. These objectives should also be specific, so that you can assess your level of personal development at the end of the year.

- **Learning objectives**: these are the skills and knowledge you would like to acquire over the coming year, and you should specify how the desired results will be achieved. This might include training courses, self-study, project work, a period of secondment to another department, obtaining a qualification, etc.

After the meeting

After the performance interview, either you or your manager will fill in the agreed objectives on the documentation. This is also an opportunity to record your overall comments about the review meeting itself, the objectives set, or any other aspect of your discussions with your manager.

Even if you do not wish to record any comments, you should sign and date the form to confirm that the meeting took place, and then pass the documentation back to your manager for their comments. When your manager has added the final comments, you will be given a copy of all the documentation, and your manager will also keep a copy. It is then your joint responsibility to ensure that all the actions agreed at the appraisal are followed up as planned, and to review your progress towards meeting your objectives, at regular follow-up meetings.

If you are unhappy with the way the meeting was carried out, or you have strong objections to the content of the form, do speak to your manager. If you are unable to resolve this, refer to the firm's grievance procedure. This is contained in the staff handbook. [Do remember that, at the end of the day, it is your manager's view of your performance that is being recorded. You may not agree with this view, but this alone does not necessarily justify raising a grievance.] You may also use the grievance procedure when your manager does not carry out regular performance review meetings with you. This will ensure that you get the feedback you are seeking on your performance.

Annex 5T

Pre-appraisal questions for appraisee

Please reply to the following questions: [*or select from these if you would like a shorter form*].

1.   What skills do you believe are necessary to carry out your job?

2.   What personal qualities are needed to carry out your job?

3.   Which part of the job interests you most?

4.   Which part interests you least?

5.   How do you feel you have performed in the last six months/year?

6.   Which tasks do you think you could have performed more effectively and why?

7.   Which tasks do you feel you have performed particularly well?

8.   Are there any improvements which could be made to the way in which you work that would make you more efficient?

9.   Do you possess skills, knowledge or experience acquired elsewhere of which we do not make full use?

10.   Which areas of your job are you unclear about?

11.   Does your job description properly describe your duties and responsibilities?

12.   Do you feel that you could take on other responsibilities, such as supervision, administrative duties, etc.

13.   Where would you like to be in one year and five years' time?

14.   Are there any general matters that you would like to discuss?

[*This preparation form could either be required to be submitted a day or two before the appraisal meeting or it could be brought to the meeting by the appraisee. Users may consider limiting questions to the more important ones – this is quite a long list*]

Annex 5U

Alternative pre-appraisal questionnaire

In order to prepare for your appraisal meeting, please spend a little time considering the issues raised in this form. You should note your comments so that you will be able to discuss the issues raised. This form will not be taken in by the person conducting your interview and does not form part of the formal record of the interview.

The appraisal meeting is your opportunity to:

(a) discuss your work and how it fits in with the work of the team that you belong to and the firm as a whole;

(b) agree on possible improvements to your role and the means by which improvements will be achieved;

(c) decide what training might be appropriate during the year ahead.

At your appraisal meeting a report form will be filled in. You will see this report and you should sign it only if you agree with the comments contained in it.

| Name of appraisee: |
| Job title: |
| Department: |
| Appraiser's name: |

1. Job description

You will find attached to this form a copy of your current job description. Is this a fair and correct description of your role or does it need amendment? If so, how?

2. Your work

What do you like best about your job?

And what do you like least about your job?

(Fee earners and managers only)

If possible, list two tasks which you think you achieved particular success in.

If possible, list two tasks which you did not perform as well as you should have, and state why.

3. Your team

How could your job be reorganised to make it more satisfying for you and/or more effective for the firm?

Would you benefit from changed supervisory arrangements? If so, what changes would you suggest?

4. Your development

Are there any personal goals that you would like to set for yourself over the next year? If so, what are they?

In which areas would you welcome training, if any?

Annex 5V
Partner review/appraisal form – small firm

Partner reviewed:

Reviewed by:

Date of review:

---

1. Job responsibilities

[add specific responsibilities not reflected in job description]

2. Professional issues: challenges arising in area of practice

3. Personal objectives for next 12 months

4. Legal training requirements

5. Management training requirements

Signed .... Date ....
Reviewer

Signed .... Date ....
Partner under review

Annex 5W
Partner review/appraisal report form (with optional ratings)

Partner reviewed:
Reviewed by:
Date of review:

Business performance	
Fees billed in year individually	
Fees billed in year by team (if applicable)	
Comments	
Objectives	
Professional responsibilities	
Knowledge and expertise	
Problem solving	
Areas for professional development (see also later: Training)	
[Rating]	
Client handling skills and marketing	
Organisation and support for marketing functions and activities	
Personal profile in local or client community	
[Rating]	
Managerial and supervisory qualities	
Leadership: setting directions and goals for team	
Motivation: ability to inspire team	
Application of quality system	
Co-ordination of team or department (if applicable)	
[Rating]	

Personal qualities	
Sensitivity for personnel welfare	
Flexibility	
Resilience	
Personal motivation and enthusiasm	
[Rating]	
Overall rating	
Business performance	
Professional responsibilities	
Client handling skills and marketing	
Managerial and supervisory qualities	
Personal qualities	
Overall rating	
Personal development objectives	
	by when?
	by when?
	by when?
Training to undertake	

Signed

Reviewer (1) .... Date.................................

Reviewer (2) .... Date.................................

Appraisee .... Date.................................

Annex 5X

Fee earner appraisal (without ratings) – short form

Name:
Date of review:
Job title:

Main purpose of job	
Main task(s) of job 1. 2. 3. 4. 5.	**Skills, knowledge, abilities and experience required to undertake these tasks**
Aspects of my job that I most enjoy	
Aspects of my job that I least enjoy	
Aspects of my job where I could improve	
Personal objectives for next 12 months 1. 2. 3.	
Training (if any) that will enable me to achieve these objectives by when? by when? by when?	

Signed .... (appraiser)

Signed .... (appraisee)

Annex 5Y

General appraisal/review form (without ratings)

This form is confidential once it has been completed but will be discussed between each of the people in the appraisal meeting. It will then be a formal record of the review meeting. Appraisers should not record comments unless they have been discussed and, preferably, agreed. If agreement is not possible please set out the different views held.

Appraisees are asked to sign the form at the end and put in their own comments if appropriate.

Name of appraisee:
Job title:
Department:
Appraisers:

---

1. Job Description

   Do you consider that the current job description is in need of amendment? If so, please note the required changes here:

---

2. Technical ability (fee earners)

   Secretarial skills (secretaries)

   Job expertise (administrators)

   Comment:

---

3. Volume of work and reliability

   Comment:

---

4. Knowledge of the firm

   Please comment on knowledge of the firm and compliance with quality procedures:

5. **Personal organisation**

Please comment on:
- Organisation of work
- Ability to meet deadlines
- Reliability of administration

6. **Problem solving and decision making (fee earners only)**

Comment on ability to inspire confidence in clients in respect of the above:

7. **Relationship with colleagues**

Comment:

8. **Communication**

Please comment on communication, both written and oral, with colleagues, clients and others:

9. **Personal objectives**

In light of the above, please try to agree a number of performance objectives. Please be as specific as possible and put a time limit on each.

(1)
(2)
(3)
(4)

10. Training

What training might assist in achieving the objectives set out above?

(1)
(2)
(3)
(4)

Summary comments by appraiser

Date:

Summary comments by appraisee

Date:

Notes: Managing partner/head of department/staff partner/personnel manager

Date:

Future action (if any)

Signed ....(appraisee)

Annex 5Z

Training feedback form

| Title of course: |
| Date of course: |

Your comments on the above course will be appreciated and acted upon. Thank you for your time and trouble. Please return to the presenter or your training manager as requested. Please provide an assessment as follows:

1 = Less than adequate
2 = Satisfactory
3 = Good
4 = Excellent

Please also add any comments in the box provided. Please continue any comments overleaf if necessary.

	1	2	3	4
Pre-course information				
Contents of the session				
Quality of presentation				
Use of visual aids, if any				
How well my interest was addressed				
Please also comment on:
What I liked most about this session
What I least liked about this session
How I would like to take these areas further, if at all

Name .... Date ....

Annex 5ZA

Sample disciplinary procedure

Policy

The aim of the firm's disciplinary policy is to ensure that the terms and conditions of employment are met and to comply with the law. Where the firm's standards are not being met by an employee, consultation with the employee will take place to ensure corrective action is taken. If the issue is not resolved following consultation, disciplinary action will be taken. The aim is to bring about the required improvement to the firm's standards and should not be viewed as punitive.

When disciplinary action is considered, the firm will ensure that the facts of the matter are investigated and established, that any disciplinary action taken is appropriate and consistent and that the employee concerned knows the reason for proposed disciplinary action and the procedure for appealing against the proposed action. Investigative meetings do not form part of the disciplinary procedure.

Employees' rights

At all stages of the procedure (see 'Warning procedure' below) the employee has the following rights:

- to be told of the complaint against him/her;
- to state his/her case;
- to be accompanied by a firm colleague or trade union representative of his/her choice;
- to be given the reason for any penalty imposed;
- to use the appeals procedure.

Reasons for disciplinary action

1. Misconduct, lack of capability or performance

   - Failure to obey a reasonable request
   - Failure to work to agreed procedures
   - Unsatisfactory performance
   - Unauthorised absence or absenteeism
   - Infringement of safety rules
   - Smoking on firm premises
   - Abusive or insulting behaviour to colleagues/public

This list is non-exhaustive.

For the above, the appropriate action would normally be the warning procedure.

2. Gross misconduct

- Violence or the threat of violence in the course of employment
- Assault or indecency, or foul or abusive language
- Theft or other dishonesty, or deliberate damage to firm's property
- Commission of any criminal offence that may affect the employee's ability to carry out his/her job
- Possession of illegal substances
- Disclosure of confidential firm information to a third party
- Breach of computer security policy
- Breach of the firm's policies relating to the use of computers, e-mail, and access to the internet
- Breach of the alcohol and illegal substances policy
- Incapability through alcohol or being under the influence of illegal drugs
- Sexual, racial, age or disability-related harassment at work
- Any action likely to bring the firm or its clients into disrepute

This list is non-exhaustive.

The above may lead to summary dismissal without notice depending upon the nature and severity of the offence. Only a senior partner or his/her appointed deputy has the authority to dismiss summarily (i.e. without notice or payment in lieu).

Warning procedure

Every effort will be made to deal with minor matters through informal counselling initially. The formal procedure will be used where the informal approach has not had the desired effect, or the issue is more serious and the informal route is not appropriate.

Stage 1 – verbal warning

A verbal warning will be given by a manager or head of department. This will be recorded on the personal file of the individual. If there is no further reason for action in respect of the disciplinary matter in question, this warning will be disregarded for disciplinary purposes after six months.

Stage 2 – first written warning

If there is a repetition of the first offence or there is a more serious first offence, a further warning will be given. The employee will then receive a written warning. This letter will indicate the details of the disciplinary issue, and the employee will be requested to sign and return a copy of the warning.

This warning will be placed on the individual's personal file. If there is no further reason for action on the offence(s) in question, this warning will be disregarded for disciplinary purposes after 12 months.

Stage 3 – final written warning

If there is no improvement or there is a more serious first offence a final warning will be issued and the employee will receive a final written warning. This warning will be placed on the individual's personal file. If there is no further reason for action on the offence(s) in question, this warning will be disregarded for disciplinary purposes after 18 months.

If the breach of discipline continues, the employee will become liable to dismissal, demotion and/or transfer.

An employee may be dismissed only after the permission of the senior/managing partner or his/her appointed deputy has been obtained.

Although provision is made for discipline by stages, the procedure may be implemented at any stage, according to the seriousness of the alleged offence. There may be occasions when misconduct is considered to be sufficiently serious to warrant only one written warning, which, in effect, will be both first and final.

Appeal procedure

If an employee disagrees with any disciplinary decision, a decision to dismiss him or her, or the imposition of any other disciplinary penalty, he/she may appeal in writing, stating the reason for the appeal, within five working days of the receipt of the written warning/notice of termination to [name or title].

The appeal will normally be heard by a partner, or in his/her absence by an appointed deputy, within 10 working days of the appeal being lodged.

The result of the appeal will normally be communicated to all the parties within two working days of the appeal being heard.

The partner may vary the sanction, although its severity cannot be increased, and his/her decision will be final.

New employees

For new employees in their probationary period the full disciplinary procedure may not be appropriate and dismissal may be preceded by one verbal warning for poor performance or misconduct. The appeals procedure would apply.

Suspension with pay

It may be necessary during the investigation of a disciplinary offence to suspend an employee with pay. This suspension will not normally exceed 10 working days.

Annex 5ZB

Sample grievance procedure

The object of the grievance procedure is to enable employees who consider they have a grievance or complaint arising from their employment with the firm to have it dealt with at the nearest appropriate level within as short a time as possible. Anyone wishing to use this procedure can do so freely and without prejudice to his/her position in the firm. It applies to all employees, irrespective of job or grade.

At all stages of the grievance procedure you may be accompanied by a fellow worker or a trade union official of your choice. Each step of the grievance procedure will be processed without unreasonable delay.

Before commencing this formal process, you are encouraged, wherever possible, to try and resolve the matter with your immediate Manager through informal discussions. Only where that has been tried, or the matter is too serious, should the formal procedure be used.

Step 1

In the first instance all grievances must be submitted in writing to your immediate superior, who will attempt to deal with the matter after making such consultations as are necessary.

Step 2

Every opportunity will be given for your grievance to be stated and thoroughly discussed. You will be invited to attend a meeting to discuss your grievance. As appropriate, further investigation may take place and action taken. After the meeting, you will be informed of the result, and what further action will be taken where appropriate. A decision will be given within [10] working days of the meeting, unless further investigation is required or where this has been extended by mutual consent. If you are not satisfied with the response, you can appeal against the decision in writing within [5] working days of being informed of the outcome of the grievance.

If the complaint or grievance relates to your immediate superior, (or you feel unable/unwilling to raise it with them) the grievance can be raised with [*name or title*] or through the human resources department.

If the matter is not resolved to your satisfaction within a reasonable time, you can raise it with [*name or title*].

Step 3

If you wish to appeal, you will be invited to a further meeting. This will be heard by a more senior manager where this is reasonably practicable. You will have the right to be accompanied and to make submissions for consideration.

After the appeal meeting, you will be informed of the firm's decision. This decision is final and the grievance procedure is exhausted following this stage.

Annex 5ZC

Sample retirement policy

At [name of firm] we are keen to offer flexible working and retirement options, which enable people to work up to, and beyond state pension age of 65 should they choose to.

We aim to do this by taking the following approaches to retirement:

- base retirement policy on the needs of the firm and relevant legislation;
- give individuals as much choice and notice as possible;
- evaluate the loss to the firm of skills and abilities and plan how to replace or retain these;
- use flexible retirement schemes;
- make pre-retirement support available;
- allow staff to take their pension and continue to work.

The normal retirement date for employees is their 65th birthday. You can request retiring early or working beyond this date, and any request will be given full and positive consideration.

The partners are committed to flexible working and will consult with you about your proposed retirement date well in advance. The availability of flexible working is subject to your being capable of continued work and not being subject to any current disciplinary warnings.

Pre-retirement support

The firm will help employees prepare for retirement as follows:

- providing financial guidance;
- providing the opportunity to attend workshops;
- from the age of 60 onwards, or where ill health is a factor, the firm tries to offer employees flexibility over both retirement date and working patterns, for example a reduction of hours, gradual retirement, lower grade or less stressful work. This is always subject to suitable work being available.

Pre-retirement checklist

In the run up to retirement there are a number of items that need to be discussed and agreed by the firm:

1. Between 12 and 6 months before your 65th birthday the firm will write to you advising you of the due date of retirement, your 65th birthday. If you wish to be considered for work after your due retirement date you should notify [name or title], in writing, not later than three months before your due retirement

date. Your request should state how long you wish to work beyond your 65th birthday – is it until a set date, a set period, e.g. six months, or is it a request to work on indefinitely?
2. Six months before your retirement date [*name or title*] will contact the firm's pension providers to notify them of your leaving date.
3. Three months before retirement, [*name or title*] will check that you have received a notification from the DWP regarding the payment of the state pension, and if not, will chase the DWP for it.
4. One month before retirement, [*name or title*] will review the situation regarding any loans, outstanding holidays, statutory sick pay, etc., and advise you about any adjustments that may need to be made.
5. Employees will not normally be permitted to remain in the company beyond their [*specify*] birthday.

Preparation for retirement

Pre-retirement interviews

All staff who are retiring should be offered a pre-retirement interview with [*name or title*]. This should take place at least six months before the employee's retirement date. The member of staff should have the option to be accompanied by a colleague or family member. At the interview, you may wish to cover the following and may also seek advice as to:

- formal agreement of actual retirement date;
- pre-retirement training courses/information;
- alternative employment options (including phased retirement/part-time working, etc.);
- voluntary work;
- extension of contract – a request to work on.

Pre-retirement seminars/courses

Pre-retirement seminars and courses might be available locally and the support of the firm will be provided in permitting reasonable paid absence for the employee to attend. Consideration will also be given to payment of or a contribution towards the fees of any such course.

Flexible retirement

Flexible, phased retirement helps the firm to prepare for the loss of employee skills. It also allows you to alter the balance of your working and personal life and prepare for full retirement, should you wish to do so.

Options that could suit employees who are close to retirement include:

- part-time working, including job share;
- short-term contract working;

- flexible location working, including from home;
- seasonal working;
- a secondment to a different role;
- outplacement with another employer or a charitable organisation.

The three schemes the firm operates are:

1. **Winding down.** Winding down is an alternative to retiring – you can reduce your hours in your current post in ways that do not reduce pension benefits.

2. **Stepping down.** Step Down is an option to move to a less demanding role in a way that preserves pension entitlement from the higher-level post.

    This will only be possible if there is a suitable role to step down into. You should discuss this option with [*name or title*] and can also seek advice as to what the implications are.

3. **Retire and continue.** In this option, you 'retire' and start receiving your pension but return to carry on with part-time or full-time work in the long or short term.

We are keen to retain the skills and knowledge of those who are considering retiring early or who have recently retired. If you want to work for the firm on a temporary basis the partners will be happy to consider your application.

There are no significant obstacles to staff resuming work after retirement – for full-time, part-time or for short periods.

Request to continue working – procedure

Should the employee wish to carry on working beyond normal retirement age, as stated above, such a request must be put in writing to [*name or title*]. This should be between three months and six months before the planned retirement. The letter should state whether this request is for a set period of time, to a set date or indefinite.

[*Name or title*] will then invite the employee to a meeting to discuss the request. The employee has the right to have a colleague or trade union representative as a companion. This meeting will be arranged as soon as reasonably possible, and will normally be within two to four weeks of the employee request. Only in exceptional circumstances will it take more than four weeks to arrange a meeting.

If the request is agreed, [*name or title*] will confirm this in writing. If the request is rejected, the employee has the right to make one appeal. This appeal must be in writing, no later that two weeks after the rejection letter. [*Name or title*] will deal with this, and again the employee has the right to be accompanied. This appeal meeting will be arranged as soon as reasonably possible, and will normally be within two to four weeks of the employee's appeal letter. Only in exceptional circumstances will it take more than four weeks to arrange an appeal meeting.

The final decision will be confirmed in writing. If the request has been turned down, the letter will confirm the planned retirement date of the employee.

The firm reserves the right to refuse a request to work beyond the normal retirement age of 65 and will normally provide the business reasons for this decision. An employee can make only one request.

6 Supervision and risk management

This section examines supervision of fee earning work and the linked issue of operational risk management – the reduction of complaints and claims against the practice. There is more of an element of professional compliance now in this section as a result of the 2007 Code, Rule 5 (Business management in England and Wales). Rule 5 creates a new duty 'for the effective management of the firm as a whole' and then goes on to require (see subrule 5.01) that arrangements are in place for a number of supervisory issues including 'the management of risk' (subrule 5.01(1)(l); see also the accompanying guidance notes 2–13 on supervision and 39–40 on the management of risk). Lexcel (4th edition) again links the topics of supervision and operational risk management. Whether to gain a potential advantage in relation to indemnity insurance or to ensure that the practice is able to evidence compliance with Rule 5, this area is likely to remain the single most persuasive reason for a Lexcel application.

Lexcel has some specific risk management procedures which have mostly been drawn up in the light of the Turnbull guidance on risk management (*Internal Control: Guidance for Directors on the Combined Code*, published by the Institute of Chartered Accountants in England and Wales). The starting point, however, should be a thorough review of supervision in the practice. This, in turn, can be examined in terms of the structures and then the personal interests and skills of those that have a supervisory role.

So far as supervision is concerned, Lexcel requires a designated supervisor for each area of the firm's work. The provisions are that supervisors must 'have appropriate experience of the work supervised and be competent to guide and assist others'. There is no requirement that supervisors must be members of panels or have certain specific experience, in contrast to the more rigid requirements in the SQM. There are also requirements of supervisors under the 2007 Code, subule 5.03(3) where it is provided that work must be checked by 'suitably experienced and competent persons'.

6.1 Supervision

6.1.1 Supervision is achieved through the departmental structure which is outlined in the organisational chart that appears at annex 6A. It is important that all fee earning work is directed to the appropriate department so that it is conducted subject to proper quality control. In all cases the head of department is the nominated supervisor of all work in their department unless otherwise indicated.

6.1.2 The departments are:

[*Specify and describe their range of activities*]

The departmental heads, with responsibility for the expertise and development of their departments are:

Conveyancing	Head of department	[*Name*]
	Other partners	[*Names*]
Crime	Head of department	[*Name*]
	Other partners	[*Names*]

[*Include details of other areas of work as appropriate*]

The responsibility for policies and plans is as follows:

Risk management	[*Name or title*]
Quality policy	[*Name or title*]
Equality and diversity	[*Name or title*]
Money Laundering Reporting Officer	[*Name or title*]
Health and safety	[*Name or title*]
Community and social responsibility	[*Name or title*]
Business planning	[*Name or title*]
Marketing	[*Name or title*]
Services plan	[*Name or title*]
Business continuity	[*Name or title*]
Financial management	[*Name or title*]
Information and communication technology	[*Name or title*]
Human resources (personnel) plan	[*Name or title*]
Training and development	[*Name or title*]
Client care	[*Name or title*]

Other important managerial and administrative roles are:

Managing partner	[*Name*]
Finance partner	[*Name*]
Risk management partner	[*Name*]

Chief cashier	[*Name*]
Assistant cashier	[*Name*]
Health and safety manager	[*Name*]
Librarian	[*Name*]
Buildings and equipment supervisor	[*Name*]
Post room/general office supervisor	[*Name*]
Training partner/director/manager	[*Name*]
IT partner/director/manager	[*Name*]

6.1.3 It is the responsibility of the supervisor to provide an appropriate level of supervision to their group, department or team, having regard to the work undertaken, the seniority and experience of the personnel under supervision and the case management controls in place. The supervisor is expected to be available to deal with issues requiring their attention and will make arrangements for a deputy to be available when this is not possible. In addition the supervisor will:

- maintain lists of work that is and is not undertaken within their group, department or team. If work is declined, the client should receive such explanation as is appropriate and every effort should usually be made to signpost them to another firm that will be able to undertake the work;
- maintain and keep under review lists of risk associated with the work undertaken under their control, ensuring that new developments are raised in an appropriate manner with all relevant personnel;
- ensure the maintenance of appropriate professional expertise and standards in the area that they supervise;
- determine whether instructions should be accepted. In most instances the signature of any partner on any matter opening form will be acceptable as evidence that the work can and should be handled by the firm. Fee earners must, however, refer matter opening forms to the supervisor, or a deputy in their absence, if there is any doubt as to the propriety of the instructions or the ability of the firm to undertake the work given the expertise required or the resources available;
- allocate work within the department/section/team to ensure that matters are handled with sufficient expertise and under appropriate supervision;
- review the performance and workload of fee earners whom they supervise through monthly 'one-to-one' review meetings at which a computer print-out of all matters under the control of the fee earner will be checked or discussed, re-allocating work if necessary;
- undertake all file reviews within their area of work, or monitor the process if this is undertaken on their behalf, and address all general issues arising from file reviews as well as the corrective action that might be required from the reviews;
- act as the risk manager for the area of work that they supervise [*elaborate here on what this might mean – e.g. to attend meetings of a risk management committee*].

6.1.4 In addition to the above, the designated supervisors in litigation areas have the responsibility for the specific risk assessment where conditional fee arrangements are being considered.

6.1.5 The signature of a partner is needed on every matter opening form as evidence that the matter should be undertaken by the firm and can be handled by the designated matter handler.

6.2 Systems of supervision

■ The following procedure is a useful 'mop-up' to cross-refer to the total pattern of supervision throughout the practice. Not all firms will wish to adopt all of the procedures that follow, but it may be useful to consider them. The same is true of most of the provisions under section 6.1.3 above.

6.2.1 Supervision is effected by:

- the allocation of all work to the appropriate department and specialists;
- all incoming post, including faxes, being seen by the supervisor or another partner/senior manager (for monitoring of e-mails see section 4A.4);
- all fee earners of up to two years' post-qualification experience having to copy letters of substantive advice to their immediate supervisor at the time that it is created;
- monthly departmental meetings, when technical problems can always be discussed;
- the monthly print-out review by head of department, with particular emphasis on the number of live files, values of work in progress, bills outstanding and any apparent inactivity on files;
- regular file reviews and audits;
- in publicly funded work, reviews of the exercise of any devolved powers;
- open door periods for consultation in the day.

6.3 Work allocation

■ The allocation of instructions (and subsequent re-allocation when needed) is a critical risk control. The following general procedure envisages partner involvement in every new matter, but this will probably be seen as unhelpful in volume departments where, as long as the work fits a general pre-designed pattern, it can be safely accepted and allocated at a lower level. If this is the case in the firm, or certain parts of it, some modification to the following procedures will be needed.

6.3.1 Work is to be allocated by a partner in all cases. The signature of a partner on the matter opening form is evidence that the partner considers that:

- this is the type of matter the firm should accept;
- the matter can be fairly allocated to the person named as matter handler;
- the partner agrees with the risk assessment that will need to be completed before the form is signed by the partner.

6.3.2 Particular care is needed with internal transfers of work. A fee earner wishing to involve a colleague in another department should always refer to the head of department or another partner in that department and not to an assistant directly.

6.4 Maintaining progress

▓ Section 6.4 of Lexcel provides that there must be 'processes' for checking for inactivity. Since it is not a 'procedure' that is required the firm is free to comply in any valid way and not necessarily as prescribed in the manual. Nonetheless, it is useful to set out the requirement in the manual and some illustrations follow.

6.4.1 Fee earners are under an obligation to ensure that there is no undue delay on the matters that they are handling and this will involve regular checks of all files. This will usually take the form of a regular 'trawl' of the filing cabinet.

[*or*: As a matter of principle all files should be subject to ongoing review at least once a month by the fee earner responsible for that file. Reviews should consider whether the client's instructions are being adequately met and whether action is needed to implement instructions or if contact is needed with the client to vary the case plan or instructions in any way. They are therefore both technical and procedural. The evidence of this personal check will be the initials of the fee earner on his/her monthly matters print-out. The fee earner is required to retain the last three print-outs which also form the basis of the monthly 'one-to-one' review with the supervisor. The date of this meeting must be noted on the print-out in question.]

[In addition, heads of department will check regularly for inactivity through the monthly matter print-out review/receipt of reports on all matters where over three months have elapsed since time was recorded, etc.]

6.4.2 In publicly funded work it is the responsibility of the designated supervisor or, in their absence, [the deputy supervisor/another litigation partner] to consider and approve all exercises of devolved powers, having regard to the guidelines in force from the Legal Services Commission. Any consideration of the exercise of devolved powers will be recorded on the form appearing at annex 6B. This form must be filed on the matter file and in a central file of all such decisions.

6.5 File reviews

▓ It is likely that the need for file reviews will prove one of the most problematic elements of the 2007 Code, Rule 5 for larger firms in particular. It is important to examine the need for checking in subrule 5.03(3) in some detail, which provides that 'The system for supervision under 5.03(1) and (2) must include appropriate and effective procedures under which the quality of work undertaken for clients and members of the public is checked with reasonable regularity by suitably experienced and competent persons within the firm, law centre or in-house legal department.' File reviews will be one very obvious way to meet this provision and are, in any event, a requirement under both Lexcel and the SQM.

Lexcel has always allowed file reviews to be substantive or procedural, or both, and it is to be hoped that the same will apply to this new rule and its requirement that the 'quality of work' is checked with 'reasonable regularity'. File reviews will be one way to meet this provision, though a pattern of work under which there is ongoing partner involvement in matters could be an alternative. Although file reviews are often seen as being one of the most problematic aspects of a Lexcel programme, most fee earners will agree that such reviews do form an essential component of effective supervision. The firm may decide the frequency and, to a degree, the depth of the reviews. There is no reason why file reviews have to happen as a set exercise once a month or quarter – they can be performed progressively as supervisor and fee earner meet.

Under Lexcel all fee earners need to be subject to a file review process, including the supervisor. It is not a requirement that all file reviews are conducted by the supervisor in person, though he or she should have overall control of it.

6.5.1 The firm operates a system of occasional, independent file reviews. The frequency of file reviews is [two/three files per month for nought to three years admitted and legal executives, and one file per month/quarter for all partners, senior executives and fee earners over three years admitted]. Files are selected [at random, from the monthly activity reports [*specify other*]].

6.5.2 This is a task that will usually be undertaken within the department in order that substantive issues can also be discussed. The selection of files should be generated by the monthly matter print-out and it is likely that files with high WIP (work in progress) value or long periods of inactivity will be selected. Where the fee earner undertakes a range of different work type matters the selection should be representative of the fee earner's work spread.

6.5.3 A file review form (annex 6C) will be completed when any such independent file review occurs. Copies will be put on to the matter file and on to a central departmental list of all review sheets to verify that reviews are occurring as planned, and that any corrective action identified as being necessary is being taken. When corrective action is specified as being required it is the responsibility of the matter handler to undertake the corrective action specified within the time specified, and in no case will this be longer than 28 days. The reviewer must then verify to his or her reasonable satisfaction that the corrective action has been performed and then sign off the form at the next monthly review.

6.5.4 As to the responsibility of the supervisor to monitor the process and to ensure that issues emerging from file reviews are addressed see section 6.1.3 above (responsibilities of supervisors).

6.5.5 It is the responsibility of [*name or title*] to review all file review data at least annually and include an analysis and recommendations based on the data that emerges from such review into the annual review of the operation of the quality management system.

6.6 Managing risk

- This section addresses the need for management of risk as set out in section 6.6 of the Lexcel standard. This in turn embodies most of the Turnbull guidance on operational risk management. The key recommendation in this report is that there should be one person who has ultimate responsibility for the management of risk. This person should:

  - understand the practice;
  - have appropriate delegated structures in place;
  - understand the nature of the risks to which the firm is exposed;
  - ensure that internal controls are established and remain effective;
  - establish communication lines to ensure that the partnership or senior management is made aware of the risk profile as it develops;
  - review plans for future developments to see what implications they may have for risk profile;
  - install warning systems and ensure that appropriate action is taken.

  Insurers tend to prefer that procedures do not differ greatly between complaints and claims and that both are instead dealt with as 'risk events'.

  Section 6.6.3 provides some terms of reference for a risk committee. There is no need to appoint such a body, but it can be helpful in larger firms. An alternative in many firms is to specify responsibility to review risk as being part of the role of heads of departments' meetings.

6.6.1 The fees for the firm's annual indemnity insurance represent a considerable item of expenditure for the firm and are geared very heavily to its risk profile, which in turn is judged largely on its claims record. In any event, if the firm is committed to providing the best legal advice possible it needs to consider its responsibilities to clients to avoid the loss and inconvenience that could arise from its negligence and the harm that would be effected to its reputation.

It has to be accepted that the firm cannot possibly operate a 'risk-free' practice. It is important, however, for the firm to take all reasonable steps to minimise the risk of a claim or a complaint against it. This has to involve all personnel.

6.6.2 The main thrust of the firm's risk management policy is that prevention is better than cure. [*Name or title*] is responsible for the management of the firm's risk profile. In this respect (s)he will:

- keep under review the firm's policy, procedures and arrangements for the management of risk;
- call meetings of the risk committee as appropriate, and in any event every six months, to discuss issues of concern;
- receive risk notices (see annex 6D) and take such action in respect of them that seems appropriate;
- monitor new aspects of risk that could develop and report accordingly to the [partnership/management board];
- negotiate and liaise with the firm's professional indemnity insurers/brokers;
- take whatever action that seems appropriate to ensure that risk is identified, anticipated and guarded against, so far as possible;

- arrange training, in conjunction with [the training partner/director/manager] on risk issues if appropriate.

6.6.3 The [*specify role*] is helped in these duties by a committee representing every department. This is comprised of:

[*name members or say where they could be identified – e.g. phone list*]

It is the responsibility of the risk committee members to:

- monitor developments in their practice area(s);
- maintain lists of risks associated with the work types of the department and ensure that these are brought to the attention of members of the department;
- maintain lists of work that the department will and will not accept;
- stipulate [in conjunction with the head of department [*if this individual is not one and the same*]] arrangements that will need to be made if work is accepted which is judged to be high risk.

6.6.4 It is the responsibility of [everyone in the practice/all fee earners] to report without delay anything that could give rise to a claim for compensation, however minimal and whatever its merit. Similarly, if a client threatens legal action against the firm, all personnel are obliged to report this without delay, even if they do not believe the threat. You must not try to deal with the situation yourself – still less ignore the problem and hope that it will go away. It should also go without saying that you should not make any statement that could be construed as an admission of fault, nor are you entitled to offer compensation, including a discount on any bill that has been issued. Any failure by the firm to meet the requirements of its insurers could lead to penalties against it. Failure to report any such circumstances without delay could therefore potentially be treated as a disciplinary offence.

6.6.5 There may be occasions when you are not sure whether you should deal with a problem as a potential claim or a complaint. The approach of the practice is that this doesn't matter, as long as you do report it.

6.7 Reporting risk

6.7.1 The level of risk presented by every file needs to be considered by the fee earner. Risk is an issue before, during and after action is taken in every matter. It is quite clear that the proactive management of risk issues will reduce the incidence of claims and complaints in most firms.

6.7.2 Before any person acts an initial risk assessment must be made as part of the file opening procedures. This is noted on the file opening form (see annex 8C). All fee earners must tick to show whether the matter is 'ordinary' or 'high' risk. It should not be left to secretaries to make this judgement if they are assisting in the administrative steps of opening the file. The accounts department will not allocate a client/matter number until a duly completed file opening form has been received, which must include an entry to this section.

6.7.3 A matter should be judged to be 'high' risk if:

- there is a novel or unusual aspect of law involved;
- a foreign jurisdiction may be involved (e.g. probate where the deceased held property abroad);
- the value of a potential claim is unusually high (consider advising on the maximum claim that the firm is covered for);
- the client has transferred this matter to the firm in circumstances where they were dissatisfied with the advice or service provided by their previous advisers.

6.7.4 In conditional fee matters a specific costs risks assessment should be conducted under procedures established in the litigation department.

6.7.5 The [*specify role*] must have all high risk assessments brought to their attention when the file is opened. They can then review whether the firm should accept these instructions and, if so, what precautionary steps in relation to responsibility, supervision and review should be imposed.

6.7.6 **During** a matter it has to be accepted that a risk profile could change at any time. This might involve greater risk to the firm or the client – for example, third parties become involved in litigation, thereby increasing the risks on costs, or unfavourable advice is received from counsel. A change of circumstances so far as the client is concerned will need to be raised with the client: if there is any suggestion that the firm could be at risk from the changed circumstances, especially if the accuracy or appropriateness of advice to date could now be questioned, a risk notice must be completed (see annex 6D) and forwarded to [*name or role*] without delay.

6.7.7 Any adverse costs orders made against the firm must be promptly reported to the client and to the appropriate [*specify role*].

6.7.8 **After** a matter is finished there needs to be a concluding risk assessment. This is noted on the file closing sheet/file closure section of the file summary sheet (see annex 8D). If it is considered that the firm should have done better for a client, and that they could fairly complain about the service provided or make a claim, the fee earner must complete a risk notice and forward it to the appropriate [head of department/departmental risk committee member, with a copy to the risk partner]. On receipt of such a notice a view will have to be taken as to what action should be taken with the client and the future handling of the matter, and whether the firm is required under the terms of its indemnity insurance contract to make a report.

6.7.9 In summary, if you have a concern before, during or after any matter, share it with your colleagues and make sure that it is reported if there could be a complaint or a claim.

6.8 Risk review

6.8.1 It is the responsibility of [*name or title*] to undertake a review of the operation of the quality and risk system at least annually. This will occur [*state cycle or time of year*] and will comprise a review of:

- claims made and circumstances reported;
- file reviews;
- client complaints;
- client surveys.

A report will be prepared and considered at the annual strategy day [*specify other*].

Annex 6A

Sample organisational chart

The partnership

Management committee
(Managing partner and two elected partners)

Departments:	Private Client/Conveyancing	Family	Litigation	Commercial	Crime
Partners:	Jack Parker	Karen Dobson John Morley	Mohammed Aziz Sally Tomalonis	John Royle Emma King	Bill Horsfield
Assistants:	Geoff Wingate	Marcus Hall Duncan Wilson legal executive	Janet Glass	Martin Evans	Pam Jones
Trainees:	There are two trainee solicitors who are not assigned to any particular department				
Secretaries:	3	2	3	2	1

In addition there are two office assistants; chief cashier; two other members of the accounts department; two receptionists; and one general office supervisor.

Total personnel: 8 partners, 6 assistant fee-earners, 2 trainees, 11 secretaries, 8 administrators (35 in all)

Annex 6B

Consideration of devolved powers

Client name

Matter number

Devolved power under consideration

Matter code

Explanation

Wording code

Power exercised? ☐Yes ☐No

Date and particulars of decision

Date

Record here the appropriate scope limitation

Record here the costs limitation

Comments

Signed _____

Signed _____

Matter Handler _____

Supervisor _____

Date _____

Date _____

Annex 6C

File review form

File name

Matter number

Department

Fee-earner handling

	Yes	No	N/A	Comments
File opening				
Procedures followed	☐	☐	☐	
Accounts label attached	☐	☐	☐	
Identity checked	☐	☐	☐	
Note of instructions	☐	☐	☐	
Instructions confirmed	☐	☐	☐	
Costs information	☐	☐	☐	
Conflicts considered	☐	☐	☐	
Appropriate risk assessment	☐	☐	☐	
State of file				
Appropriately filed	☐	☐	☐	
Key dates noted on file and in back-up system	☐	☐	☐	
Summary sheet completed	☐	☐	☐	
All related files identified	☐	☐	☐	
Separate papers/items identified	☐	☐	☐	
Progress of matter				
Case plan apparent	☐	☐	☐	
Case plan updated	☐	☐	☐	
Progress fully noted	☐	☐	☐	
Costs updated	☐	☐	☐	
Client informed of progress	☐	☐	☐	
Counsel and experts				
Client consulted	☐	☐	☐	
Approved if used	☐	☐	☐	
Properly briefed	☐	☐	☐	
Advice considered	☐	☐	☐	
Unsatisfactory advice noted	☐	☐	☐	
Advice				
Appropriate advice provided	☐	☐	☐	
	☐	☐	☐	

Short-term corrective action

By when?
Confirmed

Long-term corrective action

☐ Corrective action taken   Matter Handler   Date

☐ Corrective action verified   Reviewer   Date

Annex 6D

Risk notice

Client matter number

Fee-earner handling

Stage of matter (please summarise)

Nature of risk now arising

Action already taken

Action that you consider is now needed

Signed _____   Matter Handler   Date _____

Received   Risk Partner   Date _____

7 Client care

Much has been made in recent years of the importance of client care for the profession as a whole. In an ever more consumerist environment poor standards of service will not be tolerated. With clients increasingly likely to change advisers in response to poor experience and reputation, maintaining high standards of client care needs to be a priority for all practices.

Quite apart from the business case for effective client care processes, there is a compliance angle as well. The provisions on client care have been overhauled in the 2007 Code, with a new 'Client relations' Rule 2 replacing the former Practice Rule 15 and its accompanying code. The rule is mandatory for solicitors in private practice and certain sections will also be applicable to in-house departments. Rule 2 goes further than the former Practice Rule 15 in a number of respects, with the revisions process being used as an opportunity to embrace a number of miscellaneous rules and principles that were formerly covered elsewhere in *The Guide to the Professional Conduct of Solicitors*. A good example of this is the obligation not to accept work that the firm does not have the resources to perform, in terms of either expertise or personnel. This now appears at subrule 2.01 (Taking on clients) and is reflected in the sample client care policy that follows at section 7.1. It should also be borne in mind that compliance with Rule 2 is one of the management 'arrangements' required at 5.01(e).

The starting point is to develop a client care policy. It is important to elevate the written policy from good words in a manual to a reality within the workings of the firm. The policy statement could be framed and displayed in the reception area and on staff notice boards, or perhaps even be used as a screen saver on the IT system. Likewise, it should appear on the firm's website, if it has one, and in any brochures and client literature. The draft policy that folllows is based on the obligation under subrule 1.05 to provide a 'good standard of service to your clients'.

It could be argued, of course, that client care is the main theme of this book. The end objective of all management policies, systems and procedures is likely to be to improve the efficiency of the firm and thereby to enhance profitability. It follows that one of the ways to test whether a project to introduce the Lexcel standard to the practice has been successful is to measure improvements to client satisfaction and financial performance.

See also the Law Society's best practice guide, 'Your clients – your business' (third edition, October 2007) at **www.lawsociety.org.uk**.

7.1 Policy on client care

7.1.1 [*Name of firm*] is committed to providing a good service to all clients. The firm's services should be recognised as being expert, accurate and appropriate. The firm strives to ensure that its advice is cost effective and communicated in a manner that is appropriate for each client. The firm is also committed to providing a truly professional service, meaning that all personnel must act with integrity in all their dealings with clients. This is in part achieved by ensuring that everyone complies with the provisions of the 2007 Code, Rule 2 (Client relations). All personnel should at all times consider the need to perform to the 'four Cs', namely: competence, confidentiality, commitment and courtesy.

Competence

7.1.2 The firm will accept instructions only where it can meet its commitment to the provision of an expert and professional service to clients. Where instructions would be beyond the expertise or the capabilities of the firm they will be declined. All heads of department maintain lists of work that the firm will and will not undertake; in any cases of doubt as to the ability of the firm to act appropriately for the client, the appropriate head of department should be consulted.

Confidentiality

7.1.3 All solicitors are bound by the professional rules which require confidentiality to be maintained in all dealings with clients. This means that nobody may reveal to any outsider the nature of instructions provided or advice given to any client, other than in the pursuit of the client's instructions. In most circumstances it will also be inappropriate to reveal that the firm is in receipt of instructions from any named client. This is particularly the case in litigation, especially crime or divorce. If you are aware that friends or other people that you know are instructing the firm it may be tempting to reveal this information to others; do not do so. If you are ever in doubt as to whether you should reveal whether the firm acts for a given client, or give out his, her or its address, check with a partner. Breaches of confidentiality could cause considerable problems for the firm and will usually be treated by the partners as a serious disciplinary offence. (See also section 8.15.)

> On the need for clients' consent to their address being revealed other than in the course of acting for them see the 2007 Code, guidance note 9(b) to Rule 4.

Commitment

7.1.4 Clients seek legal advice for a variety of reasons, but many approach a solicitor when they are vulnerable and in turmoil, whether in their personal lives or in their business activities. Clients are entitled to expect a genuine commitment from all personnel in handling their instructions, and for the firm to attach appropriate priority to their requirements.

Courtesy

7.1.5 All clients are entitled to be dealt with in a respectful and courteous manner. This will have many implications, from not keeping clients waiting in the reception area without explanation, to showing them the way to and from meeting rooms, to returning telephone calls and e-mails as a priority, and generally taking an interest in them and their problems. All personnel should show a genuine concern for the firm's clients by doing their best to help them.

7.2 Dress and demeanour

7.2.1 It is important that the firm should at all times project a sense of professionalism in its dealings with clients. First impressions gained by clients do matter. All personnel should dress in a manner that is appropriate for a professional practice, and in particular avoid [*specify, e.g. jeans, tops with prominent logos, etc.*]. Please also try to conduct yourself in a way that will reassure clients. This can be achieved by appropriate behaviour around the office and a smile or a 'good morning' or 'good afternoon' to those clients you encounter in the office. Please try to be as helpful as possible to all clients of the firm – not just those that you happen to be dealing with.

7.3 Client confidentiality

▨ The topic of client confidentiality is one of the most significant additions to the new professional rules. The 2007 Code, Rule 4 adds to the duties of confidentiality (subrule 4.01) and disclosure (subrule 4.02) and introduces a duty to decline to act where one client has an 'interest adverse' to another client (subrule 4.03). These are, along with the linked issue of conflicts of interest at Rule 3, the most complex of the rule changes. The new rules on conflicts of interests are intended to be de-regulatory – i.e. they purport to enable firms to act in more situations than might have previously been possible. This is almost bound to mean that there will be more borderline situations where it is arguable as to what the firm could and should do. The indications are that the SRA will monitor compliance more strictly than might have been the case before, meaning that firms will have to address the application of the new rules with care and under appropriate supervisory arrangements.

The sample procedures that follow merely reflect the more straightforward provisions. Subject to the work types of any given practice someone should make it their task to consider how these rules impact on the practice.

7.3.1 The firm is under a duty to keep all client dealings properly confidential, other than in certain limited and exceptional cases. It is easy to fall foul of this important duty by thoughtless conversations and quick meetings in the reception area. Please keep any discussions of client business in the reception area to a minimum and, wherever possible, take clients into a meeting room when they come in to sign a document or bring in papers that need to be explained or discussed. What should be a short visit can easily change if the client asks questions and they should be entitled to do so out of the earshot of other clients or visitors.

7.3.2 You are also asked to keep personal conversations in the reception area to a minimum. The impression gained by clients overhearing conversations – especially if about the firm or other clients – in the reception area can be very negative.

▨ See also 8.8(c) of Lexcel on the duty of confidentiality more generally.

7.4 Fee earner responsibilities

7.4.1 The firm is more likely to project an organised and professional image if fee earners take responsibility to:

- advise reception of all appointments;
- make a reservation as soon as possible when meeting rooms are required;
- book car parking spaces with reception;
- ensure that clients are not kept waiting;
- ensure that clients are shown hospitality, are provided with appropriate refreshments, coffee, tea, biscuits, etc., and are shown to and from any room used for a client appointment;
- inform their secretary (if any) of their whereabouts in the building;
- ensure that reception and their secretary (if any) are informed if they leave the firm's premises other than at lunchtime, telling them when they are leaving and their expected time of return.

7.5 Receptionists' responsibilities

7.5.1 The reception area is the firm's 'shop window' and is critical to the first impression that visitors will gain of the firm. The receptionists should take responsibility to ensure that:

- the reception area is clean and tidy;
- newspapers and magazines are up to date and are neatly arranged;
- the firm's publicity material is made available to clients and is kept in presentable condition, and that floral displays are kept fresh.

7.5.2 If there is a delay of more than 10 minutes before the fee earner/staff member arrives, the receptionist should endeavour to:

- keep clients informed of the reasons;
- provide clients with suitable refreshments, coffee, tea, biscuits, etc.;
- offer an apology and explanation after 20 minutes' delay and suggest a different appointment time, or organise the fee earner's secretary to do so.

(See also section 4B1.1–4B1.2 in relation to the reception area generally.)

7.6 Confirmation of instructions

The 2007 Code, Rule 2 draws a clear distinction between the retainer with the client (see subrule 2.02) and the costs position (subrule 2.03). It is most important that the client's requirements and 'objectives' are noted and confirmed, also the important terms of business and – under subrule 2.03(1) the 'best information possible about the likely overall cost'. The following procedure, which should be read in conjunction with the general client care letter format at annex 7A, lists the various issues that need to be confirmed under subrules 2.02 and 2.03 respectively, the provisions of which are also Lexcel requirements by virtue of section 7.2 of the standard which requires compliance with Rule 2 on client relations.

On the confirmation of name and status of person dealing with the matter see *Pearless de Rougemont & Co v. Pilbrow* [1999] 3 All ER 355.

On limitations that should be advised to clients see subrule 2.02(2)(e) and the accompanying guidance notes 16 and 17; and on the importance of raising mediation or alternative dispute resolution (ADR) in contentious matters see guidance note 15 and the case law quoted.

On the need for written confirmation under Rule 2 see guidance note 12, requiring the information on the retainer to be provided in a 'clear and readily accessible form' and guidance note 25, which states that you 'should consider giving the information in writing even though this is not a requirement'. Lexcel requires confirmation of instructions to be 'ordinarily in writing' at 8.4. Note also guidance note 13 to Rule 2: 'Over complex or lengthy terms of business letters may not be helpful.' Preventing letters from being thus, given the issues that need confirmation, often seems quite a challenge.

7.6.1 The general rule is that at or near the outset of every matter the client should receive confirmation of:

- the name and status of the person acting, along with details of the person responsible for the overall supervision of the matter;
- the client's and the adviser's responsibilities;
- details of the appropriate point of contact in the event that the client is concerned with the progress or some element of the handling of the matter;
- specific advice on the costs implications of the instructions received and the advice provided;
- the general terms of business under which the firm acts and the level of service that the firm proposes to provide;
- any limitations to the service to be provided, such as conditions imposed on the firm by third party funders;
- in disputes, whether mediation or some form of ADR would be more appropriate options.

This is achieved by use of the general client care letter (annex 7A) and the firm's standard terms and conditions (annex 7B). The confirmation of instructions, including the steps to be taken by the firm and the client, is dealt with at section 8.7. These issues are, however, also covered in the general client care letter at annex 7A.

7.6.2 The client care letter at annex 7A can be tailored to the particular instructions received within the departmental precedents. Although its precise wording is not mandatory in all cases any material variations must be approved by a partner and must still comply with the professional requirements of the 2007 Code, Rule 2 (Client relations). This is most likely to apply where the client is a close friend or a relation to the adviser, but care is needed before any major variation of terms is agreed. The friend or relation becomes a normal client in all other regards and may be just as likely to complain or make a claim in the event of a problem with the services received. The view of the partners is therefore that variations from the approved precedents should be very much the exception rather than the rule. In all cases this letter should be sent out as soon as possible after instructions have been taken (guidance note 18 to Rule 2).

> ▨ There is a general exception at subrule 2.02(3) for circumstances where 'you can demonstrate that it was inappropriate to meet some or all of these requirements' and see guidance note 22 to Rule 2, which provides possible examples as cases of 'one-off advice' and those involving a 'long-standing client who is familiar with your firm's terms of business and knows the status of the person dealing with the matter'.

7.6.3 Compliance with Rule 2 will not always require provision to the client of all the information in the firm's client care letter. Where the firm has established a settled pattern of dealings with regular clients formal terms should be established which can relate to all new matters opened for that client. Agreed terms are reviewed annually by the client partner, with special reference to any variation of fee levels. Since most such clients are commercial clients, the head of the commercial department maintains the formal agreements with regular clients which can be understood to apply unless the contrary is agreed. The list of such clients and the letters setting out agreed terms can be consulted on [*provide computer system reference*].

7.6.4 The other situation where a normal client care letter might not be sent out is where professional considerations would make it inappropriate. Such cases will be exceptional, but could include:

- where the client is illiterate or has learning difficulties;
- certain instances of mental health work where the client might be distressed to receive such correspondence;
- instances of limited and 'one-off' advice;
- some cases of domestic violence, where a letter that is intercepted could aggravate any problems;
- the deathbed will.

In any such instances a full note must appear on the file setting out the reasons why a client care letter has not been sent out and detailing any alternative action that has been taken.

7.6.5 It is important that the client receives, in addition to client care information, confirmation of their instructions and objectives, and also the action that will be taken on their behalf (see section 8.7.7).

> ▨ The annexes contain various approaches to the issue of compliance with Rule 2. The standard letter at 7A is a client care letter and would generally need supplementing with some specific terms and conditions, as in relation to payment of invoices. The terms and conditions at annex 7B are a much more thorough approach and deal with many more eventualities. There is no need under SRA requirements to set out the full complaints procedure when confirming instructions and doing so has generally been discouraged by Practice Standards Unit advisers. There is, however, a need to have a

written complaints procedure. It is an issue for every firm to determine its approach to compliance.

The terms and conditions at annex 7B are reproduced by kind permission of Tony Girling to whom thanks are due. If adopting any of these precedents please consider them carefully for their appropriateness for your firm and your clients; also please monitor changes to law and procedure, especially on the issue of costs recovery. Please also see the disclaimer of liability in respect of this and all precedents contained in the preface to this book.

7.7 Complaints handling

The 2007 Code, subrule 2.05 requires all solicitors in private practice to operate an effective complaints handing system. The problems of backlogs of complaints have been a continuing source of friction between the government and the profession for many years. The Law Society established the Practice Standards Unit several years ago in an attempt to address the issues in a more proactive manner. If all firms could address client complaints with true resolve to address the client's difficulty and to learn from the experience to lessen the risks of repetition in the future, the profession as a whole would save substantial sums of money and improve its public profile.

If a firm enters the arena of complaints handling with real determination to uncover the problems encountered by clients and thereby to encourage feedback, an increase in complaints reported to the firm is likely. This is recognised within the area of quality management where the adage is that 'if you've had no complaints, you're not asking the right questions'. What matters is, therefore, not so much how many complaints are received, but how well they are processed and, if possible, resolved.

The Lexcel standard makes the requirement that firms should define what they mean by a complaint. Section 7.4(b) of the Lexcel standard requires that firms should record and report centrally all complaints received from clients. The effort in doing this can be considerable if a wide definition of 'complaint' is adopted, such as 'any expression of client dissatisfaction, however it is expressed'. An alternative, which would have the advantage of making the management of complaints handling more workable, is to filter out the problems that can be easily resolved. This narrower definition of a complaint has been adopted in the alternative in the model procedure that follows. Firms should be wary of introducing unfair hurdles as to what can be accepted as a complaint: a requirement that all complaints must be in writing would usually be seen as inappropriate. The obligation not to obstruct complaints in the 2007 Code, subrule 20.05, should also be noted.

7.7.1 None of us likes to be the subject of a complaint, but if the firm is truly committed to providing a quality service to clients all personnel need to pick up on client dissatisfaction when it does arise and address it as best they can. The firm therefore operates a complaints handling process that seeks to ensure that it:

- knows about client dissatisfaction when if and when it does arise;
- takes all reasonable steps to ensure that the dissatisfaction is addressed and resolved wherever possible;
- reassures all clients who do complain that the firm will address their concerns without delay and that it takes all complaints seriously;
- learns from experience to lessen the risk of complaints in the future.

7.7.2 A complaint is [any expression of client dissatisfaction however it is expressed [*use if wide definition required*]/any expression of client dissatisfaction which the fee earner is unable immediately to resolve [*use if narrow definition preferred – see notes above on implications of a wide or narrow definition of complaints*]]. Some degree of common sense is needed in the application of the complaints handling procedure. If a client says 'you solicitors charge a lot for what you do' it would not usually be sufficient to amount to a complaint. If, however, the client claims that a quote or agreed costs ceiling has been exceeded without notice to them it almost certainly will be. If, on checking the file, the fee earner is able to advise the client that a letter that the client had overlooked had been written to warn that the costs would be greater than previously discussed, the problem would probably have been dealt with and there would be no need to report the complaint as such. In all cases, however, it is necessary to take a view on how the client is reacting to the particular circumstances. The firm's overriding objective is to address client dissatisfaction.

7.7.3 All firms are obliged to make a copy of their complaints procedure available on request. The existence of the policy is referred to in the firm's client care letter and the full version can be found [on the firm's website/other]. If appropriate, you must refer the client to the policy, or print a copy off and send it to them if they might have difficulty in acquiring it for themselves.

[*Sample procedures can be found at annex 7C*]

7.7.4 If it is necessary to report a complaint please complete the complaints report form at annex 7D and forward it to [*name or title*]. Client complaints will usually involve no risk of loss to the firm or the client, but if there is any chance that the complaint could amount to circumstances that should be reported to the firm's insurers you must stay on the side of safety by reporting it as such.

7.7.5 As required by our complaints policy [*name or title*] will consider any complaint received in as objective a manner as possible and seek to resolve the dissatisfaction. In particular they will offer to meet with the complainant when possible and suggest appropriate redress. In so doing they will also consider if a notification need to be made to the insurers and also consider if any aspect of the quality system needs amendment.

Complaints referred by the Legal Complaints Service (LCS)

7.7.6 It is possible that a client may complain direct to the LCS (formerly the Consumer Complaints Service, and before that the Office for the Supervision of Solicitors) without first following the procedures given in the previous paragraphs. In such circumstances the LCS will immediately refer the complaint to [*name or title*] who is the designated liaison partner. The normal complaints procedures will then be followed.

Complaints review

7.7.7 [*Name or title*] will maintain records of all complaints received and action taken on them. [*Name or title*] is also responsible for conducting a review of all complaints records in [*month*] of each year to enable [him/her] to report to the firm on any trends. This will form part of an annual management review which is considered by the partners and reported to all staff. It is essential that all personnel learn from their experience and address any underlying problems. In this way the firm can use its complaints data to help to prevent future difficulties.

Making complaints

7.7.8 There may be occasions when a complaint may be made by the firm, either against another solicitor through the LCS or through other procedures. The agreement of [*name or title*] is needed before doing so in order that the professional and commercial standing of the firm can first receive proper consideration.

7.8 Client surveys

> The Lexcel standard contains a requirement that firms should review, at least annually, whether the firm's commitment to client service is being met in the perception of clients. This could be achieved in various ways. In most firms a simple client satisfaction survey, as appears in annex 7F, will be appropriate. Many domestic conveyancing departments use such forms as a matter of course. An alternative, which may be more appropriate with referrers of work or more significant commercial clients, could be a face-to-face meeting. In firms that decide to compile a register of standing terms (see section 7.6.3 above) a client satisfaction survey questionnaire could be filled in at or before the annual review meeting which is envisaged by that process.
>
> Many firms have also found that their staff – especially the support or administrative staff – can provide valuable insight on where they feel that the firm could improve: see the form at annex 7G.

7.8.1 An occasional survey is conducted on client satisfaction. All heads of department can decide when this should be conducted at any time of year, but most will conduct a survey in [*month*] to provide information for the firm's annual review in [*month*]. The survey is conducted by use of the client survey form at annex 7F and in interviews with key clients and referrers.

7.8.2 The partners are aware that asking questions of clients increases expectations and the results of the survey will be published internally, together with any decisions and recommendations, in order that everyone can assist in any improvements that are called for.

Annex 7A

General format of client care letter

Dear

[Description of matter]

Thank you for instructing this firm to act in relation to this matter.

> ▨ Confirmation is needed here or elsewhere (unless it is one of the exceptional situations under subrule 2.02(3) of the 2007 Code where some or all of the information is not being confirmed) of the following:
>
> - the client's objectives in the matter (2.02(1)(a));
> - the issues involved – give a clear explanation of these issues and the options available to the client. Those options should include the feasibility of mediation or some form of ADR in instructions involving the resolution of a dispute (2.02(1)(b)) and see guidance note 15 to Rule 2;
> - the next steps to be taken (2.02(1)(c));
> - your responsibilities (2.02(2)(b));
> - the client's responsibilities (e.g. to safeguard documentation for discovery and to produce it for your use) (2.02(2)(c));
> - any limitations or conditions resulting from a relationship with a third party – e.g. a funder, fee sharer or introducer (2.02(1)(e)), guidance notes 16 and 17 and, on referrals, Rule 9.
>
> It should also be borne in mind that there are also responsibilities under subrule 2.02 to agree 'an appropriate level of service' (2.02(2)(a) and also to keep the client informed of progress (2.02(1)(d)).

Costs

There are some important matters that I would like to confirm at this early stage, particularly in relation to costs. Our charges in this matter will be based on the time we expend on your behalf, as outlined in the accompanying terms and conditions leaflet. There may also be expenditure we incur directly on your behalf (disbursements). Value added tax, at the current rate, has also to be added to our bills. At this stage I would not envisage any particular items that would need to be brought to your attention but I will do so if and when they do arise. Please read through the enclosed terms and conditions and contact me if you would like clarification of any of its contents.

I am sure that you will appreciate some guidance on the likely overall costs. It is impossible to predict the costs accurately at this stage as there are so many variable factors in the progress of a matter such as this, but I would assess the eventual figure is likely to be in the region of [£[amount] (or between £[amount] and £[amount]). This figure includes disbursements such as [specify] which we can expect to incur on your behalf. VAT at 17.5% has to be added to our fees and all disbursements. [*Change this paragraph if providing a fixed quote or estimate*] I will review this indication of costs periodically and advise you if there is likely to be any material change. These figures are based primarily on the time spent on your instructions, on which please see more details in the accompanying leaflet. The rates that will apply to the work to be done for you on this occasion are: [*details of the hourly rates are needed here or in an accompanying document, if hourly rates are relevant to the fees to be charged*].

[In cases that go to court the usual rule would be that, in all cases involving more than minor sums, the successful party gets a contribution towards their costs. Since there is a prospect of going to court in this matter please take into account that if you succeed the contribution to your costs that the court is likely to make is unlikely to be cover all of my/this firm's costs and that if you are unsuccessful a contribution towards the other side's costs will probably be ordered in addition to this firm's costs.] [*Conditional fee arrangements would need further details, as will the implications of legal aid for the client, or in relation to costs contributions if the opponent is legally aided*]

Although it is difficult to predict precisely the progress of any legal matter I would not envisage that there will be any further payments to outside advisers or agencies such as barristers, but I will notify you if this position changes/I would envisage [*provide details*].

▨ The obligations of a client who is in receipt of public funding would also need to be confirmed where appropriate, Likewise, the availability of other funding sources or options needs to be considered under subrule 2.03(1)(d) and it might be advisable to confirm any such points here.

In order to meet any initial expenditure you have agreed to provide £[*amount*] on account of costs and I look forward to receiving this from you. [*This must always be discussed with the client first*].

▨ Confirmation of the cost-effectiveness of any proposed instructions needs consideration (see the 2007 Code, subrule 2.03(6)).

Client care

We strive to provide a quality service to all our clients. In the event of any concern about the services provided or the process that you are involved in, please do not hesitate to contact me. Further details of our client care policy, including our complaints procedure, are contained in [the accompanying booklet/the terms of business leaflet/on our website].

I shall be the person with responsibility for your matter. I am a [partner/associate/ assistant solicitor/legal executive/senior manager/junior manager/paralegal/trainee solicitor]. I shall be assisted by [*name*]. [My work is under the direct supervision of [*name*].] We have arrangements to ensure continuity of cover in the event of my being absent from the office. Please note that my secretary, [*name*], will generally have access to the file in relation to your matter and will usually be able to answer any query that might arise.

[*Set out here any preferences that you have in relation to how you work with clients – e.g.* By and large you are more likely to be able to contact me by telephone of you wait until after [*time*] *or* When we meet to discuss your matter you are likely to be offered an afternoon appointment since I am often in court in the morning, *etc.*]

Quality standards

The firm is working towards/is registered under the Lexcel quality standard of the Law Society. As a result of this we are or may become subject to periodic checks by outside assessors. This could mean that your file is selected for checking, in which case we would need your consent for inspection to occur. All inspections are, of course, conducted in confidence. If you prefer to withhold consent, work on your file will not be affected in any way. Since very few of our clients do object to this I propose to assume that we do have your consent unless you notify us to the contrary. We will also assume, unless you indicate otherwise, that consent on this occasion will extend to all future matters which we conduct on your behalf. Please contact me if I can explain this further or if you would like me to mark your file as not to be inspected. If you would prefer to withhold consent please put a line through this section in the copy letter for return to me.

Summary of action by yourself

[May I finally confirm the steps which I need you to take or the documentation which I will require to process matters on your behalf [*specify*].]

I look forward to being of assistance to you.

Yours sincerely,

> ▦ *Note:* this method of confirming the client care and retainer issues covered would require additional terms of business on such issues as payment of invoices, rights to interest, storage and retrieval charges to be covered. There are other issues that must be covered under the 2007 Code which are not covered in this letter, such as advice to the client on your right to exercise a lien for costs (2.03(10)(e)). On further information on costs issues see section 8.8.

Annex 7B

Terms and conditions

▨ These terms are produced by kind permission of Tony Girling and form an alternative or supplement to the client care letter at annex 7A. This is a general draft and will need to be considered from time to time as new issues arise. The difficult area of costs recovery is changing too fast to provide advice in this book. Precedent terms of business with some variations for departments can be obtained direct from Tony Girling Training Limited, Penbourne, Mill View Court, Barham, Canterbury, Kent CT4 6PF.

The letter accompanying the terms of business must deal with the costs estimate (or other supplemental costs information, such as any agreed costs ceiling), cost benefit, funding options and the requirements of the 2007 Code, Rule 2 such as standards of service options available to the client and the responsibilities of those involved. These do not lend themselves to standard terminology for inclusion in the Terms and Conditions.

Our aim

- We aim to offer our clients quality legal advice with a personal service at a fair cost. As a start, we hope it is helpful to you to set out in this statement the basis on which we will provide our professional services.

Our hours of business

- The normal hours of opening at our offices are between 9.00 am and 5.00 pm on weekdays. Messages can be left on the answerphone outside those hours and appointments can be arranged at other times when this is essential.

People responsible for your work

- The [job title] responsible for dealing with your work will be [name]. The assistant/secretary who may be able to deal with your queries and who will be pleased to take any message for you is [name]. We will try to avoid changing the people who handle your work but if this cannot be avoided, we will tell you promptly of any change and why it may be necessary.
- The partner of this firm with final responsibility for work done in this department is [name].

Charges and expenses

- Our charges will be calculated mainly by reference to the time actually spent by the solicitors and other staff in respect of any work which they do on your behalf. This may include meetings with you and perhaps others; reading, preparing and working on papers; making and receiving telephone calls, e-mails, faxes and text messages; preparation of any detailed costs estimates, schedules and bills; attending at court; and time necessarily spent travelling away from the office. From time to time we may arrange for some of this work to be carried out by persons not directly employed by us; such work will be charged to you at the hourly rate which would be charged if we had done the work ourselves.

- Routine letters, e-mails and texts that we send and routine telephone calls that we make and receive are charged at one-tenth of the hourly rate. Routine letters, e-mails and texts received are charged at one-twentieth of the hourly rate. Other letters, e-mails and calls are charged on a time spent basis.
- The current hourly rates are set out below. We will add VAT to these at the rate that applies when the work is done. At present, VAT is 17.5%.

	£
Partners and Consultants	195
Solicitors	173
Fellows of Inst. of Legal Executives, Senior Executives	173
Executives	145
Trainee Solicitors	106
Junior Executives/Personal Assistants	97

- These hourly rates have to be reviewed periodically to reflect increases in overhead costs and inflation. Normally the rates are reviewed with effect from 1 January each year. If a review is carried out before this matter has been concluded, we will inform you of any variation in the rate before it takes effect.
- In addition to the time spent, we may take into account a number of factors including any need to carry out work outside our normal office hours, the complexity of the issues, the speed at which action has to be taken, any particular specialist expertise which the case may demand. An increase in the rates may be applied to reflect such factors. In property transactions, in the administration of estates and in matters involving a substantial financial value or benefit to a client, a charge reflecting, for example, the price of the property, the size of the estate, or the value of the financial benefit may be considered. It is not always possible to indicate how these aspects may arise but on present information we would expect them to be sufficiently taken into account in the rates which we have quoted. Where an increase in the rates or a charge reflecting any value element is to be added we will explain this to you.
- Solicitors have to pay out various other expenses on behalf of clients ranging from Land or Probate Registry fees, court fees, experts' fees, and so on. We have no obligation to make such payments unless you have provided us with the funds for that purpose. VAT is payable on certain expenses. We refer to such payments generally as 'disbursements'.
- If, for any reason, this matter does not proceed to completion, we will be entitled to charge you for work done and expenses incurred.

Payment arrangements

- Property transactions. We will normally send you our bill following the exchange of contracts and payment is required on a purchase prior to completion; and at completion on a sale. If sufficient funds are available on completion, and we have sent you a bill, we will deduct our charges and expenses from the funds.

- Administration of estates. We will normally submit an interim bill at regular stages during the administration, starting with the obtaining of a Grant. The final account will be prepared when the Estate Accounts are ready for approval.
- Other cases or transactions. It is normal practice to ask clients to pay interim bills and sums of money from time to time on account of the charges and expenses which are expected in the following weeks or months. We find that this helps clients in budgeting for costs as well as keeping them informed of the legal expenses which are being incurred. If such requests are not met with prompt payment, delay in the progress of a case may result. In the unlikely event of any bill or request for payment not being met, this firm must reserve the right to stop acting for you further.
- Payment is due to us within 28 days of our sending you a bill. Interest will be charged on a daily basis at 4% over [*name of bank*]'s base rate from time to time from the date of the bill in cases where payment is not made within 28 days of delivery by us of the bill.
- The common law entitles us to retain any money, papers or other property belonging to you which properly come into our possession pending payment of our costs, whether or not the property is acquired in connection with the matter for which the costs were incurred. This is known as a 'general lien'. We are not entitled to sell property held under a lien but we are entitled to hold property, other than money, even if the value of it greatly exceeds the amount due to us in respect of costs.
- If we are conducting litigation for you, we have additional rights in any property recovered or preserved for you whether it is in our possession or not and in respect of all costs incurred, whether billed or unbilled. We also have a right to ask the court to make a charging order in our favour for any assessed costs.
- We do not accept payments to us in cash in excess of £200. Monies due to you from us will be paid by cheque or bank transfer, but not in cash, and will not be made payable to a third party.

Other parties' charges and expenses

- In some cases and transactions a client may be entitled to payment of costs by some other person. It is important that you understand that in such circumstances, the other person may not be required to pay all the charges and expenses which you incur with us. You have to pay our charges and expenses in the first place and any amounts which can be recovered will be a contribution towards them. If the other party is in receipt of legal aid no costs are likely to be recovered.
- If you are successful and a court orders another party to pay some or all of your charges and expenses, interest can be claimed on them from the other party from the date of the court order. We will account to you for such interest to the extent that you have paid our charges or expenses on account, but we are entitled to the rest of that interest.
- You will also be responsible for paying our charges and expenses of seeking to recover any costs that the court orders the other party to pay to you.
- A client who is unsuccessful in a court case may be ordered to pay the other party's legal charges and expenses. That money would be payable in addition

to our charges and expenses. Arrangements can be made to take out insurance to cover liability for such legal expenses. Please discuss this with us if you are interested in this possibility.

Interest payment

- Any money received on your behalf will be held in our Client Account. Subject to certain minimum amounts and periods of time set out in the Solicitors' Accounts Rules 1998, interest will be calculated and paid to you at the rate from time to time payable on [*name of bank*]'s Designated Client Accounts. The period for which interest will be paid will normally run from the date(s) on which funds are received by us until the date(s) of issue of any cheque(s) from our Client Account.
- Where a client obtains borrowing from a lender in a property transaction, we will ask the lender to arrange that the loan cheque is received by us a minimum of four working days prior to the completion date. If the money can be telegraphed, we will request that we receive it the day before completion. This will enable us to ensure that the necessary funds are available in time for completion. Such clients need to be aware that the lender may charge interest from the date of issue of their loan cheque or the telegraphing of the payment.

Storage of papers and documents

- After completing the work, we are entitled to keep all your papers and documents while there is money owing to us for our charges and expenses. In addition, we will keep your file of papers for you in storage for not less than one year. After that, storage is on the clear understanding that we have the right to destroy it after such period as we consider reasonable or to make a charge for storage if we ask you to collect your papers and you fail to do so. We will not of course destroy any documents such as wills, deeds and other securities, which you ask us to hold in safe custody. No charge will be made to you for such storage unless prior notice in writing is given to you of a charge to be made from a future date which may be specified in that notice.
- If we retrieve papers or documents from storage in relation to continuing or new instructions to act in connection with your affairs, we will not normally charge for such retrieval. However, we may make a charge based on time spent at the junior executive hourly rate for producing stored papers or documents to you or another at your request. We may also charge for reading, correspondence or other work necessary to comply with your instructions.

Financial services and insurance contracts

- If, while we are acting for you, you need advice on investments, we may have to refer you to someone who is authorised by the Financial Services Authority, as we are not. However, as we are regulated by the Solicitors Regulation Authority, we may be able to provide certain limited investment services where these are closely linked to the legal work we are doing for you.

- We are not authorised by the Financial Services Authority. However, we are included on the register maintained by the Financial Services Authority so that we can carry on insurance mediation activity, which is broadly the advising on, selling and administration of insurance contracts. Insurance mediation activities and investment services, including arrangements for complaints or redress if something goes wrong, are regulated by the Solicitors Regulation Authority. The register can be accessed via the Financial Services Authority website at www.fsa.gov.uk/register.

Termination

- You may terminate your instructions to us in writing at any time but we will be entitled to keep all your papers and documents while there is money owing to us for our charges and expenses. If at any stage you do not wish us to continue doing work and/or incurring charges and expenses on your behalf, you must tell us this clearly in writing.
- If we decide to stop acting for you, for example if you do not pay an interim bill or comply with the request for a payment on account, we will tell you the reason and give you notice in writing.
- Under the Consumer Protection (Distance Selling) Regulations 2000, for some non-business instructions, you may have the right to withdraw, without charge, within seven working days of the date on which you asked us to act for you. However, if we start work with your consent within that period, you lose that right to withdraw. Your acceptance of these terms and conditions of business will amount to such a consent. If you seek to withdraw instructions, you should give notice by telephone, e-mail or letter to the person named in these terms of business as being responsible for your work. The Regulations require us to inform you that the work involved is likely to take more than 30 days.

Limited companies

- When accepting instructions to act on behalf of a limited company, we may require a Director and/or controlling shareholder to sign a form of personal guarantee in respect of the charges and expenses of this firm. If such a request is refused, we will be entitled to stop acting and to require immediate payment of our charges on an hourly basis and expenses as set out earlier.

Tax advice

- Any work that we do for you may involve tax implications or necessitate the consideration of tax planning strategies. We may not be qualified to advise you on the tax implications of a transaction that you instruct us to carry out, or the likelihood of them arising. If you have any concerns in this respect, please raise them with us immediately. If we can undertake the research necessary to resolve the issue, we will do so and advise you accordingly. If we cannot, we may be able to identify a source of assistance for you.

Identity, disclosure and confidentiality requirements

- We are entitled to refuse to act for you if you fail to supply appropriate proof of identity for yourself or for any principal whom you may represent. We may arrange to carry out an electronic verification of your identity if we consider that a saving of time and cost will be achieved by doing so. The cost of any such search will be charged to you. If the amount is in excess of £10 including VAT, we will seek your prior agreement.

- Solicitors are under a professional and legal obligation to keep the affairs of the client confidential. This obligation, however, is subject to a statutory exception: legislation on money laundering and terrorist financing has placed solicitors under a legal duty in certain circumstances to disclose information to the Serious and Organised Crime Agency. Where a solicitor knows or suspects that a transaction on behalf of a client involves money laundering, the solicitor may be required to make a disclosure. If, while we are acting for you, it becomes necessary to make such a disclosure, we may not be able to inform you that it has been made, or of the reasons for it, because the law prohibits 'tipping-off'. Where the law permits us, we will tell you about any potential money laundering problem and explain what action we may need to take.

- Our firm may be subject to audit or quality checks by external firms or organisations. We may also outsource work. This might be for example typing or photocopying or costings, or research and preparation to assist with your matter. Information from your file may therefore be made available in such circumstances. We will always aim to obtain a confidentiality agreement with the third party.

- In order to comply with court and tribunal rules, all documentation relevant to any issues in litigation, however potentially damaging to your case, have to be preserved and may be required to be made available to the other side. This aspect of proceedings is known as 'disclosure'. Subject to this, we will not reveal confidential information about your case except as provided by these terms of business and where, for example, your opponent is ordered to pay your costs, we have to meet obligations to reveal details of the case to them and to the court.

Communication between you and us

- Our aim is to offer all our clients an efficient and effective service at all times. We are proud that we hold the accreditation of [Investors in People] and our clients and our staff are of first importance to us. We hope that you will be pleased with the work we do for you. However, should there be any aspect of our service with which you are unhappy, please raise your concern in the first place with [fee earner name]. If you still have queries or concerns, please contact our Client Services Manager, [name], at [address]. [Name] is the Client Care Partner to whom any final difficulty can be reported.

- We will aim to communicate with you by such method as you may request. We may need to virus check discs or email. Unless you withdraw consent, we will communicate with others when appropriate by e-mail or fax but we cannot be responsible for the security of correspondence and documents sent by e-mail or fax.

- The Data Protection Act requires us to advise you that your particulars are held on our database. We may, from time to time, use these details to send you information which we think might be of interest to you.
- Where we act for two or more clients jointly it is on the clear understanding that we are authorised to act on instructions from either, both or any of them.

Terms and conditions of business

- Unless otherwise agreed, and subject to the application of then current hourly rates, these Terms and Conditions of Business shall apply to any future instructions given by you to this firm.
- Although your continuing instructions in this matter will amount to an acceptance of these Terms and Conditions of Business, it may not be possible for us to start work on your behalf until one copy of them has been signed and returned to us for us to keep on our file.

I confirm I have read and understood, and I accept, these Terms and Conditions of Business.

Signed ....   Date ....

Annex 7C

Sample complaints procedures

A Model complaints procedure for partnerships

Our complaints policy

We are committed to providing a high-quality legal service to all our clients. When something goes wrong we need you to tell us about it. This will help us to improve our standards.

Our complaints procedure

If you have a complaint, please contact [name], our Client Care Partner. [In multi-office firms: You can write to [him/her] at [address]: In large departmentalised practices: [Name] will pass your complaint to [name of head of department], the partner in charge of the department involved in your complaint.] If we have to change any of the responsibilities or the timescales set out below we will let you know and explain why.

What will happen next?

1. Within three days we will send you a letter acknowledging your complaint and asking you to confirm or explain any details. If it seems appropriate we will suggest a meeting at this stage. We will also let you know the name of the person who will be dealing with your complaint.

*2. We will then record your complaint in our central register and open a file for your complaint. We will also investigate your complaint by examining the relevant file.

3. If appropriate we will then invite you to meet [name] to discuss and hopefully resolve your complaint. We would hope to be in a position to meet with you in this way no longer than 14 days after first receiving your complaint. If you would prefer not to meet, or if we cannot arrange this within an agreeable timescale, I will write fully to you setting out my views on the situation and any redress that we would feel to be appropriate.

*4. Within three days of any meeting we will write to you to confirm what took place and any suggestions that we have agreed with you. In appropriate cases we could offer an apology, a reduction of any bill or a repayment in relation to any payment received.

*5. At this stage, if you are still not satisfied, please let us know. We will then arrange to review our decision. We would generally aim to do this within 10 days. This will happen in one of the following ways.

- [Name] will review [his/her] own decision
- We will arrange for someone in the firm who has not been involved in your complaint to review it.
- [Name of senior partner] will review your complaint within 10 days.

- We will ask our local law society or another local firm of solicitors to review your complaint. We will let you know how long this process will take.
- We will invite you to agree to independent mediation. We will let you know how long this process will take.

6. We will let you know the result of the review within five days of the end of the review. At this time we will write to you confirming our final position on your complaint and explaining our reasons. We will also give you the name and address of the Legal Complaints Service. If you are still not satisfied, you can contact them about your complaint. We very much hope that this will not be necessary.

* Delete any terms not considered to be appropriate

B Model complaints procedure – for sole practitioners

My complaints policy

I am committed to providing a high-quality legal service to all my clients. When something goes wrong I need you to tell me about it. This will help me to maintain and improve my standards.

My complaints procedure

If you have a complaint, please contact me with the details. If I have to change any of the timescales set out below I will let you know.

What will happen next?

1. Within three days I will send you a letter acknowledging your complaint and asking you to confirm or explain the details. I may suggest that we meet to clarify any details.
2. I will then record your complaint in my central register and open a file for your complaint and investigate your complaint. This may involve one or more of the following steps.

- If I acted for you, I will consider your complaint again. I will then send you my detailed reply or invite you to a meeting to discuss the matter.
- If someone else acted for you, I will ask them to give me their reply to your complaint. I will then examine their reply and the information in your complaint file. I may also speak to the person who acted for you.
- I may ask another independent local solicitor to investigate your complaint and report to me.
- I will then write inviting you to meet me and discuss and hopefully resolve your complaint.

3. At this stage I would welcome the opportunity to meet with you. I would aim to be in a position to be able to meet with you within 14 days of first receiving your complaint. If you would prefer not to meet, or if we cannot arrange this within an agreeable timescale, I will write fully to you setting out my views on the situation and any redress.

4. Within three days of the meeting I will write to you to confirm what took place and any solutions I have agreed with you. In appropriate cases I could offer an apology, a reduction of any bill or a repayment in relation to any payment received.

5. At this stage, if you are still not satisfied, please contact me again. I will then arrange to review my decision within the next 10 days. This may happen in one of the following ways.

   - I will review the decision myself.
   - I will arrange for someone who is not connected with the complaint to review my decision.
   - I will ask my local law society or another local firm of solicitors to review your complaint. This may take longer than 10 days in which case I will let you know how long this process will take.
   - I will invite you to agree to an independent mediation. This again may take longer than 10 days and I will do my best to let you know how long this will take.

[Any of the above options that are not available will need to be deleted]

6. I will let you know the result of the review within five days of the end of the review. At this time I will write to you confirming my final position on your complaint and explaining my reasons. I will also give you the name and address of the Legal Complaints Service. If you are still not satisfied, you can contact them about your complaint, but I very much hope that this will not be necessary.

Annex 7D
Client complaint report form

Client:
Private paying/public funding:
Client partner, if any:
Description of matter:
Matter no.:
Could a claim be made for any losses?
Details of complaint:
Action already taken:
Action proposed, including possible redress:
Client care partner notes:

Matter resolved:

Signed .... Date....................................

Annex 7E

Client complaints register

Model central complaints register

A central complaints record is good practice and should include the following:

- a complaint reference number;
- the date of the complaint;
- the name of the client;
- the name of the member of staff involved;
- a general description of the complaint;
- the date of any internal meeting and the names of those present;
- the date the file was examined;
- the date of any meeting with the client;
- an indication of whether the complaint is justified in the views of the firm;
- the reasons for the complaint;
- details of any suggestions to resolve the complaint and redress that might be offered;
- the dates of any letters confirming details or suggestions;
- the date of any review and the result of the review;
- the date of the final letter;
- the date the file was closed; and
- any action to be taken internally as a result of the complaint.

Complaint:

Client name:

Matter/file no.:

Fee earner handling:

Description of complaint	Client meeting date, if any	Internal meeting, if any, and who is present	Action taken	Matter resolved? If so – date If not – future action?

Annex 7F

Client survey form

Your name:	
Department:	*[completed by firm]*

	Poor	Fair	Good	Excellent
1. How would you rate our reception area and the greeting you received?				
If poor or fair, how do you think we could improve this aspect of our practice?				
2. How would you rate the personal manner of the adviser that you had the most dealings with?				
If poor or fair, how do you think we could improve their service to you?				
3. How would you assess the communication, be it by letter or e-mail, that you received?				
If poor or fair, how could we have improved this for you?				
4. How would you rate your understanding and commitment to the action that was taken on your behalf?				
If poor or fair how could this have been improved for you?				
5. In general terms, how would you assess our service for you?				
If you have any suggestions for how we could improve things that have not been dealt with above, please comment here				
Would you be likely to recommend this firm to others?	☐ Yes ☐ No ☐ Undecided			

Thank you for your time and trouble in completing this form. Please return it in the stamped addressed envelope provided.

Annex 7G

Staff survey form

1. If and when you were last aware of a client who was unhappy with the service provided what was the cause of the problem?

2. What steps do you think should be taken for the firm to improve its service to clients?

3. Would you always recommend the firm to friends and relatives? If not, why not?

4. Please add here any suggestions not covered above which could be helpful.

Thank you for your time and trouble. Please return this form to [*name*] by no later than [*date*].

Your name .... (optional)

Your department .... Date ....

8 Case and file management

This section follows the order of section 8 in Lexcel which tracks the life of a file from first enquiry to matter closing and any follow-up services that are required after the retainer has terminated. This area could be addressed in a number of ways: either one section could be drawn up for the whole firm or it might be preferable to draw up distinct sections for each department or group. The sample procedures that follow work on the basis that will be appropriate in most firms – one general set of procedures with departmental variations in an annex (see annex 8A).

A Preliminary issues

8.1 Client enquiries

8.1.1 Client enquiries about possible services are received:

- by telephone to the office;
- by telephone directly to an individual known to the client, potential client or referrer;
- by letter, fax or e-mail;
- by callers to the office.

It is essential that all enquiries as to whether the firm could or would be willing to act should be dealt with as quickly, efficiently and courteously as possible. Even if declining to act on this occasion, the firm has the opportunity to make a favourable impression for the next.

8.1.2 For procedures on general telephone enquiries and callers into the reception area see section 4B2 above.

8.2 Acceptance of instructions

▨ There is no obligation on solicitors to accept work other than within the 2007 Code, subrule 11.04 (Refusing instructions to act as advocate). Clearly, firms may not decline to act on grounds that would breach the 2007 Code, Rule 6 and thus amount to discrimination on any of the prohibited grounds. More generally, subrule 2.01 deals with 'taking on clients' and repeats a number of provisions that formerly appeared in various places in *The Guide to the Professional Conduct of Solicitors* such as the obligation to decline to act where illegality would be involved or where the firm lacks sufficient resources to deal with the matter.

8.2.1 The firm is not obliged to act in all cases. Greater consideration will need to be given to enquiries from new clients as opposed to new matters from existing clients. The firm may not decline to act on grounds that would offend its policies on anti-discrimination (see section 1.8 above). It could decline to act, however, on any of the following grounds:

- the enquiry is for a work area that the firm does not undertake or wishes to restrict;
- the client has a track record of not paying the firm's bills or has threatened or assaulted personnel within the firm;
- the client is engaged in business activities that the firm would not wish to be associated with.

In all such cases the client should be given such explanation as is appropriate in the circumstances.

8.3 Situations where instructions must be declined

8.3.1 In addition there are situations where the firm is obliged not to accept work under the 2007 Code, subrule 2.01. These situations are:

- where the firm could commit a breach of the law or professional obligations in acting, e.g. where there is, or could be, a conflict of interest (see section 8.6) or the client refuses to undergo identity checks as required by the anti-money laundering procedures;
- where the firm lacks the expertise or the resources to represent that client effectively, or the instructions would put at risk current commitments to that client or others;
- where the firm has reasonable grounds for believing that the instructions are affected by duress or undue influence and do not represent the client's wishes.

8.3.2 When the firm is in receipt of instructions from joint clients it is important to check that all clients agree with the instructions. On the duty of disclosure between joint clients and the need for consent to disclosure of instructions from joint client see the 2007 Code, guidance note 4 to Rule 6.

8.4 File opening

8.4.1 A 'file opening' form must be completed whenever a matter is to be commenced. The client and matter number provided by the accounts department, coupled with the identification of work types, ensures that all dealings for clients are clearly distinguishable.

8.5 Miscellaneous files

8.5.1 New matters often emerge from current matters and it is not always apparent when an issue is first raised as to whether a distinct new matter will develop. Fee earners must be aware of the need not to run separate matters under the same file and must be prepared to open a new file, perhaps transferring any papers to a colleague, as soon as it becomes clear that the issue is something other than a minor incidental issue related to the matter in hand.

8.5.2 Similarly, general files for commercial clients must not be used as a means of bypassing the normal file opening procedures. It is acceptable, however, for commercial fee earners in particular to run 'miscellaneous' files for a particular client where a composite bill will eventually be raised, or for miscellaneous enquiries from different clients where a record of the conversation or communication is needed but it is not appropriate to open specific files.

8.6 Conflict of interests

The professional rules on conflict of interests were overhauled in the review process leading to the new Solicitors' Code of Conduct 2007. Along with the accompanying rules on confidentiality and disclosure they were implemented in May 2006, in advance of other parts of the 2007 Code. The new Rule 3 limits what will amount to a conflict of interests, the key change being that the conflicts must usually relate to the 'same or related matters'. This will mean that the firm can now often accept instructions where it would previously have had to decline them, as long as there are no related confidentiality problems. The new rule would even allow the firm to act against a current client in litigation if the new instructions are unrelated, though guidance note 15 to Rule 3 recognises that many firms will choose not to do so on grounds of 'professional embarrassment'. The implications of this are that conflicts checking will require more partner or senior attention than has often been the case before.

It should also be borne in mind that conflicts checking is one of the issues listed in Rule 5 as needing 'arrangements' to be in place (subrule 5.01(1)(d)). These arrangements need to address the conflicts problems that arise as the matter progresses. A procedure that deals with the issue only at the outset of procedures is unlikely to be adequate.

Any procedures that are particular to an area of work will need to be highlighted. It may well be that more strenuous checks are needed in some areas of the practice than in others. If the practice embraces conveyancing work it might set out its approach to the circumstances where seller and purchaser can both be represented, if at all.

Under Lexcel there will need to be a record of conflicts having been considered. This could be achieved by requiring fee earners to tick the file opening form to show that it has been considered. In the circumstances that there is a possible issue of conflict an attendance note would need to be added to state what steps the practice has taken to consider the issue.

Although the standard envisages that professional conflicts of interests should be the subject of these provisions, commercial firms in particular may wish to extend their procedures to embrace commercial conflicts: i.e. the situations where the firm would not wish to act for fear of being conflicted out of other work in the future.

8.6.1 Conflict of interests must be considered at the earliest opportunity before accepting instructions and then throughout the matter as it progresses. The evidence that this has been considered is a tick by the fee earner instructed in the conflict of interests box on the matter opening form. Any further deliberations must be the subject of an attendance note on file outlining the considerations and action taken, with any such note being referred to on the matter opening form [*where the matter opening form is stored on the file – if not, the file summary sheet*].

8.6.2 It is the fee earner's responsibility to check for conflicts of interest and to monitor the risk of conflicts arising after the matter has commenced. The accounts department will check in all matters whether a conflict of interest appears to exist by checking the name of any opponent against the computer database of existing relationships. It is important that all possible variations of names and identities are supplied. The accounts department will bring any concerns to the attention of the fee earner, whose responsibility it is to take the issue up with their supervisor in all difficult or unresolved circumstances.

8.6.3 Commonsense checking for conflicts should never be disregarded. A fee earner having a concern that will not necessarily be highlighted by an accounts department check should consider an e-mail around the firm to see if any colleague knows of any reason why the practice should not act. It should be stressed that for the firm to act where it should not do so could be seen as a professional offence and lead to disciplinary proceedings; the firm is also open to a claim for compensation or lost fees and the risk of at least one alienated client.

8.6.4 Where a conflict is found or believed to exist, any doubts as to the propriety of accepting instructions should be considered by the [head of department/supervisor/other]. If it is felt that instructions should be declined the client should be informed of this as soon as possible and they should be offered such explanation and recommendation as in all the circumstances is professionally appropriate.

8.6.5 Fee earners must be alert to the risk that a conflict may develop after a matter has started and must bring any such concerns to the [head of department/supervisor/other] as soon as possible.

B Taking instructions and early action

8.7 Taking and confirming instructions

> There is more emphasis on the retainer with the client being established and confirmed in the 2007 Code than was the case under previous professional rules. There has been criticism from insurers that firms can sometimes overlook the basics of what it should be doing for the client in dealing at length with the terms of business. All files must 'tell the story' of what the firm is doing for the client, and this should start with a clear note of initial instructions, confirmed to the client unless exceptional circumstances prevail.

8.7.1 It is essential that all fee earning personnel act upon the client's full, considered instructions. Instructions may be received by letter, telephone or at a meeting. If they are received other than at a meeting they should be acknowledged promptly, having regard to the sensitivity of the matter and its urgency to the client and legal process. Particular attention must be given to circumstances where instructions are received by one fee earner and then passed to another for attention.

8.7.2 Any instructions taken by telephone must be confirmed to the client in writing. Where this is done contemporaneously with the call the copy letter/e-mail on file could function as an attendance note of the conversation.

8.7.3 Any particular methods of taking instructions, as through the use of checklists on a case management system, are noted in the additional departmental procedures and precedents.

8.7.4 It is important that instructions receive critical analysis on receipt. The 2007 Code requires at subrule 2.02(1) that the client's 'objectives' must be identified and the client must be provided with a 'clear explanation of the issues involved and the options available to the client'. (See section 7.6.)

8.7.5 If the instructions contain inconsistencies or errors, or if carrying out the instructions would involve illegality by the client or the firm, unprofessional conduct by the firm, or potentially lead to undesired results for the client, any such problem must be raised with the client as soon as possible and must be resolved before the instructions can be acted upon, though it may be possible to undertake some work in the interim. (See section 8.3 on the circumstances when instructions must be declined.)

8.7.6 At the outset of the matter the fee earner will establish the following:

- as full an understanding of the background facts as possible;
- the client's objectives and desired results and, if possible, the likely or approximate timescale;
- what the fee earner will do;
- what the client will do;
- whether the fee earner is the appropriate person to deal with the matter or whether it should be referred to a colleague;
- method of payment (see section 8.8);
- cost effectiveness of the proposed matter.

8.7.7 All of the points in 8.7.6 should be confirmed to the client, usually in writing, along with advice on the options available to the client and, if possible, the suggested action to be taken. See section 7.6.3 for what is required where there is a clearly established pattern of dealing on such instructions with that client or in certain instances of one-off advice.

8.8 Costs information

8.8.1 The 2007 Code requires confirmation of the costs position to be provided to the client in most instances. Subrule 2.03(1) requires the client to be given the 'best information possible about the likely overall cost of a matter both at the outset and, when appropriate, as the matter progresses'. This means that hourly rates must be set out where they are to be used as the basis for the fees to be charged, along with further guidance so that the client can understand their exposure to fees and other costs. The general rule is that all costs information 'must be clear and confirmed in writing' (subrule 2.03(5)). The policy of the firm is to ensure that these provisions are complied with, notwithstanding the exception at subrule 2.03(7) that the full information might not always be required.

8.8.2 The difficulties of assessing helpful costs information at the outset of many more complex matters are recognised. Guidance note 36 to Rule 2 provides that in such cases it is required that you 'provide the client with as much information as possible at the start and that you keep the client updated'. The note goes on to suggest agreeing a ceiling figure or review dates in such instances.

8.8.3 You will be prompted to provide the necessary information if you adopt the client care letter format at annex 7A (see section 7.6.2 on the use of this precedent).

8.8.4 There are other issues to consider in litigious matters in particular. These include:

- available sources of funding: there is an obligation on the firm to check whether the client has insurance in place or might qualify for legal aid (public funding).This is done through use of the costs and funding checklist at annex 8B;
- the client's exposure to the costs of the other side(s) in a dispute, especially where an opponent is legally aided;
- in legal aid matters, the operation of the funding code;
- the suitability of mediation or some other form of ADR (see section 7.6.1).

8.8.5 On the need to keep costs information up to date see section 8.17.

8.9 Consent to inspection

Since matter files are confidential to the client their consent is needed for an inspection to occur. For the approved wording on client consent to inspection by Lexcel or other external assessors (the same principle would apply to ISO 9001) see the *Lexcel Assessment Guide*.

8.9.1 As a general principle, the client's consent to inspection of files is necessary at any assessment for Lexcel. You should note that the firm will obtain a confidentiality undertaking from the assessor, but in pursuance of Law Society guidelines the firm asks for the client's consent by use of the standard wording on the point in the client care letter (see annex 7A).

8.9.2 Where the client has indicated that they do not consent to inspection this should be clearly marked on the file and any information that would enable the assessor to know what the firm is doing for that client (e.g. matter print-outs) must not be disclosed.

8.9.3 Where the client has not refused consent the firm is entitled under Law Society guidelines to assume that consent has been obtained. In such circumstances, however, if the fee earner feels that matters have developed in such a way that the client would not now approve of disclosure, or if the firm feels that it would not be appropriate because of particularly sensitive aspects of the file, the firm may decline to submit the file to inspection.

8.10 Key dates

With missed time limits remaining one of the principal causes of claims against solicitors, the importance of this procedure will be readily apparent. The requirement is that the key date should be noted on the file, but also 'backed up' in some system that will be available in the event of the fee earner's absence or illness. There is no approved list of what will amount to a key date in all areas of work, but the obvious examples include:

- striking out;
- appeals;
- limitation dates;
- time limits for reviews, renewals, surrenders, and termination of leases;
- time limits in probate matters;
- dates by which options to purchase and rights of pre-emption must be exercised;
- dates by which share offers must be taken up.

Some firms have overlooked the need to have effective procedures to ensure that key dates are checked and signed off. It is important to consider how the information will be monitored and actioned. Having the record is one thing; making sure it is used in an effective manner also needs consideration. A fairly full procedure follows – many firms might find something less elaborate just as satisfactory.

8.10.1 The firm is required to maintain a backup system for all key dates. Key dates should be regarded as any date, the missing of which could give rise to a cause of action in negligence. The list of key dates is to be found in departmental guidelines appearing in the appropriate departmental appendix (see annex 8A for the conveyancing example).

8.10.2 It is the responsibility of all fee earners to notify [*name or title*] of any backup dates and to ensure that an entry is made to the key dates diary. The entry for any expiry of time periods such as limitation periods must be twofold:

- the date in question (e.g. the last day for issue of proceedings);
- the date sufficiently in advance of the actual key date to enable appropriate action to be taken. This is a specific fee earner responsibility ('countdown' dates). It is recognised that some dates do not require countdown dates, but others (e.g. limitation periods) may require several warnings.

8.10.3 It is the responsibility of the [*name or title*] to notify the fee earner responsible for any matter listed of an entry. This is done on a weekly basis. In the absence of [*name or title*] the [head of department/other] will ensure that someone deputises for [him/her]. The notice is to be treated by the fee earner as incoming post and must be replied to. During the absence of any fee earner the notice therefore passes to another fee earner supervising that colleague's activities in their absence and must always be actioned.

8.10.4 On occasions the fee earner may wish to amend a key date after it has been entered into the backup key date reminder system. If so, the procedure is as follows:

- the existing entry must be clearly crossed out and initialled and the update or correction must be clearly shown;
- if approval was obtained for the change, this should also be marked and the partner approving the change identified by his or her initials;
- in no circumstances should any amendment be made by correction fluid (if in hard copy format).

8.11 Matter planning

All matters require a strategy or plan of action. In addition, a 'project plan' is needed in respect of complex cases. In Lexcel see 8.5 on this requirement. Legal aid lawyers should consult section F2.1 of the SQM on the circumstances when a complex case plan is required.

8.11.1 As a matter of principle every matter should have a clear strategy apparent from the file. This plan should show that thought has been given to how each client's needs will be acted upon. It is recognised that it will often be difficult to finalise this in detail at the outset of a case or transaction because it may be impossible to assess the likely response of any other parties. It is essential, however, that clients are presented with a strategy for meeting their instructions as soon as possible with an explanation of how and why this might need to be varied.

8.11.2 In most cases the plan will simply be either a letter to the client or a separate memorandum on file. If the plan is by memorandum steps must be taken to ensure that the client is made aware of it and their agreement is obtained. In other cases a more detailed ' project plan' will be required. It is a matter of professional judgement for the partner or fee earner in charge of the matter to determine whether a first letter or detailed project plan is required. The following issues must be considered and dealt with:

- written description of matter and person(s) dealing;
- responsibility and supervision;
- frequency of team meetings, if any;
- agreed objectives of legal action;
- main steps to be taken by firm and client;
- frequency of supervisory reviews;
- billing frequency and procedures.

C File maintenance

8.12 File maintenance

Ensuring proper standards of file maintenance across the firm may well be one of the most obvious benefits of a Lexcel and/or risk management programme. It is recommended that each work type area or department consider its own rules of how files should be maintained. There are obvious efficiency gains in improving the state of files generally, especially when covering for colleagues on holiday or sick leave. The following procedure suggests that full files should be maintained, but in many firms that undertake more substantial matters it might be naïve to suppose that all information can be stored on a traditional paper file. Increasingly e-mails are not printed out. The test is whether information can be retrieved and the practice can be confident that all of the communication and dealings on the file are known about and available.

8.12.1 The file should be a complete record of dealings on that matter. This means that all communications should be noted on the file, or be readily accessible if this is not the case. It is the responsibility of the fee earner handling the matter to ensure that the file is well maintained and, in particular that the file:

- notes all conversations and communications of any substance with the client or otherwise on the matter;
- is kept up to date with regular and careful filing;
- is kept tidy, with the progress readily apparent to any colleague who might need to check the position on the matter (as on holiday cover);
- is maintained in accordance with any departmental guidelines appearing in the appropriate departmental appendix (see annex 8A for the conveyancing example).

Well-maintained files reduce wasted time and effort for all and are likely to enable the firm to portray a more professional and organised image to clients and others.

8.13 File summary sheets

Section 8.8(d) of Lexcel requires that 'the status of the matter and the action taken' should be capable of being checked by other members of the practice. In most matters the use of a file summary sheet is a good way to achieve this, but this may be too simplistic in very lengthy litigation or commercial files. A summary sheet in itself is not essential, but the firm may wish to stipulate that if they are in use they must be completed.

8.13.1 If a file summary sheet is mandatory, it must be used on all matter files and kept up to date at all times by the fee earners handling that matter. This ensures that the state of the matter will be readily apparent to anyone else checking the file.

8.14 Attendance notes

8.14.1 Attendance notes are vital to provide a record of advice given, instructions received, or decisions made about which there may be a dispute. Attendance notes are also the primary evidence of time expended on a matter and are therefore vital for billing, notwithstanding the computerised time records.

8.14.2 Secretaries are frequently in direct contact with clients and others concerned with professional work, especially when a fee earner is not available. It is therefore equally important that secretaries should record written attendance notes on all issues that progress a client matter. All attendance notes must be filed on the correspondence clip to date order as soon as possible. Handwritten notes must be intelligible to the writer and others.

8.15 Traceability and confidentiality

■ This is one of the many areas where 'arrangements' are required by the 2007 Code, subrule 5.01 on the need for effective supervision of work done within the firm. See subrule 5.01(1)(g) on 'the safekeeping of documents and assets entrusted to the firm'.

8.15.1 All papers, documents and items in relation to client work must be traceable within the office through their being filed or stored on the matter file at all times. This involves use of the client matter numbering system and the computer identification of all documentation. The location of all items and papers that are not kept within the file must be clearly recorded on that file. Items of evidence that are in the possession of the firm, or other physical items that the firm is required to retain in pursuance of instructions, must be labelled with the appropriate matter number and the client's name.

8.15.2 Deeds and files are to be stored and tracked [*specify procedure*].

8.15.3 Consideration should always be given to copying items of sensitivity where their loss could cause particular difficulty for the firm or the client.

8.15.4 Proper care must be taken of files removed from the office. If taking files home the fee earner is required to leave a note on their desk or in their diary of which files have been taken. This is to minimise the time that can be wasted by looking for files that are not in the office. Please take particular care about files in cars. In no circumstances should you leave files in an unlocked car, or overnight. Please also ensure that any work done on a client file on train journeys does remain confidential. In this respect please also consider who might overhear your telephone calls on mobile phones in trains or in public places.

D Progressing matters

8.16 Maintaining progress

▨ In relation to the need to maintain progress see the 2007 Code, subrule 2.02(1)(d) requiring the client to be kept informed of progress 'unless otherwise agreed'. On the position where you wish to cease to act for a client see subule 2.01(2) and its requirements for 'good reason' and 'reasonable notice'.

8.16.1 All matters must be progressed in an appropriate manner, having regard to the importance of the matter to the client, any instructions that they have provided on desired or necessary timescale and the constraints of the process concerned. In particular, fee earners will:

- provide regular and reasonable information to clients on progress or the reasons for the lack of it;
- respond to any telephone calls or communication from clients promptly;
- reply in a professional manner to solicitors acting for the opponent or other parties;
- check all matters regularly for progress (see section 6.4).

8.16.2 On occasions the firm will reach the unfortunate conclusion that it cannot continue to act for a client on a matter. Such circumstances could include the refusal of a client to provide instructions, the non-payment of an invoice or a breakdown of the necessary relationship. In all cases a partner must consent to the termination of a retainer and must provide reasonable notice to the client of the decision in writing.

8.17 Matter progress reports and costs updates

▨ On the need to keep the client informed on progress see the 2007 Code, subrule 2.02(1)(d). On the costs position note that the former requirement in the Solicitors Costs Information and Client Care Code for regular updates on costs which needed to be at least six-monthly under Rule 6a has now been replaced with a general requirement that the client should be informed about changes to the costs position as 'appropriate'. See the *Lexcel Assessment Guide* for further guidance on this change. Legal aid lawyers should bear in mind that six-monthly costs updates remain an element of the SQM, notwithstanding the change in the 2007 Code. See SQM F2.3.

8.17.1 Any changes to the matter plan should be made in a full and appropriate manner, such as by letter documenting the agreed amendments and agreed with the client. Any development that would cause the fee earner to doubt the costs information already provided should be reported to the client without delay.

8.17.2 The costs position should be reviewed and reported to the client as appropriate by way of a costs update unless they have agreed otherwise, as where the work is being done to a fixed quote. As a general rule the costs position must be discussed with the client before an estimate or agreed upper limit is exceeded. It is important to monitor progress towards costs estimates or other limits in order to raise the issue with the client in a timely manner.

8.17.3 The client must be informed in writing if there is a change of fee earner handling the matter or the designated supervisor, or if there are any other material changes within the firm that affect the handling of their matter.

8.18 Undertakings

Undertakings are another issue for which the firm must have 'arrangements' under the 2007 Code, subrule 5.01. Poorly worded or ill-advised undertakings have caused substantial losses for firms and their insurers. Failure to observe an undertaking is a professional offence and it is well worth checking the obligations on undertakings which now appear in Rule 10 (Relations with third parties) at subrule 10.05.
The main provisions in an office procedure for undertakings should be to:

- require partner or senior manager consent to the giving of non-routine undertakings;
- set out clear procedures on who may give routine undertakings (as most obviously to exchange contracts or discharge mortgages in conveyancing);
- provide for the effective discharge of undertakings;
- make it clear that the firm will not be liable for personal undertakings arising outside the scope of the work of the practice.

Some firms find a central register of undertakings helpful. These are sometimes a relic of earlier Legal Aid Board requirements where various auditors tended to insist on them, but they are not essential under SQM (see E1.2(d) and the accompanying guidance which states that the procedures may or may not include a central record). This means that central registers can be discarded if the firm prefers and seem unlikely to be a mandatory element of satisfactory 'arrangements' for the sake of Rule 5.01(1)(f).

8.18.1 Undertakings are an important consideration for the firm. Guidance note 24 to Rule 10 of the 2007 Code defines an undertaking as 'any statement, made by you or your firm, that you or your firm will do something or cause something to be done, or refrain from doing something, given to someone who reasonably relies upon it'. The following points should be noted:

- There is no rule that the undertaking has to be written, though it may be difficult to prove an oral undertaking.
- An undertaking is binding even if it is to do with something outside the solicitor's control.
- Ambiguous undertakings are generally construed in favour of the recipient.
- Solicitors who fail to honour an undertaking could be seen to be guilty of professional misconduct.

8.18.2 The first rule is not to offer undertakings unless necessary. The second rule is that all undertakings require a partner's consent or approval. The exceptions to this rule are set out in the departmental appendices and are limited to:

- the giving of routine conveyancing undertakings;
- undertakings that are offered to court.

8.18.3 In all cases great care must be taken to ensure that the firm will be able to honour any undertaking given. It is vital that the firm limit undertakings to those for which it is competent. For example, the firm may not give an undertaking to repay a loan if this depends upon a third party paying the monies to it. Do not give open undertakings; make each one for a specific amount and as detailed as possible. Furthermore, the wording of undertakings needs to take into account that the firm will only do what is within its power: do not offer undertakings that the client will do a stated action.

8.18.4 Non-routine undertakings are noted by use of an undertaking sticker which must be placed on the outside front cover of the file and initialled by the partner giving or approving it. On the discharge of the undertaking the person doing so must initial to show that it has been discharged. No file may be archived until all undertakings have clearly been discharged.

8.18.5 An undertaking by e-mail must not be accepted.

8.19 Experts and counsel

Where outsiders are involved in the services delivered to clients it makes sense that they should be subject to controls to make sure that they support the firm's commitment to deliver quality services. Many firms will take the view that the most useful list is the 'non-approved' list of experts and counsel that should not be instructed in future. Earlier editions of this book suggested a 'B' list for experts and others where there was some reservation about them, and a 'C'; list for non-approved advisers. This distinction has been removed from this edition. Lists are increasingly computerised and any reservations about a name are likely to be flagged up against that name on one simple list. The use of non-approved names (the 'C' list in previous editions) seems to be declining and that list has therefore been removed from this edition. Where such a list is still in use the combined effects of data protection rights and defamation are such that firms should be very careful about its usage.

In larger firms it will be best to entrust the task of maintaining lists to the departments or groups. In smaller practices one firmwide list should be quite acceptable.

8.19.1 The choice of counsel or other external expert should always be based on matching the client's needs and priorities with the most suitable person for the role, having regard to the complexity of the service required, the timescale within which the report or service is required and the costs constraints of the client or their funder if they are to pay for the report or service or might need to do so. The choice of external adviser should never be influenced by preferences on the part of the adviser or the client that are prejudicial in a manner that is prohibited by our policy on equality and diversity (see section 1.4).

8.19.2 The first point of contact should be the list of approved counsel and experts, which is maintained by [*clarify arrangements*]. But it is always possible to choose an adviser not on this list if this is felt to be necessary or more appropriate. It is the responsibility of [*name or title*] to keep up to date the list of approved counsel and other professional contacts.

8.19.3 All recommendations for entry to or removal from the list should be made by submitting a form (see annex 8E) to [*name or title*].

8.19.4 The performance of those on the approved list will be constantly monitored. If anyone feels that the approved expert fails to meet the required standards details are to be recorded on the matter file and a recommendation to remove that expert from the list should be considered.

8.19.5 Where appropriate, clients should be consulted on both the decision to involve experts and the selection of them. In the unlikely event of a client choosing an expert that the firm would not approve of the reservations of the firm should be mentioned, but the client has the right to override the firm's reservations, subject to normal professional standards on the propriety of all actions taken for clients. Where the client expresses a preference that is contrary to the firm's equality and diversity policy their instructions will be challenged. If the instructions are not varied the firm should decline to act further in the matter. In all cases, however, a client may require that a particular medical examiner not be used on grounds of previous personal experience.

8.19.6 The client should be advised of the name and status of the expert/counsel, the likely timescale before a response will be received and the likely cost if the client will be expected to pay, or could be asked to do so.

8.19.7 Experts will receive instructions through letter, brief, telephone conversation or at a meeting. Where instructions are provided orally they must be confirmed subsequently in writing. In all cases a note of instructions or a copy of them must appear on the matter file.

8.19.8 On receipt of advice from any counsel or expert the fee earner receiving it must consider its suitability and value. If (s)he considers it inappropriate (s)he should refer it back to the adviser with a detailed request for the improvement that is felt to be necessary to bring it into line with the firm's expectations. If the standard of advice remains unsuitable, consideration should be given to the non-payment of the fee and to recommending the removal of that individual from the approved list. The failure of a barrister or expert to meet the firm's standards must be noted on the matter file and the central record.

8.19.9 As and when experts' fees notes are received they are met and settled if before the end of the case unless a deferred payment arrangement is in place.

E Matter closing

8.20 File closing

8.20.1 As soon as a client matter has been fully completed, the fee earner handling that matter is to close the file so that it can be archived. The archive form at [annex 8D] is to be used.

▨ A simple file closing checklist is contained in the file summary sheet at annex 8D.

8.20.2 The fee earner must ensure that all ledger balances have been reduced to nil otherwise the matter cannot be archived on the accounting system. The fee earner is also to assess and record the year for the eventual destruction of the file.

8.20.3 The file is then to be passed to [*name or title*] who will archive the file on the accounting system and store the file in [*location*]. The process will allocate to the file a sequential storage number which will be recorded in the client matter details for future reference. The archiving process prevents any further postings to be made to the client or time ledgers and shows the matter as being closed, but all detailed entries including the matter details will be retained permanently in the accounting database and can be printed out if required later.

8.21 Final review

8.21.1 Before a file is archived there must be a final written review of the matter to see whether the client's objectives were met and, if not, why not. There should be a final report to the client which will usually accompany any final invoice or receipt against monies held on the client's behalf. The final review sheet questions on the file summary sheet must be initialled in order that the file can be archived – [*name or title*] has been instructed to return any files where this has not been done. Likewise, files that have obviously not been 'thinned' will be returned to the fee earner concerned.

8.21.2 Clients may need advice on storage of documents and files and of review dates that they should note. If it is felt inappropriate for any reasons not to provide a final report to the client (e.g. the firm is acting for a minor) this must be explained in a file note that details what alternative steps, if any, have been taken.

8.21.3 On the need for a concluding risk assessment see section 6.7.8.

8.21.4 Formal after-care does not feature as a major element of the firm's work, but such arrangements as do exist are dealt with in departmental instructions (for example, wills reviews and company secretarial work). The client will be advised of any future action they need to take.

8.22 Archiving

[*State here arrangements for file storage, including who has responsibility and where the files are stored. In deciding appropriate storage times the applicable limitation periods should be considered, as well the need to maintain records under the Money Laundering Regulations*]

Annex 8A

Format of departmental appendix (conveyancing)

1. The range of work undertaken by the department
2. Generic risks of conveyancing work
3. Conflicts in conveyancing work: if and when the firms would act for both parties and compliance with 2007 Code, Rule 3
4. List of key dates in conveyancing work
5. Departmental arrangements for noting key dates
6. Procedures for alerting fee earners of key dates and responses required
7. Undertakings: authority of fee earners to provide 'routine' undertakings and instructions to be followed: Law Society formula for exchange, etc.
8. Rules on how files must be maintained: e.g. colour-coding of files, what goes where on files, use of summary sheets
9. Issues particular to work type: e.g. handling and noting requests for quotes, including monitoring success rates
10. Any after-care provisions – work done after the matter is completed (unlikely)
11. Arrangements for departmental meetings
12. Any special departmental file review arrangements

Annex 8B

Costs and funding checklist

Client matter number

Client name

	Method of funding		
1.	Could this client qualify for public funding?	☐Yes	☐No
2.	Does the client have household or business protection insurance ('before the event' insurance)?	☐Yes	☐No
3a.	Could this matter be conducted under a conditional fee agreement (CFA)?	☐Yes	☐No
3b.	If Yes, has this been discussed with the client and explained to them?	☐Yes	☐No
4.	Does the matter involve goods or services that could be covered by credit card insurance?	☐Yes	☐No
5a.	Is the client a member of a trade union?	☐Yes	☐No
5b.	If Yes, could cover be available?	☐Yes	☐No
6.	Has consideration been given to the availability and suitability of 'after the event' insurance?	☐Yes	☐No
7.	Are contingency arrangements appropriate in this case?	☐Yes	☐No

I confirm that:

- The above funding options have been discussed with me

- I know of no possible source of funding that I have not mentioned

- I wish

to act for me on the basis set out in their letter of the   to me confirming instructions

Client's signature _____   Date _____

Annex 8C

File opening form

Client surname

First names

Previous names (if relevant)

Company name	
Trading name	
Contact name	
Status	

Address	

Work contact details

Telephone number	
Fax	
e-mail	
Mobile	

Home contact details

Telephone number	
Fax	
e-mail	
Mobile	

Special circumstances (e.g. notify by fax)

Matter description

Names of any other connected parties for conflicts check

Work code

I consider this matter to be

☐ High risk   ☐ Ordinary risk

Unusual circumstances — instructions

Identity checks already conducted?

☐ Yes   ☐ No

If Yes, state date on system

If No, form ML1 **must** accompany this form.

Do you agree to this matter being opened?

☐ Yes   ☐ No

Initials _____

Date _____

Annex 8D

File summary sheet

(to be placed on file when opened and kept up to date)

Client matter number

Client name

Client partner (if any)

Useful contacts

Name	Address	Telephone number

Conflicts of interest?

Special instructions from client

Tick if no consent to audit inspection ☐

	Instructions			In all cases note below any concerns
1.	Note of instructions on file?	☐ Yes	☐ No	
2.	Funding code in public funding?	☐ Yes	☐ No	
3.	Cost benefit discussed with client?	☐ Yes	☐ No	
4.	Does this work involve high risk for the firm?	☐ Yes	☐ No	
5.	Evidence of identity?	☐ Yes	☐ No	
6.	Full instructions taken from client?	☐ Yes	☐ No	
7.	Regular client?	☐ Yes	☐ No	
	If Yes, identify the terms which apply			
	If No, show date of client care letter			
8.	Version of terms and conditions sent			
9.	Other reason client care letter not sent			

File reviews

File review date

Corrective action?
If any, confirm taken

File review date

Corrective action?
If any, confirm taken

Final review (must be completed before archiving)

Objectives met? (if not report to supervisor in writing)	
Future review date	
Nil balances	
File thinned	
Client advised regarding storage	
Further action notified	
Papers/items returned to client	
Destroy date	

Annex 8E

Experts/Counsel recommendation form

To the Departmental Supervisor

From

Details of expert/counsel

Name

Telephone

Address

Mobile

Fax

e-mail

I recommend that this expert/counsel should be

☐ added to the fully approved list

☐ removed from the approved list

If recommending inclusion as approved, details of qualifications/recommendation received, etc.

I have used this expert/counsel on matter number

My experience was (consider oral report if negative experience)

If recommending the use of this expert/counsel, I would add the caveat that (if any)

☐ Agreed   ☐ Not agreed

Signed _____   Signed _____

Position _____   Departmental Supervisor

Date _____   Date _____

Appendix 1

Cross references to Lexcel procedures

Lexcel ref		Manual ref	Notes
1	**Structures and policies**		
1.1	(a) Documentation on legal framework	1.2	Governance paperwork would not usually form part of a manual
	(b) Business structure	1.3	
1.2	Risk management policy	1.7	1.7 is a general risk management policy
	(a) Strategic risk	Section 2	Strategic risk is addressed in business planning activity
	(b) Operational risk	Section 6	Operational risk is dealt with in conjunction with supervision
	(c) Regulatory risk		Regulatory risk is a theme of the whole publication, but see section 7 in relation to compliance with 2007 Code, Rule 2; also 8.8 on confirming terms of business in particular
1.3	Quality policy	1.4	There is likely to be overlap between the quality and client care policies
	(a) Role of quality in overall strategy	1.4.3	
	(b) Process to suggest improvements	1.6.1	
1.4	Policy on avoidance of discrimination and promotion of diversity	1.8	
	(a) Employment, etc.	1.8.2	
	(b) Delivery of service;	1.8.1	
	(c) Instruction of counsel and experts	1.8.1	
1.5	Policy on anti-money laundering	1.9	It should be noted that not all firms are subject to the Money Laundering Regulations, so exemptions might be appropriate
	(a) Appointment of MLRO	1.9.6	
	(b) Disclosure process	1.9.9	See also internal report form at annex 1B

Lexcel ref		Manual ref	Notes
	(c) Identification checking	1.9.13	The MLR 2007 extend the need for ID checking
	(d) Training of personnel	1.9.6, 1.9.7	Obligation of MLRO to arrange training and personnel to attend
	(e) Records	1.9.17, 1.9.18	Record keeping provisions are also subject to possible change under MLR 2007
1.6	Avoidance of mortgage fraud	1.10	
1.7	Health and safety policy	1.11	Supplemental detailed procedures set out at annex 4D
1.8	Community and social responsibility policy		This is an optional element of Lexcel
2	**Strategy, the provision of services and marketing**		
2.1	Marketing and business plan	2.1	
2.2	Documented services offered	N/a	Usually met by brochure or website
	(a) Client groups to be served		
	(b) how services to be provided		
	(c) How services designed to meet client needs		
2.3	Documented review of plans every six months	2.1.1	
2.4	Business continuity plan	2.2.1	See guidance at 2.2
	(a) Evaluation of potential threats		
	(b) Ways to reduce, avoid and transfer risk		
	(c) Processes for testing and checking the plan		
3	**Financial management**		
3.1	Responsibility for overall financial management	3.1	
3.2	Evidence of financial management processes	N/a	These records would not usually feature in an office manual
	(a) Annual budget		
	(b) Variance analysis of income and expenditure		

	(c) Annual profit and loss/income and expenditure accounts (d) Annual balance sheet; (e) Annual cash or funds flow forecast (f) Quarterly variance analysis at least of cashflow	3.21
3.3	Time recording process for billing	Necessary for billing only, recommended for management information
4A	**Information management**	
4A.1	Practices to have ICT plan (a) Application of ICT facilities (b) Role of ICT in client service	The plan could be contained in text in the manual or the manual might refer to the plan
4A.2	Data protection policy (a) Registration with the Information Commissioner (b) Training of personnel	
4A.3	Information management policy (a) Relevant information assets of practice and clients (b) Risk to these assets (c) Procedures for protection and security of assets (d) Process for training personnel	
4A.4	E-mail policy (a) Scope of permitted and prohibited use (b) Procedures for monitoring use	

Lexcel ref		Manual ref	Notes
	(c) Procedures for proper management and security		
	(d) Procedures for proper storage and destruction		
4A.5	Website	4A.5	
	(a) Document approval and publishing		
	(b) Scope of permitted and prohibited use		
	(c) Security and contents		
4A.6	Internet access policy	4A.6	
	(a) Scope of permitted and prohibited use		
	(b) Monitoring access		
4B	Facilities	4B	
4B.1	Documented office facilities		
	(a) Use of premises and equipment	4B.1	And see 4E on office facilities
	(b) Clients visiting premises	4B.2	
	(c) Communication arrangements	4B.3, 4B.4 and 4C	Phone and post/communications
	(d) Handling financial transactions	Section 3	
4B.2	Legal research and updating	4E.3	
4B.3	Office manual or intranet	1.1.4	There is also a reference to the fact that Lexcel requires all policies and plans to have a designated person to control them. See also 6.1.2
	(a) Control office manual or intranet	1.1.4	
	(b) Annual review	1.1.4	
	(c) Updating manual or intranet	1.1.4	

5	People management		
5.1	Plan for		
	(a) Recruitment	5.5	
	(b) Training and development	5.8	A training plan could emerge from the appraisal/review process or might form part of the strategic plan, or office or departmental plans
5.2	Person specifications	5.5.2	See precedent examples
5.3	Recruitment and selection procedures		
	(a) Identification of vacancies	5.5.3	
	(b) Drafting of job documentation;	5.5.3	
	(c) Methods of attracting candidates	5.5.4	
	(d) Selection methods	5.5.5	
	(e) Storage, retention and destruction of records	5.5.5	
	(f) ID checking and medical examination	5.5.5	
	(g) Fee earners' disciplinary record.	5.5.5	
5.4	Induction process	5.6	See also induction checklist at annex 5Q
	(a) Management structure and job responsibilities;		
	(b) Terms and conditions of employment		
	(c) Immediate training requirements		
	(d) Key policies		
5.5	Training and development policy	5.8	
	(a) Provision of appropriate training	5.8.1	
	(b) Supervisors and managers	5.8.1–5.8.3	
	(c) Process to evaluate training	5.8.8	See annex 5Z
5.6	Review system	5.7	The term 'review' is favoured in place of appraisal

Lexcel ref		Manual ref	Notes
6	Supervision and operational risk management		
6.1	Management structure	6.1.1	See also annex 6A
6.2	Named supervisor for each area of work	6.1.2	
6.3	Active supervision	6.2.1	Envisages limiting of checking of outgoing post by experience
	(a) Checks on incoming and outgoing correspondence	6.2.1	
	(b) Departmental, team and office meetings and communication structures	6.2.1	
	(c) Reviews of matter details	6.3.1	
	(d) Devolved powers in publicly funded work	6.2.1	
	(e) Availability of supervisor	6.1.3	
	(f) Allocation and reallocation of work	6.1.3, 6.3.1	
6.4	Inactivity checks	6.4	
6.5	Regular, independent file reviews	6.5	
	(a) Define file selection criteria	6.5.1	
	(b) Number and frequency of reviews	6.5.1	
	(c) Records of review	6.5.3	
	(d) Corrective action	6.5.3	
	(e) Designated supervisor to monitor file review data	6.5.4	
	(f) Annual review of file review data	6.5.5	
6.6	Risk procedures		
	(a) Designate one overall risk manager	6.1.2, 6.6.2	
	(b) Reporting arrangements	6.7	
	(c) Lists of work undertaken and steps taken when work is declined	6.1.3	

	(d) Details of the generic risks communicated	6.1.3
	(e) Manage instructions with high risk profile	6.7.5
6.7	Analysis of risk assessment data	
	(a) Indemnity claims	6.8
	(b) Client complaints trends	
	(c) File review data	
	(d) Identification of remedial action.	
6.8	Operational risk to be considered and recorded	6.7
	(a) Client/matter acceptance	6.7.2
	(b) Risk profile of all new instructions	6.7.2
	(c) Change to risk profile	6.7.6
	(d) Clients to be advised of adverse costs order	6.7.7
	(e) Concluding risk assessment	6.7.8
	(f) Notify risk manager of circumstances	6.7.8
7	**Client care**	
7.1	Policy for client care	7.1
7.2	Processes for compliance with Rule 2	7.1.1
7.3	Record of standing terms of business	7.6.3
7.4	Written complaints handling procedure	7.7
	(a) Defines complaint and sets out how to identify and respond	7.7.2
	(b) Records and reports centrally all complaints	7.7.4
	(c) Identifies cause and offers redress, correcting any unsatisfactory procedures	7.7.5
	(d) Reviews of complaints data and trends	7.7.7
7.5	Process to monitor client satisfaction	7.8

Lexcel ref		Manual ref	Notes
8	File and case management		
8.1	Client enquiries	8.1	
	(a) Telephone enquiries		
	(b) Clients in person		
	(c) Correspondence and e-mail		
8.2	Acceptance of new instructions	8.2, 8.3	
8.3	Conflicts of interests	8.6	
8.4	Outset of the matter	8.7	See also annexes to section 7, 7A in particular
	(a) Client's requirements and objectives	8.7.6	
	(b) Clear explanation of issues raised and advice given	8.7.6, 8.7.7	
	(c) What fee earner will do and timescale	8.7.6	
	(d) Establish method of funding	8.7.6, 8.8.4	
	(e) Cost-benefit analysis		
	Above to be confirmed to client, ordinarily in writing	8.7.7	
8.5	Matter strategy	8.11	
8.6	Matters progressed		
	(a) Key information on file	8.12	
	(b) Key dates	8.10	
	(c) Monitoring key dates	8.10.3	
	(d) Timely response	8.16.1	
	(e) Continuing costs information	8.17	
	(f) Clients informed in writing if change of fee earner or point of contact	8.17.3	

8.7	Undertakings	8.18	
8.8	Documented procedure		File opening procedure also likely in full accounts manual
	(a) Listing open/closed matters for single client, linked files and funders	8.4	
	(b) Tracing documents, files, deeds, wills, etc.	8.15	
	(c) Safeguarding confidentiality	8.15.4	
	(d) Checking status of matter and action taken	8.13	
	(e) Ensuring documents stored in an orderly way.	8.12	
8.9	Use of barristers and other external advisers	8.19	
	(a) Use of clear selection criteria	8.19.1	
	(b) Consultation with client and advice to client	8.19.5	
	(c) Details to client of name and status of adviser, time to respond, and cost if paid by client	8.19.6	
	(d) Records of barristers and experts used	8.19.2	
	(e) Evaluation of performance	8.19.8	
	(f) Clear instructions	8.19.7	
	(g) Checking of opinions and reports	8.19.8	
	(h) Payment of fees.	8.19.9	
8.10	End of matter		
	(a) Reports to client on outcome and further action required	8.21.1	See also annex 8D
	(b) Accounts for outstanding money	8.21.1	
	(c) Returns to client of documents and property	8.21.2	
	(d) Advice on storage and retrieval	8.21.2	
	(e) Future review	8.22.4	
	(f) Archiving and destruction	8.22	

Appendix 2

Compliance with Lexcel and the Specialist Quality Mark
of the Legal Services Commission

Introduction

This book has been drawn up primarily to enable practices to develop procedures for compliance with Lexcel, but there will be many firms that will also be concerned with the Specialist Quality Mark (SQM) of the Legal Services Commission. This appendix shows where the relevant section of the SQM is dealt with in relation to Lexcel v.4 and this Manual. It should be borne in mind that there can be no guarantee that the procedures contained in this manual will be sufficient for any particular assessor under either the SQM or Lexcel, but they should form a useful illustration of the sort of provisions that might apply.

The SQM is the third edition of a legal aid quality standard. The current version edition of SQM is dated 2002 (issue 1.1, reprint August 2005). There are no current plans to review it. In some places the SQM is based on Law Society rules no longer in force, especially in the area of costs information. It should not be assumed that simply because the professional regulations have changed that the SQM will follow suit.

The following table shows overlaps between Lexcel and the SQM and where sample procedures can be viewed in this book. Many of the overlaps are not precise and a more detailed comparison of the two standards and, therefore, the applicability of the suggested procedure might be necessary.

1. Table of overlaps between SQM, Lexcel and references in this Manual

SQM section	Summary	Lexcel reference	Manual reference	Comment
A1.1	Your business plan	2.1	2.1	
A1.2	Reviewing your business plan	2.3	2.1.1	
A2.1	Providing service information	N/a	N/a	
A2.2	Logo guidance	N/a	N/a	
A3.1	Non-discrimination in provision of services	1.4	1.8	
A3.2	Targeting specific client group	N/a	N/a	
B1.1	Staff knowledge: signposting and referral	N/a	N/a	
B1.2	Signposting and referral procedure	N/a	N/a	
B1.3	Referral records	N/a	N/a	
B1.4	Up to date supplier information	N/a	N/a	
B2.1	Community Legal Service Partnerships (CLSP) protocols	N/a	N/a	The LSC has withdrawn from Community Legal Service Partnerships and abolished Regional Legal Services Committees; but the SQM has not been amended to reflect this
C1.1	Staff structure	6.1	6.1.1	
C1.2	Key roles and decision-making structure	6.1	6.1.2	Guidance suggests office manual should set out details
C1.3	Organisational standards	N/a	N/a	
C1.4	Status enquiries	N/a	N/a	
C1.5	Independence	N/a	N/a	
C2.1	Financial responsibilities	3.1	3.1	
C2.2	Financial processes	3.2	N/a	Finance reports listed do not usually form part of an office manual
C2.3	Independent financial review	N/a	N/a	
C2.4	Internal financial reviews	3.2	N/a	
C2.5	Professional indemnity insurance	N/a	N/a	
D1.1	Job description and person specification	5.2	5.5.2	Requirement in Lexcel now limited to person specification

SQM section	Summary	Lexcel reference	Manual reference	Comment
D1.2	Key responsibilities and objectives	5.2	5.5.2	
D1.3	Key responsibilities in selection, treatment and for behaviour of staff	1.4	1.8	LSC requires disciplinary sanctions breach. This is implicit in the need for a policy in the 2007 Code, subrule 6.03
D1.4	Operating an open recruitment process	5.3	5.5.3– 5.5.6	An open recruitment process is defined as one where selection can be demonstrated by reference to objective and consistent assessment
D2.1	Induction	5.4	5.6	
D2.2	Performance review and feedback	5.6	5.7	
D2.3	Individual training and development plans	5.5	5.8	The format is prescribed and must outline what is to be achieved, how it is to be achieved and the timescale
D2.4	Training records	5.5	5.8.6	
D3.1	Named category supervisor	6.2	6.1.2	
D3.2	Supervisors' legal competence	6.2	N/a	The SQM is more specific than Lexcel in relation to the criteria by which someone becomes and remains a category supervisor
D3.3	Supervisory skills	6.2	N/a	The manual assumes that the heads of department nominated as supervisors would have sufficient expertise and ability to guide and assist others
D3.4	Supervisors' legal training	N/a	N/a	Supervisors under Lexcel are simply subject to normal training requirements and CPD needs; the SQM is more specific
D3.5	Conditions for supervision	6.3	6.1.3	
D4.1	Case allocation	6.3(f)	6.3	
D4.2	Systems of supervision	6.3	6.2.1	
D4.3	Limits of competence and referral	7.2	N/a	The need to turn instructions away where the firm lacks the resources or expertise to handle them is implicit in 7.1.1 which commits the firm to observing Rule 2 (Client relations) of the 2007 Code
D4.4	Access to reference materials	4B.2	4E.3	

SQM section	Summary	Lexcel reference	Manual reference	Comment
D4.5	Updating legal information to staff	4B.2	4E.3	
D5.1	Training requirements for casework staff	5.5(a)	5.8.1–5.8.3	
D5.2	Legal qualification or minimum hours	N/a	N/a	
E1.1	File list	8.8(a)	N/a	
E1.2	File management procedures			
E1.2(a)	Conflicts	8.3	8.6	
E1.2(b)	Tracing documents	8.8(b)	8.15	
E1.2(c)	Key dates backup	8.6(b)	8.10	
E1.2(d)	Undertakings	8.7	8.18	
E1.2(e)	Inactivity checks	6.4	6.4.1	
E1.2(f)	Linking files	8.8(a)	8.4	
E1.3	Case files logical and orderly	8.8(e)	8.12	
E2.1	File reviews	6.5	6.5	
E2.2	Process management	6.5	N/a	
E2.3	File reviewers	N/a	N/a	See also 2007 Code, 5.03(3)
E2.4	Review and corrective action on file	6.5	6.5.3	
E2.5	Review records	6.5	6.5.3	
E2.6	Monitoring file reviews	6.5(e)	6.5.4	
F1.1	Recording and confirming basic information	N/a	N/a	
F1.1(a)	Instructions	8.4	8.7	The 2007 Code, subrule 2.02(1) requires the client's objectives to be identified and other information to be confirmed
F1.1(b)	Advice and/or action	8.4	8.7	
F1.1(c)	Name and status	7.2	7.6.1	See subrule 2.02(2)(d)
F1.1(d)	Costs information	7.2	7.6.1 and 8.8	See subrule 2.03
F1.2	Recording and agreeing further information in writing	8.4	7.6	
F2.1	Complex case plans	8.5	8.11	Now referred to as project plans in Lexcel
F2.2	Updating issues and case progress	8.6	8.17	

SQM section	Summary	Lexcel reference	Manual reference	Comment
F2.3	Updating costs information	8.6(e)	8.17	
F2.4	Legal aid eligibility	N/a	N/a	
F2.5	Responsibility for the client's case	7.2	Annex 7A	See client care letter
F3.1	Confirming information at the end of the case	8.10	8.21	
F4.1	Confidentiality procedure	N/a	N/a	But – is a conduct rule
F4.2	Consent to file audits	N/a	N/a	
F4.3	Privacy	N/a	N/a	
F5.1	Non-discrimination – suppliers	1.4	1.8.1	
F5.2	Selection of suppliers	8.9	8.19	
F5.3	Evaluation of suppliers	N/a	8.19	
F5.4	Information to the client	8.9(c)	8.19	
F5.5	Content of instructions	8.9(f)	8.19	
G1.1	Information on how and to whom to complain	7.2	7.7 and Annex 7A	Implied in Rule 2 – see client care letter
G1.2	Complaints procedure	7.4	7.7.1	
G1.3	Central record and annual review	7.4(b)	7.7.7	
G2.1	Client feedback procedure	7.5	7.8	
G2.2	Annual review and outcome	7.5	7.8.1	Guidance suggests feeding this into the annual risk review – see 6.8 in manual
G3.1	Appointing a quality representative	6.6(a)	1.1.4	
G3.2	Up-to-date quality procedures	4B.3	1.5.1	
G3.3	Process control	N/a	N/a	
G4.1	Having a quality manual	4B.3	1.4.4	
G4.2	Manual availability	4B.3	N/a	Guidance in manual
G4.3	Quality Mark forms	N/a	N/a	
G4.4	Quality Mark information	N/a	N/a	

2. Internal SQM Audit Checklist

The following list gives the main requirements of the SQM that should be checked annually and prior to an audit. Sufficient time should be provided for to enable appropriate action to be taken, e.g. a review of the business plan. References are to the current version of the SQM (first edition April 2002, issue 1.1, reprint (August 2005).

1. Franchise representative

Has the LSC been notified of any change of franchise representative?

[*This became a quality representative under SQM G3.1; but has been renamed Liaison Manager under the Unified Contract 2007 (Clause 3).*]

2. Welfare benefits

[*Former requirements for compulsory set training now relaxed and awareness training only required where appropriate to the caseworker's clients and cases.*]

3. Family mediation

[*Former requirements for compulsory set training now relaxed as above.*]

4. Status enquiries

If applicable, has the LSC been notified of any adverse findings made by the OSS [sic, *in the SQM, now Legal Complaints Service*] or other regulatory body? (C1.4 – duty to report within 28 days)

5. Business plan

Has the business plan been reviewed at least every six months and have the reviews been documented (A1.2)?

Did reviews include an analysis of financial performance in terms of income and expenditure (C2.2)? What evidence is there?

6. Management structure

Has the written management structure been reviewed, and updated if necessary (C1.1)? See also A1.1 – a summary of caseworkers' experience and qualifications.

7. Job descriptions

Are there current up-to-date job descriptions for all staff and partners who are involved in legal aid work (D1.1)?

8. Recruitment

Has required recruitment documentation been retained (D1.4)? [*Also note the need for an open recruitment process.*]

9. Induction

Are there induction records for all new members of staff (D2.1)? [*SQM requires this to begin within 2 months of joining.*]

10. Appraisal

Have appraisals been fully carried out for all staff and partners who are involved in legal aid work (D2.2)?

11. Training

Are there training records for all staff and partners involved in legal aid work and are the records up to date (D2.4)? [*All training must be recorded.*]

Have training and development needs been assessed **for all** staff at least annually (D2.3)? [*See also D5.1 on caseworker training requirements.*]

Have supervisors met the minimum training requirements (D3.4)? [*Now six hours in each category supervised.*]

12. Finance

Does the firm maintain the financial information required at C2?

Is there clear evidence to demonstrate how the firm undertakes its financial management, e.g. budgetary control (C2.2)?

Is there a statement from the firm's accountant that verifies that the firm has a set of audited accounts relevant to the financial period (C2.3)? [*Note that preferred suppliers may be required to show their accounts to the LSC's relationship manager; but any such requirement will remain controversial.*]

13. Supervision of work

Have qualified supervisors been appointed for each category of work or contract (D.3.1)?

Have the details of the supervisors submitted self declaration forms and have any changes in supervisor been advised to the LSC (D3.1)?

Is the operation of supervision [all supervisors] working effectively (D4)? Is there evidence?

Is there evidence that cases are allocated to staff on the basis of skills, competence and capacity (D4.1)?

14. File reviews

Are file reviews being carried out properly (E2.1)?

Is there clear evidence of file reviews (E2.4)?

Have observations raised on reviews been reviewed for possible trends/weaknesses (E2.6)? Has corrective action been taken (E2.1(d))?

Are the number of files being reviewed for each fee earner still appropriate? (E2.1(a))?

15. File management

Are files managed in accordance with:

- F1.1   Confirmation of instructions/advice/case funding – one-off advice
- F1.2   Conformation of key information
- F2.1   Case plans in complex matters
- F2.2   Update and progress reports
- F2.3   Costs updates (at least six-monthly)
- F2.4   Changes to Legal aid eligibility
- F2.5   Any change of adviser notified
- F3.1   Closing issues – at end of matter
- F4.1   Confidentiality procedures
- F4.2   Client consent to inspection [*This requirement was introduced in anticipation that the LSC would accredit private files to the SQM. This development did not take place. The LSC considers that by signing the acceptance of funding, the client also consents to the audit of his/her case file.*]
- F.4.3 Privacy arrangements
- G.2.1 Client satisfaction feedback procedures – although part of SQM section G, a record of a request for client feedback is usually maintained on the client's file.

16. Counsel and experts register

Has the central register of counsel/experts been reviewed and updated as necessary (F5)?

Is there evidence that the performance of counsel/experts is monitored?

17. Complaints register

Has the central register of complaints been reviewed and analysed (G1.3)?

18. Office manual

Has the office manual been updated as necessary with properly recorded amendments (G3.2)?

19. Legal reference material

Does the firm have current legal reference material (D4.4)?

Are fee earners updated on changes to law, practice and procedures (D4.5)?

Do all caseworkers have qualifications or 12 hours/week (D5.2)?

20. SQM/CLS issues

Have you provided service information to LSC for CLS Direct (A2.1)?

Are staff informed/trained in signposting and referral (B1.1)?

Does a procedure exist for this (B1.2)?

Are records of referral maintained (B1.3)?

Is the latest CLS/CDS directory up to date (**www.clsdirect.org.uk** or 0845 345 3 345) (B1.4)?

Signed (Quality representative):

Date:

3. Quality data review

Although not directly required by SQM an annual management review is advisable to ensure that all aspects are kept under review as they need to be. Bear in mind that at least an interim review of the business plan must occur each six months between annual main reviews.

This form highlights all the areas where some form of monitoring is required by the firm or is desirable. The references are to the requirements in the SQM.

An agenda for a smaller firm could include partner appraisals. It might even be worth holding such a review six-monthly.

Agenda

1. General developments – relationship with LSC, etc. (consider the use of Contract Management Review Criteria and Quality Profile which may be obtained from the LSC on request).
2. Patterns of matter starts, matter completions, and turnover time.
3. File reviews (see E2.6 on the need for a centralised record).
4. Complaints records and trends (see G.1.3 on the need for analysis and review).
5. Changes to documentation (see G.3.2 on annual review).
6. Client feedback review (see G.2.2).
7. Partner objectives for next period and appraisal (D2.2).
8. Review of business plan (A1.2).
9. Pattern of referrals (B1.3).
10. Management structure (C1.1) – changes to be incorporated within three months.
11. Evaluation of suppliers (i.e. counsel and experts) (F5.3).
12. Annual review of risk (G5.4) (optional).

Appendix 3

Solicitors' Code of Conduct 2007: table of main references

Many practices will be concerned to check their manuals against the requirements of the Solicitors' Code of Conduct 2007 which took effect as of 1 July 2007. In some instances the inclusion of an appropriate procedure in the manual will be a suitable way of showing compliance with the provisions of the 2007 Code, especially in relation to the 'arrangements' needed under subrule 5.01 (Supervision and management responsibilities). In other areas firms might wish to see what should be in place to ensure that personnel meet the requirements that are imposed, of which the best example is Rule 2 (Client relations). Compliance with this latter rule is also a specific Lexcel requirement as a result of 7.2.

The following table shows references in this book to the 2007 Code, including those guidance notes that are mentioned. For a comparison table showing similarities and changes between *The Guide to the Professional Conduct of Solicitors* and the 2007 Code of Conduct see **www.web4law.biz/code** or Peter Camp, *Companion to the Solicitors' Code of Conduct 2007* (Law Society Publishing, 2007).

Code ref	Subject	Manual ref
2.01(1)	Circumstances when instructions must be declined	8.3; see also 7.1.2 on inadequate resources
2.01(2)	Ceasing to act: termination of retainer	8.16 and annex 7B
2.02(1)	Client retainer: instructions and steps to be taken	8.7 on client objectives, also annex 7A in general
2.02(2)	Client retainer: level of service and responsibilities	7.6.1 and annex 7A in general. On client being informed of progress see 8.16
2.02(3)	Compliance with all requirements of Rule 2 not always needed	7.6.3
2.03(1)	Costs information, including: (a) basis of charging (b) if rates to be increased (c) likely payments (d) means of payment, including public funding and insurance (e) advice on lien for unpaid costs (f) potential liability for other party's costs (g) possibility of costs insurance	8.8 in general, see also: annex 7B annex 7A annex 7A annex 8B annex 7B annexes 7A and 7B annex 8B
2.03(2)	Conditional fee arrangements	Noted at annex 7A

Code ref	Subject	Manual ref
2.03(3)	Legal aid (public funding) information required by Legal Services Commission	Noted at annex 7A
2.03(5)	Costs information to be clear and confirmed in writing	8.8
2.03(6)	Cost-effectiveness of legal cases	Annex 7A
2.03(7)	Full information in subrule 2.03 not always required (see also guidance note 28)	8.8
2.05	Complaints systems	7.7 and annexes 7C–7E
Guidance notes to Rule 2		
12	Communication on retainer to be in 'clear and readily accessible form' (see also note 25)	7.6.1
13	Discourages 'over-complex or lengthy terms of business'	7.6.2 and 7.6.3
15	Obligation to advise on mediation and ADR	7.6.1, 7.6.2
18	Retainer information to be sent 'as soon as possible after you have agreed to act'	7.6.1 and 7.6.2
20	Clients to be informed on change of matter handler and other 'material' alterations	8.17.3
22	Circumstances when inappropriate to confirm retainer information required by subrule 2.02	7.6.3
36	Difficulties of confirming costs information at the outset and action to be taken	8.8.2
Rule 5.01(1)	Need for 'arrangements for the effective management of the firm as a whole'	
	(a) Adequate supervision	6.1.3 and 6.1.4
	(b) Money laundering regulations, where appropriate	1.9
	(d) Identifying conflicts of interests	8.6
	(e) Compliance with Rule 2 (Client relations)	See above in table
	(f) Control of undertakings	8.18
	(g) Safekeeping of documents and assets	8.15

Code ref	Subject	Manual ref
Rule 5.01(1)	(h) Compliance with Rule 6 (Equality and diversity)	1.8
	(i) Training	5.8
	(j) Financial control of budgets	Section 3
	(k) Continuation of practice	2.2
	(l) Management of risk	On operational risk see 6.6–6.8
5.03(1)	Need for a system for supervising clients' matters	6.1, 6.2, 6.3
5.03(3)	Need for checking of quality of work	File reviews: see 6.5
Rule 7	Prohibited publicity methods	Section 2 guidance
7.07	Requirements on e-mail format and letterhead	4A.4.4 on use of e-mails

Index

Lexcel Assessment Guide

Fourth edition

Lexcel Assessment Guide

Fourth edition

The Law Society

The Law Society

First edition published in 1997 as *The Assessment Guide*
Second edition published in 2001 as *Lexcel Assessment Guide*
Third edition published in 2004 as *Lexcel Assessment Guide*

This fourth edition published in 2007 by the Law Society
113 Chancery Lane, London WC2A 1PL

ISBN: 978–1–85328–678–0

Typeset by Columns Design Ltd., Reading
Printed by TJ International, Padstow, Cornwall

Contents

Foreword

Practice management excellence is a crucial element for any effective law firm or in-house legal department. Those within practice should be committed to the promotion of service excellence in every aspect of their professional life. By doing so society, practices and the profession can all benefit through the achievement of best practice.

Lexcel, the Law Society's practice management quality mark, is not only aimed at providing a goal for practices to aspire to, but as an aid in developing management techniques. Legal practices – accredited or not – are utilising Lexcel's framework approach to achieve greater cost efficiencies, reductions in risks and client service excellence.

Lexcel can help practitioners fulfil their obligations in the increasingly complex regulatory environment. The continuing pressure is eased with accreditation as the structure promoted within Lexcel ensures that solicitors analyse their business operations on a regular basis. This can, in particular, help a practice to comply with areas within the Solicitors' Code of Conduct which came into effect on 1 July 2007. Specifically, rule 5 (Business management) requires practitioners to 'make arrangements for the effective management of the firm as a whole'. The guidance to the Code goes further and stipulates that practices will need to 'produce evidence of a systematic and effective approach to management' which may be evidenced by quality standards such as Lexcel.

Practices can use Lexcel's standards to demonstrate a framework which facilitates compliance with multiple requirements within the new Code. The standard does go further, however, requiring policies and procedures to enhance practice beyond what is asked for in certain areas of the Code. Risk management is an area that continues to be an ever developing concern for solicitors. In this case, the Lexcel framework can improve the identification and implementation of preventative action quickly to minimise risks to the practice and its clients.

Lexcel can help any practice, regardless of size or type of work undertaken. Sole practitioners to large private practices and legal departments alike can all benefit. The flexibility the standard offers can suit a wide range of practices develop management techniques that help manage risk and enhance service. I thoroughly recommend it to you.

Andrew Holroyd
President (2007–8)
The Law Society

Preface

Lexcel v.4 provides legal practices of all varieties and sizes with a framework to manage their practice in accordance with best practice principles. In addition, the framework will support compliance with the Solicitors' Code of Conduct 2007 and other regulation. This means that practitioners must now be continually vigilant with regard to factors that can affect their practices. As a result, practice management is an area of increasing focus for the majority of legal practices in England and Wales.

The Lexcel practice management quality mark is designed and developed to benefit those within legal practice. Lexcel can be achieved by any practice, regardless of its size or type of work undertaken. The sole practitioner with little or no staff can benefit, as can larger practices or legal departments.

The Lexcel Office will continue to review the application and assessment processes involved with becoming accredited. For up-to-date information, contact the Lexcel Office.

This publication

The *Lexcel Assessment Guide* (fourth edition) provides information that will be required by practices, assessors and consultants who want to meet or assess against the requirements in Lexcel v.4. This book replaces the previous edition of the *Lexcel Assessment Guide* which forms part of the *Lexcel Practice Excellence Kit*.

The revisions to Lexcel 2004 were conducted over an eighteen-month period by a revisions committee. The Lexcel Office wishes to thank each member of the revisions committee, the Lexcel Assessment Panel and all the working parties for their contributions through the revisions process.

The Lexcel Office is thankful to all those practices and assessors who participated in the pilot of the new standard.

Advice and information

The Lexcel Office will continue to supply and enhance the materials provided to legal practices that focus on implementing best practice. These include practical advice for the differing range of practice types applying or seeking accreditation. Training is also available for those working in legal practice, such as managing partners, quality managers, practice managers and risk managers. Courses are particularly useful for those who are supporting their practices with the implementation of the Lexcel quality mark.

More details, advice and information, including informative materials and events focusing on the practical challenges and solutions for specific types of practices, can be obtained by contacting the Lexcel Office. For updates on events and guidance, please visit the Lexcel website.

The Lexcel Office would like to thank Matthew Moore and Rupert Kendrick of Web4Law for their contribution to the writing of the *Lexcel Assessment Guide*.

Lexcel Office
The Law Society
Telephone: 020 7320 5933
E-mail: Lexcel@lawsociety.org.uk
Website: **www.lexcel.lawsociety.org.uk**

August 2007

Introduction

The objective of Lexcel is to enhance the service given by a practice to its clients, to improve the management of the practice and the morale and motivation of its staff. Lexcel encourages practices to consult with clients to ensure that the views of the users of legal services have an impact on the way the service is delivered. There is an emphasis within the standard on continuous improvement.

The application of the requirements will vary from practice to practice and will need to take into account the circumstances of each organisation. Most organisations will document all procedures within an office manual, but there is no reason why they should not be set out in a number of different sources.

The standard consists mostly of mandatory requirements which are indicated by the use of the words 'will' or 'must'. There are also some optional requirements which will be appropriate in most cases but are not mandatory; these are indicated by the use of the word 'should'.

There is reference in the standard to 'policies', 'processes', 'procedures' and 'plans'.

- A 'policy' is a general approach taken within the practice to the issue in question. A policy defines why a particular approach is adopted by the practice.
- A 'process' is a description of the sequence of related activities required to achieve desired outputs. A process must be observable even if there is no documented procedure requiring it to occur.
- A 'procedure' is a written description of how an activity will occur within the practice. A procedure describes the steps that staff should follow in order to complete an activity. At an assessment, a procedure can only be said to be complied with if the assessor can observe that the procedure contained in the practice's documentation is in effective operation.
- A 'plan' is an outline of where a practice desires to be in the future and describes how it intends to arrive at that destination. A plan can be described as a map which supports practices to arrive at their desired destination in the future. In general the Lexcel standard permits practices to develop plans in the manner and detail that the practice considers appropriate, assuming a basic level of adequacy.

For ease of reference the term 'practice' is used throughout the standard. This should be taken to include any organisation that can be subject to the standard, including partnerships, limited liability partnerships, sole practices, incorporated law firms and legal departments. Various provisions of the standard may be inapplicable to certain types of practice, in which case they should be excluded, e.g. time recording may not be applicable in a local authority practice.

The Lexcel Office can provide guidance on the application of the standard to particular forms of practice.

The Lexcel standard

The standard requires practices to have a number of policies and plans. Please note that practices must document the person responsible for each policy and plan. In addition, a documented review of all policies and plans must take place at least annually.

As sole practitioners will be responsible for all policies and plans it is not necessary for them to document this information.

1 STRUCTURES AND POLICIES

1.1 Practices will have documentation setting out:

(a) the legal framework under which they operate;
(b) their business structure.

1.2 Practices will have a risk management policy, which must include:

(a) strategic risk;
(b) operational risk;
(c) regulatory risk.

1.3 Practices will have a quality policy, which must include:

(a) the role that the quality system plays in the overall strategy of the practice;
(b) a process for personnel to suggest improvements to the quality system.

1.4 Practices will have a policy on the avoidance of discrimination and the promotion of equality and diversity, to include:

(a) employment and partnership, recruitment and selection, training and conditions of service and promotions within the practice;
(b) the delivery of service;
(c) the instruction of counsel and experts in all professional dealings.

1.5 Practices will have a policy to ensure compliance with anti-money laundering legislation. The policy must include:

(a) the appointment of a Nominated Officer usually referred to as a Money Laundering Reporting Officer (MLRO);
(b) a process for making disclosures within the practice and by the MLRO to the authorities;
(c) identification checking;
(d) training of personnel;
(e) the proper maintenance of records.

1.6 Practices providing services to clients in relation to property transactions will have documented procedures in relation to the avoidance of involvement in mortgage fraud.

1.7   Practices will have a policy in relation to the health and safety of all personnel and visitors to the practice.

1.8   Practices should have a policy in relation to community and social responsibility.

2   STRATEGY, THE PROVISION OF SERVICES AND MARKETING

2.1   Practices will develop and maintain a marketing and business plan.

2.2   Practices will document the services they wish to offer, including:

(a) the client groups to be served;
(b) how services are to be provided;
(c) the way in which services are designed to meet client needs.

2.3   A documented review of 2.1 and 2.2 will be conducted at least every six months.

2.4   Practices will have a business continuity plan, which must include:

(a) an evaluation of potential threats and the likelihood of their impact;
(b) ways to reduce, avoid and transfer the risk;
(c) processes for testing and checking the plan.

3   FINANCIAL MANAGEMENT

3.1   Practices will document responsibility for overall financial management.

3.2   Practices will be able to provide documentary evidence of their financial management processes, including:

(a) annual budget (including, where appropriate, any capital expenditure proposed);
(b) variance analysis conducted at least quarterly of income and expenditure against budgets;
(c) annual profit and loss or income and expenditure accounts (certificated or audited accounts);
(d) annual balance sheet;
(e) annual cash or funds flow forecast;
(f) quarterly variance analysis at least of cashflow.

3.3   Practices will have a time recording process which enables the accurate measurement of time spent on matters for billing purposes.

4   INFORMATION MANAGEMENT AND FACILITIES

4A   Information management

Practices must ensure they comply with relevant legal and regulatory provisions in relation to all policies in 4A and ensure that all personnel receive appropriate training to understand the policies.

4A.1   Practices will have an information communication technology (ICT) plan, including:
(a) the application of all ICT facilities within the practice;
(b) the role of ICT in facilitating services for clients.

4A.2   Practices will have a policy in relation to data protection compliance issues, which must include:

(a) ensuring registration with the Information Commissioner;
(b) training of personnel.

4A.3   Practices will have an information management policy, including:

(a) relevant information assets of both the practice and clients;
(b) the risks to these assets, their likelihood and their impact;
(c) procedures for the protection and security of the assets;
(d) a process for training personnel.

4A.4   Practices must have an e-mail policy, including:

(a) the scope of permitted and prohibited use;
(b) any procedures for monitoring personnel using e-mail;
(c) procedures for proper management and security;
(d) procedures for its proper storage and destruction.

4A.5   If the practice has a website, the practice must have a website management policy, including:

(a) a process for document approval and publishing;
(b) the scope of permitted and prohibited use;
(c) procedures for the proper management of its security and contents.

4A.6   If personnel in the practice have internet access the practice must have an internet access policy, including:

(a) the scope of permitted and prohibited use;
(b) any procedures for monitoring personnel accessing the internet.

4B   Facilities

4B.1   Practices will document the office facilities needed to provide a service, including:

(a) the use of premises and equipment, including security and safety issues;
(b) arrangements for clients to visit the offices;
(c) communication arrangements;
(d) procedures for the handling of financial transactions.

4B.2   Practices will have a process for legal research, including the updating and sharing of legal and professional information.
4B.3   Practices will maintain an office manual or intranet collating information on office practice, which must be available to all personnel of the practice. Practices will have a process to:

(a) control the office manual or intranet to ensure that only the current version is in use;
(b) review the manual or intranet at least annually;
(c) update the manual or intranet and record the date of amendments.

5   PEOPLE MANAGEMENT

5.1   Practices will have a plan for:

(a) the recruitment of personnel, including likely recruitment needs;
(b) the training and development of personnel.

5.2   Practices will list the tasks to be undertaken by all personnel within the practice and document the skills, knowledge and experience required for individuals to fulfil their role satisfactorily, usually in the form of a person specification.

5.3   Practices will have procedures to deal effectively with recruitment and selection, which must include:

(a) the identification of vacancies;
(b) the drafting of the job documentation;
(c) methods of attracting candidates and applicants;
(d) selection methods used;
(e) storage, retention and destruction of records;
(f) references and ID checking and any use of medical examination;
(g) checking fee earners' disciplinary record.

5.4   Practices will conduct an appropriate induction process for all personnel, including those transferring roles within the practice and must cover:

(a) management structure and the individual's job responsibilities;
(b) terms and conditions of employment;
(c) immediate training requirements;
(d) key policies.

5.5   Practices must have a training and development policy and will:

(a) ensure that appropriate training is provided to personnel within the practice in accordance with its policy;
(b) ensure that all supervisors and managers receive appropriate training;
(c) have a process to evaluate training.

5.6   Practices will conduct a documented review of the responsibilities, objectives, performance and training of all personnel at least annually.

6   SUPERVISION AND OPERATIONAL RISK MANAGEMENT

6.1   Practices will have a written description of their management structure which designates the responsibilities of individuals and their accountability.

6.2   There will be a named supervisor for each area of work undertaken by the practice. The supervisor must have appropriate experience of the work supervised and be competent to guide and assist others.

6.3   Practices will have processes to ensure that all personnel, both permanent and temporary, are actively supervised. Such processes will include:

(a) checks on incoming and outgoing correspondence, including letters, e-mails and faxes;
(b) departmental, team and office meetings and communication structures;
(c) reviews of matter details in order to ensure good financial controls and the appropriate allocation of workloads;
(d) the exercise of devolved powers in publicly funded work;
(e) the availability of a supervisor;
(f) allocation of new work and reallocation of existing work, if necessary.

6.4   Practices will have processes to ensure that all those doing legal work check their files regularly for inactivity.

6.5   Practices will have procedures for regular, independent file reviews, of either the management of the file or its substantive legal content, or both.

In relation to file reviews, practices will:

(a) define file selection criteria;
(b) define the number and frequency of reviews;
(c) retain a record of the file review on the matter file and centrally;
(d) ensure any corrective action which is identified in a file review is actioned within 28 days and verified by the reviewer;
(e) ensure that the designated supervisor reviews and monitors the data generated by file reviews;
(f) conduct a review at least annually of the data generated by file reviews, which will contribute to the review of risk assessment data.

6.6   Practices will ensure that procedures are in place to:

(a) designate one overall risk manager for the practice with sufficient seniority, to be able to identify and deal with all risk issues which may arise;
(b) establish appropriate reporting arrangements to ensure that risk issues are appreciated and addressed;
(c) maintain lists of work that the practice will and will not undertake including any steps to be taken when work is declined on grounds that it falls outside acceptable risk levels. This information must be communicated to all relevant staff and must be updated regularly;
(d) maintain details of the generic risks and causes of claims associated with the area(s) of work that is/are undertaken by the practice. This information must be adequately communicated to all relevant staff;
(e) manage instructions which may be undertaken even though they have a higher risk profile than the norm for the practice, including unusual supervisory and reporting requirements or contingency planning.

6.7   Practices will analyse at least annually all risk assessment data generated within the practice. This must include:

(a) any indemnity claims;
(b) an analysis of client complaints trends;
(c) data generated by file reviews;
(d) the identification of remedial action.

6.8   Operational risk will be considered and recorded in all matters before, during and after the processing of instructions. Before the matter is undertaken the adviser must:

(a) consider if a new client and/or matter should be accepted by the practice, in accordance with 8.2 below;
(b) assess the risk profile of all new instructions and notify the risk manager in accordance with procedures under 6.6 above of any unusual or high risk considerations in order that appropriate action may be taken.

During the retainer the fee earner must:

(c) consider any change to the risk profile of the matter from the client's point of view and report and advise on such circumstances without delay, informing the risk manager if appropriate;
(d) inform the client in all cases where an adverse costs order is made against the practice in relation to the matter in question.

At the end of the matter the fee earner must:

(e) undertake a concluding risk assessment by considering if the client's objectives have been achieved and if the client could fairly complain or make a claim for damages in relation to the service provided;

(f) notify the risk manager of all such circumstances in accordance with documented procedures.

7   CLIENT CARE

7.1   Practices will have a documented policy for client care.

7.2   Practices will have processes to ensure compliance with Rule 2 of the Solicitors' Code of Conduct 2007.

7.3   Practices must have a record of any standing terms of business with regular clients. The practice must be able to produce such terms in relation to the issues covered by this section.

7.4   Practices will operate a written complaints handling procedure that ensures compliance with Rule 2 of the Solicitors' Code of Conduct 2007 and in addition:

(a) defines what the practice regards as a complaint and sets out how to identify and respond to complaints;

(b) records and reports centrally all complaints received from clients;

(c) identifies the cause of any problem of which the client has complained offering any appropriate redress, and correcting any unsatisfactory procedures;

(d) practices will conduct reviews at least annually of complaints data and trends, such review(s) forming part of the review of risk.

7.5   Practices will have a process to monitor client satisfaction.

8   FILE AND CASE MANAGEMENT

8.1   Practices will document how client enquiries in relation to possible instructions are handled, with particular regard to:

(a) telephone enquiries;

(b) clients who enquire in person in the reception area, including confidentiality;

(c) enquiries by correspondence and e-mail.

8.2   Practices will document how decisions will be made as to whether to accept new instructions from existing clients or instructions from clients who have not instructed the practice before.

8.3   Practices will document their arrangements to ensure that conflicts of interests are identified and acted upon in an appropriate manner.

8.4   At the outset of the matter the fee earner will:

(a) establish as full an understanding as possible of the client's requirements and objectives (where incomplete, this must be supplemented subsequently);

(b) provide a clear explanation of the issues raised and the advice given;

(c) explain what the fee earner will do and in what timescale;

(d) establish the method of funding, including the availability or suitability of insurance, trade union benefits, conditional or contingency fee arrangements, or costs insurance products;

(e)   consider whether the intended action would be merited on a cost-benefit analysis and whether, in public funding cases, the guidance in the funding code would be satisfied.

The issues covered in (a)–(e) above must be confirmed to the client, ordinarily in writing, unless it would be appropriate not to do so. In all cases, a note of these issues must appear on the matter file.

8.5   Practices will ensure that the strategy for the matter is always apparent on the matter file and that in complex cases a project plan is developed.

8.6   Practices will have documented procedures to ensure that matters are progressed in an appropriate manner. In particular:

(a)   key information must be recorded on the file;
(b)   key dates must be defined and recorded on the file and in a back-up system;
(c)   there must be a process to monitor key dates;
(d)   a timely response is made to telephone calls and correspondence from the client and others;
(e)   continuing information on cost is provided;
(f)   clients are informed in writing if the person with conduct of their matter changes, or there is a change of person to whom any problem with service should be addressed.

8.7   Practices will document procedures for the giving, monitoring and discharge of undertakings.

8.8   Practices will have a documented procedure to:

(a)   list open and closed matters, identify all matters for a single client and linked files where relevant and all files for particular funders;
(b)   ensure that they are able to identify and trace any documents, files, deeds, wills or any other items relating to a matter;
(c)   safeguard the confidentiality of matter files and all other client information;
(d)   ensure that the status of the matter and the action taken can be easily checked by other members of the practice;
(e)   ensure that documents are stored on the matter file(s) in an orderly way.

8.9   Practices will have a documented procedure for using barristers, expert witnesses and other external advisers who are involved in the delivery of legal services, which will include provision for the following:

(a)   use of clear selection criteria;
(b)   where appropriate, consultation with the client in relation to selection, and proper advice to the client on choice of advocate or other professional;
(c)   clients to be advised of the name and status of the person being instructed, how long he or she might take to respond, and where disbursements are to be paid by the client, the cost involved;
(d)   maintenance of records (centrally, by department or office) on barristers and experts used, including evidence of assessment against the criteria;
(e)   evaluation of performance, for the information of other members of the practice;
(f)   giving clear instructions;
(g)   checking of opinions and reports received to ensure they adequately provide the information sought (and, in litigation matters, comply with the rules of court and any court orders);
(h)   payment of fees.

8.10   Practices will have documented procedures to ensure that, at the end of the matter, the practice:

(a)   reports to the client on the outcome and explains any further action that the client is required to take in the matter and what (if anything) the practice will do;

(b)   accounts to the client for any outstanding money;

(c)   returns to the client any original documents or other property belonging to the client if required (save for items that are by agreement to be stored by the practice);

(d)   if appropriate, advises the client about arrangements for storage and retrieval of papers and other items retained (insofar as this has not already been dealt with, for example in terms of business) and any charges to be made in this regard;

(e)   advises the client whether they should review the matter in future and, if so, when and why;

(f)   archives and destroys files in an appropriate manner.

Assessment criteria

The standard requires practices to have a number of policies and plans. Please note that practices must document the person responsible for each policy and plan. In addition, a documented review of all policies and plans must take place at least annually.

As sole practitioners will be responsible for all policies and plans it is not necessary for them to document this information.

Please see Appendix A for a table of polices and plans in relation to the above.

---

1   STRUCTURES AND POLICIES

Section 1 deals with policies that practices will need to have in place. In-house practices may be subject to organisation-wide policies and may have limited control over the formulation of such policies. In this case, however, they should be able to demonstrate how the policies apply to their practice.

1.1   Practices will have documentation setting out:

(a) the legal framework under which they operate;
(b) their business structure.

The most common type of business structure for solicitors is a partnership. The type of partnership can be varied, for example a limited liability partnership (LLP) or an unlimited company. At the time of publication multi-disciplinary partnerships are not permitted in England and Wales. Practices should keep their legal framework and business structure under review to ensure they are operating in the most effective manner.

Practices that are partnerships should have a partnership agreement. Some of the issues to consider when drafting the partnership agreement are:

(a) management and voting rights;
(b) the authorisation of individual partners or managers to bind the practice in contract;
(c) rights to share in profits;
(d) how capital contributions will be dealt with and rights to interest;
(e) how capital will be repaid;
(f) entry to and expulsions and retirements from the practice;
(g) the rights of partners to elect part-time working patterns and provisions for parental leave, including maternity provisions;

(h) the situation in case of long-term illness or incapacity;

(i) how succession will be achieved, if appropriate;

(j) continuity of the practice in the event of death or incapacity in the case of small or sole practices.

Sole practitioners should consider leaving a letter or other instructions with a fellow practitioner, if there are reciprocal arrangements, or a friend or relative to deal with their wishes for the practice in the case of death or incapacity. The Sole Practitioners Group and Solicitors Regulation Authority (SRA) have further information.

In the case of in-house departments, the documentation should set out the relationship of the legal department to the parent body and any colleague departments. This could be done by reference to organisation-wide documents or charters, or any legislative provisions.

> **Assessment note:** Practices are encouraged to provide the assessor with documentation to demonstrate the above requirements. Assessors may, however, accept interview evidence as the documentation may contain sensitive information that the practice doesn't want to disclose.

1.2   Practices will have a risk management policy, which must include:

(a) strategic risk;

(b) operational risk;

(c) regulatory risk.

The risk management policy needs to describe the practice's approach to reducing risk.

'Strategic risk' refers to risks that could have an effect on the viability and success of the business. For example, strategic risks that may need to be considered are financial decisions and succession planning.

'Operational risks' are those risks that can arise as a result of the nature of the work the business conducts, for example indemnity claims as a result of negligence.

'Regulatory risks' are any risks that need to be considered as a result of the regulatory framework that impacts on the business. For example, compliance with the Solicitors' Accounts Rules 1998 and the Data Protection Act 1998.

> **Assessment note:** Assessors will require documentary evidence of a risk policy which considers strategic, operational and regulatory risk. In addition, interview evidence will be sought from a variety of personnel to confirm that the policy has been implemented, is understood and is regularly reviewed.

1.3   Practices will have a quality policy, which must include:

   (a) the role that the quality system plays in the overall strategy of the practice;
   (b) a process for personnel to suggest improvements to the quality system.

The quality policy should detail the practice's overall approach to ensure that clients receive a good service. It is important that all personnel understand the policy in order to deliver a consistently high level quality service.

The process for personnel to suggest improvements will vary from practice to practice. In small practices, it may be in an information process where personnel make suggestions on an ad hoc basis. In a larger practice, however, it may be a more formal system of staff suggestions.

Practices should consider drawing all information from the annual reviews into the overall quality review.

Assessment note: Assessors will seek evidence of the understanding of the quality policy during the course of interviews with personnel. Additionally, assessors will encourage practices to focus on how this requirement helps the practice continually to improve the services that it offers to clients.

1.4   Practices will have a policy on the avoidance of discrimination and the promotion of equality and diversity, to include:

   (a) employment and partnership, recruitment and selection, training and conditions of service and promotions within the practice;
   (b) the delivery of service;
   (c) the instruction of counsel and experts in all professional dealings.

Equal opportunities and anti-discrimination are concepts concerned with providing opportunities and removing barriers that affect particular groups. Legislation is increasingly protecting rights of people in groups and society. Laws prohibit discrimination on the grounds of racial or ethnic origin, disability, age, gender, sexual orientation and religion or belief. Anti-discrimination legislation is designed to promote equality and fairness in relation to employment and the provision of services.

Diversity is a broader concept that builds upon the progress made through equal opportunities. Policies must encourage the development of individuals regardless of their background and irrespective of social class and education. Diversity promotes the recognition of the value that each person can bring to the workplace.

Increasingly public authorities are asking businesses to demonstrate good equal opportunities policies in order to secure contracts. Businesses that have a history of discrimination in employment or service delivery are highly likely not to be awarded any contracts.

(a) **Discrimination in employment.** Equal opportunities, anti-discrimination and diversity work together by addressing the inequalities and barriers faced by people, as well as by valuing, learning and benefiting from the diverse cultures in society. Employees have a right to expect fair and equal treatment. This expectation is supported by the law. Discrimination can in turn also deny practices of the widest range of talent. In addition, fair treatment makes good business sense as employers who treat employees fairly and flexibly will be best placed to recruit and retain staff in an increasingly diverse and competitive labour market.

Unlawful discrimination can be costly to a practice, as there is no limit to how much an employment tribunal can require a practice to pay someone if the practice has been found as an employer to have discriminated against an employee. Employers are also vicariously responsible for the actions of their employees and it is therefore important that employees know what is expected of them.

(b) **Discrimination in the provision of services.** Practices are generally free to decide whether to accept instructions from a particular client. However, any refusal to act must not be based upon discriminatory grounds.

Practices should maintain lists of experts and third parties who are regarded as suitable for instruction. A practice should ensure that the lists are compiled on the basis of the ability of those listed to undertake work of a particular type. The list should not contain exclusion, restriction or preference on discriminatory grounds as set out in the standard and legislation.

Practices may develop different policies to address anti-discrimination, equality and diversity or have one main policy. For the anti-discrimination and equal opportunities policy to be effective, it must have the support of everyone in the practice and be an integral part of the business strategy. Involvement of senior managers is vital to show commitment to the policy.

Private practices should note that they will be bound by anti-discrimination rules laid out by the Law Society. Practices are, however, responsible for the creation and maintenance of their equal opportunities policy, including any required compliance with current legislation.

Assessment note: A Lexcel assessor will look for evidence that the policy is being effectively implemented and communicated to all staff, and is regularly monitored for compliance. The assessor will expect to see evidence of an annual review of the policy. Overall, the policy should include:

- the practice's commitment to provide equality for all and an intention to encourage, value and manage diversity and avoid discriminating on the forbidden grounds;
- a commitment to fair recruitment including clear statements within any advertising, selection and recruitment processes;
- an anti-harassment provision in the policy;
- senior management's commitment to delivering equality and diversity in the workplace as well as in the provision of services.

1.5 Practices will have a policy to ensure compliance with anti-money laundering legislation. The policy must include:

    (a) the appointment of a Nominated Officer usually referred to as a Money Laundering Reporting Officer (MLRO);

    (b) a process for making disclosures within the practice and by the MLRO to the authorities;

    (c) identification checking;

    (d) training of personnel;

    (e) the proper maintenance of records.

At the time of publishing this book a new set of regulations are in draft form and practices will need to check their compliance obligations under the new regime. The Law Society guidance can be found at **www.lawsociety.org.uk**.

It is necessary to review the practice's anti-money laundering policy. When reviewing the policy some of the issues that may be considered are as follows:

- levels of reporting by office or department;
- training that has been done and is needed;
- whether any breaches of the regulations occurred;
- whether any significant incidents arose.

Assessment note: When assessing against this requirement, assessors will seek evidence that the practice is complying with the scope of their money laundering responsibilities. If the practice is within the regulated sector, the assessor will be looking to see that the practice has a reporting officer; that people have been trained; that ID checks are being carried out; and that the practice has procedures in place to maintain proper records and report suspicious circumstances.

Please note: the assessor will have gained an understanding, as part of Lexcel training, on the current Money Laundering Regulations. The purpose of the assessor's role is to assess compliance in terms of the Lexcel requirement only and not any other regulations.

1.6 Practices providing services to clients in relation to property transactions will have documented procedures in relation to the avoidance of involvement in mortgage fraud.

Private practice firms providing conveyancing services will need to provide their personnel with guidelines in relation to procedures to be followed in the event of suspicion of mortgage fraud. The requirements of the Council of Mortgage Lenders Handbook will also be a concern for most firms providing conveyancing services.

Assessment note: Assessors will be looking for documentary evidence which outlines procedures to assist in the identification of suspected mortgage fraud activities and the reporting of these to appropriate personnel. In addition, assessors will require interview evidence to confirm that personnel are aware of the procedures.

1.7   Practices will have a policy in relation to the health and safety of all personnel and visitors to the practice.

There are general duties on employers and organisations to ensure a safe working environment. In accordance with the applicable legislation, practices should adopt a policy to ensure that they are taking adequate steps to meet their obligations. A good source of information is the Health and Safety Executive's website which is **www.hse.gov.uk**.

When drafting a health and safety policy, practices may want to consider the following issues:

- equipment;
- staff handling and use of substances;
- accidents, first aid and work-related ill health;
- monitoring of conditions and systems of work;
- emergency procedures, fire and evacuation of premises.

Practices should ensure that any health and safety policies extend to include external parties and personnel who conduct work out of the office. For example, visitors to a practice's facilities and home workers should be considered.

Assessment note: Practices should be able to prove the effective communication of any health and safety policies to their Lexcel assessor. The assessor will seek evidence that an annual review of policy has been undertaken and that any amendments have been carried out.

1.8   Practices should have a policy in relation to community and social responsibility.

This requirement is optional for practices to comply with in relation to the Lexcel standard. If a practice tenders for work it is likely that its clients will expect it to document how the practice operates in a responsible fashion. Some of the issues that a practice may want to incorporate into its policy include:

- facilities;
- recycling;
- resources;
- travel;
- pro bono and charitable work.

Assessment note: As this is an optional requirement, assessors will not raise non-compliances against this requirement.

2   STRATEGY, THE PROVISION OF SERVICES AND MARKETING

2.1   Practices will develop and maintain a marketing and business plan.

A business plan should consist of:

(a) Analysis of the factors, both internal to the practice and externally, that are relevant to the future development of the practice.
(b) Key objectives and overall practice strategies for the forthcoming 12 months at least from the date of the document or review of any such document to provide a background against which the practice may measure its performance.
(c) Some outline or detailed objectives covering a further two years at least which evidence a consideration of the factors relevant to the future of the practice.
(d) For items (b) and (c) above, a finance plan, evidencing due consideration of the overall financial implications of the strategy or strategies to be adopted within the practice and setting some financial goals or objectives if not appearing elsewhere in the business plan.

Business plans

Some form of strategic document or business plan is required by this provision. In some practices this may be achieved through a combination of different documents – perhaps a main business plan for the practice along with a series of departmental plans. Factors that will determine the complexity of the strategic documentation will include:

- The size of the practice – sole and small practices will often have simpler strategies and less need for complex documentation.
- The amount of change that is anticipated over the period of the plan – a practice seeking to consolidate or stabilise its current operations will probably have less to address than one that is expanding.
- The management style of the partners or managers.
- The organisational requirements in local authorities or other in-house departments.

> **Assessment note:** Whatever the style and format of the documentation, assessors will seek evidence of analysis of significant factors – both internal and external to the practice – which will be likely to have an impact on the future of the practice. This analysis could take various forms, but could include:
>
> - staff survey;
> - internal 'brainstorming' sessions;
> - assessment within the practice of 'SWOT' factors (strengths, weaknesses, opportunities and threats);
> - consideration of proposed legislative changes or government plans;
> - consultation of local plans;
> - organisation-wide plans for in-house departments.

Performance measurement

Performance objectives are intended to provide hard data as to whether the plan has succeeded or not. Wherever possible, objectives should be 'smart', i.e.:

> Specific
> Measurable
> Achievable
> Realistic
> Time-limited

Objectives may relate to gross fee income, size of the organisation, or any performance ratios felt to be relevant, including client satisfaction.

The standard recognises that objectives for the current or next 12 months should in most cases be more detailed than those for the medium-term future.

Marketing plans

The standard does not require all recognised practices to market themselves actively – merely that they should consider the appropriate marketing activity for the practice. The practice that is content with its current supply of work, or which feels that instructions may need to be turned away because of excess demand, would not be expected to involve itself in promotion that is likely further to increase the flow of potential instructions. If a decision is made not to engage in active marketing, it must be documented in order to meet this requirement. On the other hand, a practice that sets out in its main strategy a desire to develop all or some of its practice areas would need to show that the marketing steps that will be needed have been considered.

It is a requirement that the financial implications of the marketing strategy are shown to have been considered. This will result in evidence being available of such consideration, or the establishment of financial objectives within the business or departmental plans. A finance plan is best seen as a management overview of the financial implications of the strategy in question. It is separate from, but perhaps ancillary to, more detailed budgets.

However marketing is dealt with, the documentation should cover:

(a) areas of work that the practice wishes to develop, expand, reduce or cease to provide;
(b) the benefits that the practice hopes to achieve from its marketing or promotional activity;
(c) any promotional methods that will be employed and responsibility for them;
(d) a budget for promotional activities.

Some of the issues that practices may want to consider are:

● type, length and style of desired documentation;
● possible involvement of external advice;

- staff involvement and communication to the staff;
- feasible marketing activity and its budget;
- most effective format of review.

Assessment note: In local authority and in-house practices, the assessor would expect to see a service plan or documented references to the corporate plans of the umbrella organisation. The assessor will expect the practice to have documented what it seeks to achieve, within the limits imposed by corporate or statutory prescription. It is for each practice to choose the format and style of the documentation. It follows that the length and complexity of the documentation will vary between practices.

The assessor will look for evidence that the practice has a business plan and has given due consideration to marketing. Section 2 envisages that some practices may wish to combine the business plan and marketing plan or may wish to produce two separate documents. Plans which are shortly to come into operation or which are already implemented for the current 12 months will be acceptable.

It is not a requirement of the standard that staff must be consulted on and informed of the business plan or other documentation described in this section. It is, however, increasingly regarded as good business practice to involve staff in the business planning process and to keep them informed of the practice's plans and progress.

The contents of all business or marketing plans can be retained as being confidential to the practice, if it so chooses. In such circumstances the assessor will seek evidence of the existence and understanding of such plans from interviews. Interviews are likely to be at partner or senior manager level as these are the people most likely to be involved in business strategy.

2.2   Practices will document the services they wish to offer, including:

    (a) the client groups to be served;
    (b) how services are to be provided;
    (c) the way in which services are designed to meet client needs.

It is important that the practice should consider and record the extent or scope of its services and also any limitations to them. This will be useful to:

- clients wishing to check if the practice can deal with their concerns;
- other external persons such as referrers of work;
- staff, in particular those in client-facing roles.

Since in most cases it will be clients and potential clients who have most interest in this provision, the requirements will often be met by lists and details of services as contained in brochures or on websites. The sort of special features which will commonly be listed will be the languages that advice can be offered through, the availability of home visits, wheelchair access to the offices, etc.

Practices providing publicly funded services should list the contract categories that are offered and any policy established on the acceptance of instructions given any limitations to matter starts.

In-house departments might describe or append service agreements with colleague departments, or external authorities that are advised through contractual arrangements.

Assessment note: Assessors will seek evidence from a variety of sources as to the effectiveness of any communication and updating of the practice's known capabilities. An assessor may request to see documentation that records the extent, scope and limitations in their business.

2.3   A documented review of 2.1 and 2.2 will be conducted at least every six months.

Assessment note: Practices must be able to show that all strategic and marketing documentation is kept under continual review. The evidence of such reviews could be partnership strategy papers or partnership or management group minutes. Sole practitioners must also be able to demonstrate that reviews have taken place as required, for example by way of dated notes or appendices to plans.

2.4   Practices will have a business continuity plan, which must include:

   (a)   an evaluation of potential threats and the likelihood of their impact;
   (b)   ways to reduce, avoid and transfer the risk;
   (c)   processes for testing and checking the plan.

Having a business continuity plan is a key risk management tool that has been part of the Lexcel standard since March 2007. This requirement is now an obligation under the Solicitors' Code of Conduct 2007 which came into force on 1 July 2007.

When drafting a business continuity plan it is worth considering the skills you need to implement the plan and which personnel possess these skills. It is also vital that there are clear communication channels, so that personnel and clients can be informed of any interruptions to the business. An important part of your business continuity plan is likely to be the backup and retrieval arrangements that you have in relation to IT.

In addition, you should give consideration to your practice's location and think about the risks that could realistically impact on the continuity of your business. Some of the procedures you should consider implementing to manage the risks are as follows:

- how you initially assess the disruptive situation;
- preferred method of protecting personnel, clients, equipment, information and records;
- how to report emergencies;
- how to warn employees;
- an evacuation plan;
- how to decide whether or not to shut down operations;
- how to shut down operations;
- how internal and external communications are to be handled.

Once you have identified the risks to your practice you must give consideration to how these risks can be reduced.

A key feature of this requirement is to test the plan to ensure that it works, which can be conducted in a variety of ways. The level of your testing will depend on your resources but the best should be carried out as effectively as possible. For example, you may simulate a disaster, test that the IT backup works and the information can be readily retrieved, or test the communication channels to ensure that contact details are current.

Assessment note: Practices will be required to produce documentary evidence of their business continuity plan and will be asked about what factors were taken into consideration when it was drawn up. Assessors will review the extent and scope of the plan, as well as the methods through which practices communicate and enforce any requirements contained within it to personnel. In addition, assessors may interview personnel included in the implementation of any actions outlined in the plan to ensure roles and responsibilities are understood. Assessors will also look for evidence that the plan has been reviewed at least annually.

3   FINANCIAL MANAGEMENT

3.1   Practices will document responsibility for overall financial management.

In an increasing number of private practice firms it may be an employee who has day-to-day responsibility for monitoring and correcting financial performance issues, or it may be shared responsibility between an employee and the partners or a finance or managing partner. It is vital that a partner retains overall responsibility for the supervision of the practice's finances in accordance with the Solicitors' Accounts Rules 1998.

For in-house practices responsibility for financial performance may reside outside the department – for example, a designated contact in the finance department.

> **Assessment note:** Assessors will find that practices choose to document the person with overall responsibility for financial management in a variety of ways. The practice may have an organisation chart, an office manual or job description which includes this information.

3.2   Practices will be able to provide documentary evidence of their financial management processes, including:

   (a) annual budget (including, where appropriate, any capital expenditure proposed);
   (b) variance analysis conducted at least quarterly of income and expenditure against budgets;
   (c) annual profit and loss or income and expenditure accounts (certificated or audited accounts);
   (d) annual balance sheet;
   (e) annual cash or funds flow forecast;
   (f) quarterly variance analysis at least of cashflow.

In private practice the production of a profit and loss account and a balance sheet is commonplace. Firms could often improve, however, in the area of management accounting, i.e. planning for future performance rather than reporting on the past.

> **Assessment note:** Assessors will take into account that many firms will not necessarily engage their auditors to advise on management accounting issues. They should therefore enquire as to the extent of the accountants' involvement in the firm in considering any assurance from such advisers that the requirements of this section have been addressed.
>
> Financial management data is best evidenced by showing all appropriate data or paperwork to assessors, but practices may decline to do so if they wish. In such cases the assessors will require correspondence from the practice's accountant confirming that the above requirements have been adhered to.
>
> In-house legal practices may have less control over their finances and assessors will take into account that these organisations may be set a budget which they will monitor and will be unable to meet all the requirements in 3.2.

3.3   Practices will have a time recording process which enables the accurate measurement of time spent on matters for billing purposes.

It is only mandatory to time record if time is a factor for billing purposes, otherwise it is optional. However, time recording provides valuable management data. It can help practices evaluate if fixed fee work is profitable and help management evaluate the performance of personnel. It is nonetheless acceptable that a practice could take the view that it will only time record on those matters that will need to be billed or costed on a time basis and decline to time record elsewhere. Where some matters or types of matter are not normally subject to time recording, practices may wish to carry out a time recording exercise on a sample basis. This would provide a benchmark to ensure that fixed fee or percentage-based fees are viable.

Computerised time recording has become the norm for most types of legal practice in recent years. It is not compulsory that any such system is computerised; in some smaller firms file-based or manual systems are still in use and this will be acceptable.

Assessment note: The assessor will verify that all personnel are aware of the practice's time recording process through interview evidence. Verification of the accuracy of the time recorded on files will be checked against the time recording system when relevant.

---

4   INFORMATION MANAGEMENT AND FACILITIES

4A   Information management

Practices must ensure they comply with relevant legal and regulatory provisions in relation to all policies in 4A and ensure that all personnel receive appropriate training to understand the policies.

Practices will find guidance to some of the issues raised in 4A on the Law Society's website: **www.lawsociety.org.uk** (Information Security Guidelines for Solicitors). See also Appendix B.

4A.1 Practices will have an information communication technology (ICT) plan, including:

   (a) the application of all ICT facilities within the practice;
   (b) the role of ICT in facilitating services for clients.

Practices must demonstrate a regular review of the use and development of information technology systems. The standard does not require a particular level of ICT but practices should give consideration to the use of information technology for delivering the practice's current services and any future services that it may want to offer. Each practice must decide how to address the issues set out in this section.

> **Assessment note:** Practices must demonstrate a regular review of the use and development of ICT systems. This plan may form part of the overall business plan or be a separate plan. Assessors will expect to be satisfied that the use of ICT for delivering the practice's services has received due consideration by partners or managers.

4A.2 Practices will have a policy in relation to data protection compliance issues, which must include:

   (a) ensuring registration with the Information Commissioner;
   (b) training of personnel.

The effective management of electronic data is now critical to practices in both practising efficiently and offering a competitive service to their clients.

The issues that the policy should cover are as follows:

- the different types of data that will be collected;
- the need for compliance with the eight data protection principles of the Data Protection Act 1998;
- responsibility for training and implementation;
- whom to contact if you receive a data request.

> **Assessment note:** The practice's policy in relation to data protection will need to be provided to the assessor, alongside confirmation of registration with the Information Commissioner and any records of completed training. The assessor will gather evidence of compliance against the policy through interview evidence with personnel.

4A.3 Practices will have an information management policy, including:

    (a) **relevant information assets of both the practice and clients;**
    (b) **the risks to these assets, their likelihood and their impact;**
    (c) **procedures for the protection and security of the assets;**
    (d) **a process for training personnel.**

When drafting your information management policy, it is important to decide what your information assets are, i.e. any information you have that is of value to your practice or clients. The policy must cover all assets, including those in electronic and paper format. Once the information assets have been identified, you will be in a better position to evaluate any potential risks to that information and be able to implement effective procedures to combat those risks. Some of the common risks to electronic information include:

- virus attacks;
- current personnel and former employees damaging the integrity of information through lack of knowledge or malice;
- using unlicensed software;
- sharing passwords.

The fragile nature of electronic data demands that particular care is taken to safeguard its integrity and to preserve it securely for periods required by legislation and professional rules and regulations.

Most case management systems will incorporate some provision for safe document management. However, practices will need to decide whether this is sufficient for their needs or whether a specific document management or storage system is required. In making this decision the practice will need to consider:

- the type and volume of electronic documentation;
- the length of time it has to be held; and
- the question of by whom, when and in what circumstances such documentation can be accessed when in storage.

When considering how to protect your information assets, thought should be given to how the assets are to be destroyed and whether there are any confidentiality issues that need to be addressed.

> **Assessment note:** Practices must prove to assessors that their information management policy is supported by documentary evidence relating to its implementation, control and monitoring. Assessors will seek interview evidence that personnel are aware of the policy and adhere to it.

4A.4 Practices must have an e-mail policy, including:

> **(a) the scope of permitted and prohibited use;**
> **(b) any procedures for monitoring personnel using e-mail;**
> **(c) procedures for proper management and security;**
> **(d) procedures for its proper storage and destruction.**

It will be necessary for the practice to establish its policy on the use of its e-mail system. Legal practices involved in work across a variety of industries should take particular care in effectively implementing e-mail policies and procedures. For example, those involved in matters for financial services organisations would be well placed to enforce stringent controls in the light of the ever increasing developments of regulation for the industry such as the rules set out by the Financial Services Authority (FSA).

Practices should consider incorporating e-mail policies as a condition of employment for all staff including temporary and contract employees to ensure that the policy has been properly communicated and any penalties for misuse are understood. The objective of this is to ensure that the practice and employees avoid exposing the practice to any legal liability.

Practices should further consider whether, in the event of a dispute in relation to the appropriateness of an employee's use of e-mail, the policy would be sufficiently clear to an employment tribunal to protect the practice. Care should be exercised when drafting this policy.

Practices should also be aware of the sensitivities relating to individuals' rights when writing and implementing an e-mail policy and if staff e-mails are to be monitored it is important to inform staff of this.

Assessment note: The Lexcel assessor will need proof that an e-mail policy has been effectively implemented, is monitored on a regular basis and is understood by personnel.

In-house legal departments may be bound by an organisation-wide policy. If this is the case, the assessor will seek evidence that the policy is effectively communicated throughout the legal department.

4A.5 If the practice has a website, the practice must have a website management policy, including:

> **(a) a process for document approval and publishing;**
> **(b) the scope of permitted and prohibited use;**
> **(c) procedures for the proper management of its security and contents.**

Practices operating a website should ensure that it is properly managed for the benefit of both the practice and its clients. The layout and text should be clear and concise throughout so as to reduce the risk of misinterpretation. A website carries global exposure to legal proceedings and the damage to a practice's reputation which if neglected can be significant.

Planning and documenting the structure, scope and extent of the website is advisable, particularly when implementing business and marketing plans for the practice. Practices should identify key personnel who monitor access to and control of content. This will assist in effectively managing the visible aspects of the website and allocate responsibility to all appropriate staff.

> **Assessment note:** The assessor will look for evidence of plans and reports associated with the implementation, development and review of a website policy. In addition, evidence will be gathered from interviews of personnel to verify that the policy is understood.

4A.6 If personnel in the practice have internet access the practice must have an internet access policy, including:

(a) the scope of permitted and prohibited use;
(b) any procedures for monitoring personnel accessing the internet.

The internet is a powerful business tool for research on areas of interest to personnel. The ease of access means all practices will likely be connected to the internet and should have a policy to assist personnel in understanding what is deemed appropriate use. Practices will want staff to use the internet in a proper and appropriate manner, including compliance with core policies on areas such as discrimination and the downloading of offensive material. Practices may have specialist ICT staff that assist in the monitoring of the policy; however, practices should have an authoritative figure that is responsible for the management issues associated with internet use.

As with the e-mail policy, it is considered good practice to incorporate the internet use policy into conditions for employment. This helps to ensure that all staff are aware of the policy. In addition, practices may want to set out the potential penalties for misuse.

As with e-mail policies, practices should consider the appropriateness of their internet procedures and ensure these are sufficiently clear to all employees. Details of this policy can be included in the recruitment process to promote awareness to all new members of staff.

> **Assessment note:** Lexcel assessors will look for evidence of a policy, its effective implementation, and the procedures for monitoring the conditions laid out in the policy. Interviews may be conducted with any key staff involved in the development and monitoring of the policy to verify the value of the management processes and verify that staff are aware of the policy and how it impacts on them.

4B   Facilities

4B.1 Practices will document the office facilities needed to provide a service, including:

    (a) the use of premises and equipment, including security and safety issues;
    (b) arrangements for clients to visit the offices;
    (c) communication arrangements;
    (d) procedures for the handling of financial transactions.

Some practices may choose to address these requirements through one document, while others may comply with a series of documents, co-ordinated or not. Practices may choose the style and complexity of documentation that suits them best, but in most cases these provisions will be set out in the practice's office procedures manual. It is important that the arrangements required above should be accessible to all personnel within the practice.

Many practices will have arrangements in place for the maintenance of photocopying equipment and contractual arrangements for external copying of large or multiple copies. Computer support contracts become increasingly significant as more work is entrusted to data format or conducted via e-mails.

The importance of client reactions to the offices has often been stressed. The state of the reception area, the professionalism of the welcome and the availability of refreshments should be seen as an important element of the client care policy of the practice. Practices should provide confidential facilities for clients who need to have conversations of a sensitive nature or need documents signed. In some practices, confidential information will be overheard by other clients awaiting an appointment and appropriate arrangements will need to be made (see 8.1(b)). Practices that are open to public access should also consider staff safety and how threatening or abusive behaviour should be dealt with.

The efficient use of communication facilities might require training for those personnel concerned – for example, familiarisation with the features of the practice's telephone system is likely to form part of induction.

In most practices the accounts procedures will be a significant element of the overall practice manual, which should provide worked examples of entries for payments in, cheque payments, payments of petty cash, transfers, etc. Breaches of the Solicitors' Accounts Rules 1998 are a significant risk for firms in private practice; the availability of clear instructions forms an effective safeguard in this respect and can assist in minimising wasted time between accounts and fee earning personnel.

Assessment note: Practices should document any official process or procedure relating to the use of their facilities, including details of the roles and responsibilities of anyone involved in their management. Regular monitoring should be conducted and results from these reviews must be documented. This will provide evidence of the practice's proactive approach.

4B.2 Practices will have a process for legal research, including the updating and sharing of legal and professional information.

This provision does not require the practice to have its own law library, though many do. What is important is that fee earners have reasonable access to legal research tools, which in many practices will increasingly be web-based. There should be reasonable controls regarding location of reports, books, periodicals and other journals, along with distribution arrangements for updating material if appropriate.

The reference to professional information could be interpreted to mean that consideration needs to be given to the sharing of know-how, be it:

- notes of research from within the firm;
- materials from courses attended;
- discussions at team or departmental meetings;
- counsels' opinions that might be of general interest within the practice;
- the accessibility of precedents.

Assessment note: Assessors will require interview evidence from staff to confirm that the process is in effective operation.

4B.3 Practices will maintain an office manual or intranet collating information on office practice, which must be available to all personnel of the practice. Practices will have a process to:

(a) control the office manual or intranet to ensure that only the current version is in use;

(b) review the manual or intranet at least annually;

(c) update the manual or intranet and record the date of amendments.

The requirements in Lexcel for procedures mean that some form of office procedures manual is essential, whether contained in one document or more. There is no need for such documentation to be available in hard copy; it is becoming increasingly common for practices to restrict such documentation to soft copy on the intranet only. This has obvious advantages in relation to the other provisions requiring control over the development and amendment of the manual. The main consideration is whether all personnel have adequate access to the systems and procedures that are described in the documentation. There is no need for plans to be contained in the manual and it is a matter of choice as to whether it is useful to include a summary of their provisions in the manual or not.

Although the manual is increasingly unlikely to be available in hard copy format, many practices produce an introductory guide to its provisions in their staff induction training materials. This can be very helpful in developing an overview of the more detailed procedures that are available for fuller inspection in the main documentation.

Assessment note: The office manual will often form an integral reference document for compliance with Lexcel, particularly at an assessment; however, it will be acceptable for practices to have it available on an intranet. The assessor will normally ask for a copy of the practice's manual ahead of the assessment, so that they can familiarise themselves with its content. By checking the manual or intranet, the records of review and gathering interview evidence, the assessor will be able to ascertain compliance with this requirement.

5   PEOPLE MANAGEMENT

5.1   Practices will have a plan for:

(a) the recruitment of personnel, including likely recruitment needs;
(b) the training and development of personnel.

Practices will have different ways of addressing the planning required by this provision. Some practices may address this requirement in the business plan or as separate plans, or it may fall to heads of department or team leaders to address their requirements in operational plans for which they are responsible. However your practice chooses to meet this requirement, it should be borne in mind that this information is relevant to the business plan and should be fed into the business planning process.

A sole practitioner or small practice may have no plans to recruit staff. In such cases they will need to demonstrate that the issue has been given due consideration.

> **Assessment note:** The length and complexity of the plan or plans will be for each practice to determine. However, assessors will want to see sufficient evidence of the issues raised by this provision receiving adequate consideration. This will also be ascertained with sole practitioners and smaller practices that have no plans to recruit, through interview evidence.
>
> The plan(s) may be confidential to the practice and need not be disclosed to the assessor. Practices which decline to show such documentation to assessors will have to prove compliance by other means that the personnel plan does exist and covers the necessary areas.

5.2   Practices will list the tasks to be undertaken by all personnel within the practice and document the skills, knowledge and experience required for individuals to fulfil their role satisfactorily, usually in the form of a person specification.

A person specification details the essential and required/desired skills, knowledge and experience necessary for a particular role or post. A job description details the tasks and responsibilities of the position. It is commonplace for the person specification and job description to be contained within the same document.

All personnel within the practice – including partners – will need to have a person specification or other such documentation in place. The precise format of the job documentation will be at the discretion of the practice, but typically it should recite the job title and then cover the jobholder's place in the organisation, reporting lines, the main purpose(s) of the role and a list of specific responsibilities.

It is good practice to review the job skills, knowledge, experience and description regularly. Many practices do so at each individual staff member's appraisal meeting, especially as it enables a review of the role over a suitably long timescale.

> **Assessment note:** An assessor may request to see the documentation associated with any job within the practice. Where this includes documents related to an individual's appraisal, consent from the individual will be sought first.

5.3 **Practices will have procedures to deal effectively with recruitment and selection, which must include:**

    (a) **the identification of vacancies;**
    (b) **the drafting of the job documentation;**
    (c) **methods of attracting candidates and applicants;**
    (d) **selection methods used;**
    (e) **storage, retention and destruction of records;**
    (f) **references and ID checking and any use of medical examination;**
    (g) **checking fee earners' disciplinary record.**

Effective recruitment into the practice will clearly make a substantial contribution to the quality of service by the organisation and manage the risks associated with recruiting. It is an increasing trend that recruitment and selection are open processes which are seen to be as objective and non-discriminatory as possible. In many practices there will be different arrangements for the recruitment and selection of professional staff, secretaries and trainees. Ensuring that a practice has effective recruitment procedures in place should help the practice to recruit the best person for the vacancy.

It is considered good practice to consider interview questions in advance of the interview and to document them. This can help to ensure that you gather as much information as possible during the interview and reduces the likelihood of forgetting to ask relevant questions or asking inappropriate ones. Part of the interview process may include candidates being assessed in some way. The assessment could be designed to test their technical ability or personality profile.

Practices should always maintain records of interview notes, not least to support any potential claim of unfairness in the process. Practices should note that merely having notes of the interview will not in itself defend against a claim of unfair treatment or discrimination. In order better to support equality in the recruitment process, practices should consider including criteria at relevant stages of the process – for example, interview criteria and interview assessment or score sheets.

The Employment Practices Data Protection Code (Part 1) provides that interview notes should not be kept for longer than one year.

Once the practice has selected the candidate it would like to appoint, it will ensure that it vets the person by obtaining references, confirming their eligibility to work in the European Union and verifying their identity. In addition it is worth considering getting proof of qualifications and P45.

The requirements in 5.3(g) require a practice to satisfy itself that the fee earners' disciplinary records are satisfactory to you. The means of conducting these checks is for the practice to decide – it may decide to contact the fee earner's professional body or obtain a signed declaration from the candidate confirming their disciplinary record status. Practices may want to consider checking the record of other professional personnel that they are intending to employ, for example accountants, to ensure that they have as much information about their personnel as possible.

> **Assessment note:** Practices should ensure that the responsibility for recruitment is documented. Assessors may look for evidence of such documentation as well as any other recruitment policies within the practice. Interviews of those within the practice who have been involved in the recruitment process, from both employer and employee sides, may be conducted. In addition, the assessor may ask to see records of any recruitment campaigns carried out, subject to confidentiality.

5.4   Practices will conduct an appropriate induction process for all personnel, including those transferring roles within the practice and must cover:

   (a)   management structure and the individual's job responsibilities;
   (b)   terms and conditions of employment;
   (c)   immediate training requirements;
   (d)   key policies.

It is recognised that the full induction process may be staggered over a period of time and may consist of the provision of reading materials, face-to-face meetings or the use of interactive materials on the practice's intranet. The induction process may be varied, depending on the position of the recruit and whether they are temporary, permanent or transferring from within the practice.

The induction process is a good opportunity to ensure that the person is aware of the practice's culture and the standards expected of them. Furthermore it is good practice to explain the support structures available to personnel, as well as the key policies in relation to risk, supervision and ICT use, etc.

> **Assessment note:** There is no need for a documented procedure setting out how induction training is provided, but assessors will need sufficient evidence that the induction process is in effective operation. The assessor may ask to see any records of induction and/or interview members of staff who have had an induction recently to ascertain compliance.

5.5   Practices must have a training and development policy and will:

   (a)   ensure that appropriate training is provided to personnel within the practice in accordance with its policy;
   (b)   ensure that all supervisors and managers receive appropriate training;
   (c)   have a process to evaluate training.

The training and development policy should provide all staff with an outline of the extent and options available to them, including any restrictions identified by the practice. Practices should consider detailing any financial or resource limitations to any training.

Effective training and development policies can prove valuable to practices by promoting growth of an individual. This can support the staff retention activities as well as ensure that clients are aware of the practice's desire to improve the quality of their services/products.

Supervisors and managers will receive some form of supervision/management training. The type and frequency of the training will be determined in line with the practice's training and development policy.

Assessment note: Practices should provide details of the training and development policy to their assessor. Assessors will review the depth to which the policy is supported, understood and utilised within the practice. The assessor may request records of training undertaken by personnel, as well as records of the evaluation undertaken.

5.6 Practices will conduct a documented review of the responsibilities, objectives, performance and training of all personnel at least annually.

The requirement in this section for written records and documented procedures is to ensure that any issues are addressed. Written records of the discussions and agreements emerging from the process are vital.

The review can take a variety of forms, for example mentoring, appraisals or performance reviews. An effective review scheme is core to the performance management programme of most organisations. This does not necessarily mean, however, that the same documentation should be in use for all personnel or that the process should be unduly bureaucratic. Partner schemes, in particular, may be subject to quite different arrangements from the staff scheme or schemes.

In most practices the setting of objectives will coincide with the annual review, but it does not necessarily have to. It is commonplace for financial objectives emerging from the budget, for example, to be settled before the start of the financial year and then reviewed in the appraisal meeting, or ongoing departmental or office meetings. It is good practice to consider individual objectives in relation to the overall business objectives for the forthcoming year.

It is common practice to review training needs for jobholders within the review meeting, perhaps in conjunction with other training reviews throughout the year. This information should, therefore, generate a training plan, whether on a departmental or organisation-wide level.

Review records are sensitive and will need to be subject to controls under data protection compliance considerations. The practice should make clear who has access to records and for how long they are retained.

Sole practitioners will need to review their own responsibilities, objectives and training and development plans.

> **Assessment note:** Assessors may only examine personnel records with the express consent of the jobholder in question. Records will be examined for their compliance with the practice's policy.

6   SUPERVISION AND OPERATIONAL RISK MANAGEMENT

6.1   Practices will have a written description of their management structure which designates the responsibilities of individuals and their accountability.

The description of the management structure may take many forms, from the simple list of responsibilities commonly found in the introductory sections on the intranet or office manual, to an organisational chart showing the role of departments and administrators in the overall reporting structure.

In-house departments are required to show how the legal department fits into the parent organisation and the main reporting structures within the department.

The management structure in a sole practice may be very simple as there may be only one person who is responsible for everything. All the functions for which the sole practitioner is responsible do not need to be listed.

> **Assessment note:** Documentation describing management structures must be shown to the Lexcel assessor, including any diagrams or process flows.

6.2   There will be a named supervisor for each area of work undertaken by the practice. The supervisor must have appropriate experience of the work supervised and be competent to guide and assist others.

Practices are required to designate a named supervisor for each area of work that they undertake. This information may be incorporated into the description of the management structure required in 6.1. It will be a matter of judgement in every case as to whether a limited supply of work is a distinct aspect of work in its own right or merely an incidental part of a larger area of the practice's work. One example would be that change of name deeds would usually be seen as being incidental to certain areas of practice and not a distinct area of specialisation.

There are two separate aspects to the competencies that supervisors should possess – technical experience and supervisory skills. In relation to the first of these, there are no specific requirements in the Lexcel standard. Good practice dictates that supervisors should be members of a specialist panel, if one exists for that area of work. Alternatively, supervisors could maintain a minimum number of hours of work per annum on that specialisation. Likewise, there is no requirement that supervisors must be of a certain status, such as partner or senior manager, in Lexcel. Practices should, however, consider that supervisors who are of a senior level have greater gravitas than other colleagues, which can in turn enhance the seriousness of the tasks at hand.

Assessment note: Assessors will seek evidence of appropriate experience and training. The standard of experience will vary between those who 'self-supervise' and those who are responsible for large departments within a practice, especially if staffed by more junior personnel. Where a sole practitioner does not have solicitor or other experienced lawyer colleagues, or there is only one solicitor practising in a particular area of law within a larger practice, he or she is self-supervising. In such circumstances, the solicitor will need to demonstrate how supervisory skills are applied to his or her own professional development, for example in planning the work program and analysis of training needs.

Supervisors may wish to consider preparing a brief profile of their experience and recent training in the event that the assessor wishes to explore this with them.

6.3   Practices will have processes to ensure that all personnel, both permanent and temporary, are actively supervised. Such processes will include:

(a)   checks on incoming and outgoing correspondence, including letters, e-mails and faxes;

(b)   departmental, team and office meetings and communication structures;

(c)   reviews of matter details in order to ensure good financial controls and the appropriate allocation of workloads;

(d)   the exercise of devolved powers in publicly funded work;

(e)   the availability of a supervisor;

(f)   allocation of new work and reallocation of existing work, if necessary.

Regular supervision helps practices to control the implementation and use of their policies and procedures. When applied effectively, this can create significant benefits ensuring that the practice manages risk effectively. In addition, practices often find that processes can assist in identifying staff development or issues.

Practices should be aware that the onus is on the supervisor to be available and actively supervising staff. This includes ensuring that those under supervision have a manageable workload and work being done is at an appropriate level.

Supervising e-mails can be a challenge, particularly due to the increasing volume of electronic communication and document formats. Practices may supervise e-mails in a variety of ways. For example, an e-mail could be printed off and put in the matter file.

Practices may have a policy that defines which e-mails must be reviewed before they are sent and which are not subject to prior supervision. This latter option may be done by assigning types of e-mails as risk categories.

Assessment note: Assessors will conduct interviews with staff of a variety of levels to gauge the effectiveness of the supervision processes.

6.4   Practices will have processes to ensure that all those doing legal work check their files regularly for inactivity.

It is important that files are checked regularly by those handling them to ensure that client dissatisfaction and possible claims arising from delay do not occur. This requirement is ancillary to independent file reviews since those are normally carried out by someone who has not had conduct of the matter. In addition, file reviews tend to be selective and will not, therefore, check whether all matters are being progressed in an appropriate manner.

Typical arrangements will include a weekly to monthly review by the fee earner of the contents of their filing cabinet and/or e-mail records. In addition, this may consist of a check of an accounts department's print-out of all matters per fee earner, especially if it is a report that highlights time elapsed since time recorded on the specific matter.

> **Assessment note:** The assessor will ascertain through interview evidence if the practice's processes are understood and being followed by all personnel.

6.5   Practices will have procedures for regular, independent file reviews, of either the management of the file or its substantive legal content, or both.

In relation to file reviews, practices will:

(a)   define file selection criteria;

(b)   define the number and frequency of reviews;

(c)   retain a record of the file review on the matter file and centrally;

(d)   ensure any corrective action which is identified in a file review is actioned within 28 days and verified by the reviewer;

(e)   ensure that the designated supervisor reviews and monitors the data generated by file reviews;

(f)   conduct a review at least annually of the data generated by file reviews, which will contribute to the review of risk assessment data.

Practices must decide how files will be selected for review. The files may be selected randomly or targeted for a particular reason, for example high risk matters.

File reviews need not be undertaken by the designated supervisor in person, although they often will be: for example, file reviews are sometimes outsourced. Where the supervisor does not undertake the file reviews in person it will need to be apparent that they will be made aware of the outcome of the file reviews. It is important, however, that fee earners are involved in the file review arrangements, including partners and senior managers. The frequency and depth of reviews often reflects the seniority and experience of the file handlers.

Ideally, file reviews are undertaken by someone other than the person with conduct of the case. However, in sole practices and where there is only one fee earner practising in a category of law, it may not be possible to identify anyone who could comment on legal issues. Where such is the case, a supervisor, a fee earner in another category, a suitably trained manager or an administrator may carry out the file review. If a sole practitioner is the only fee earner, the process of case management and client care activity can be reviewed by a member of support staff.

Another option is that file reviews could be outsourced, as where there are reciprocal arrangements with fellow local sole practitioners. It will be important to ensure that client confidentiality is controlled in such cases, however, and that no conflict of interests arises from the operation of such arrangements.

The review will generally embrace technical and procedural issues but it is ultimately for the practice to decide. This will be most common in sole or very small practices where there is no prospect of another person within the practice having the necessary expertise to assess the technical content of the file.

File reviews will also highlight corrective action that is needed and record when it has been completed. Corrective action will usually be checked by the reviewer or the fee earners may confirm that it has been carried out. Alternatively, the corrective action might be checked at a future file review.

The mechanism for the corrective action is for the practice to decide; however, it should be borne in mind that the corrective action must take place within a maximum of 28 days. The term 'verified by the reviewer' contained within 6.5(d) is intended to mean that the file review is subsequently signed off by the reviewer, to indicate that the corrective action has been correctly carried out. File review data should be analysed for trends and will need to be included in the analysis of data for the annual risk review.

> **Assessment note:** Assessors will need documentary evidence of the procedures in place and their effective implementation and communication throughout the practice. Interviews may be conducted with any personnel involved in file reviews, particularly fee earners, partners, senior managers and supervisors. The assessor will want to see the central file review record to ensure compliance, and will discuss the requirement with personnel during interviews.

6.6   **Practices will ensure that procedures are in place to:**

   (a)   **designate one overall risk manager for the practice with sufficient seniority, to be able to identify and deal with all risk issues which may arise;**
   (b)   **establish appropriate reporting arrangements to ensure that risk issues are appreciated and addressed;**
   (c)   **maintain lists of work that the practice will and will not undertake including any steps to be taken when work is declined on grounds that it falls outside acceptable risk levels. This information must be communicated to all relevant staff and must be updated regularly;**
   (d)   **maintain details of the generic risks and causes of claims associated with the area(s) of work that is/are undertaken by the practice. This information must be adequately communicated to all relevant staff;**

(e) **manage instructions which may be undertaken even though they have a higher risk profile than the norm for the practice, including unusual supervisory and reporting requirements or contingency planning.**

The main requirement is that one designated person should have overall control of the risk exposure of the practice. This is not to say that that person needs to have all of the responsibility, for example, in many practices different personnel will have the roles of handling complaints, claims and money laundering reporting. In such instances the overall risk manager might be the managing or senior partner in private practice, or one of those with a particular responsibility.

The overall risk manager should have sufficient seniority and influence within the practice to be able to ensure that risk matters are treated with the importance that they deserve. Often these critical responsibilities are combined under the auspices of a compliance partner, sometimes the senior partner.

In-house practices will not usually have professional indemnity insurance in place and will, in effect, self-insure. However, there may still be risks that need to be managed, for example adopting an effective media strategy in potentially sensitive matters. Therefore, in the interests of providing a reliable and satisfactory service to clients, the requirements of this section must still be addressed.

One familiar suggestion in risk management is that the organisation should be more selective in the work that it takes on. There should be evidence that consideration is always given to whether the practice has sufficient resources and expertise to meet the client's reasonable expectations. Practices should maintain lists of types of work that they will and will not undertake.

Practices will need to compile and keep under review lists of the risks implicit in the work that they undertake. This should be based primarily on the experience of the practice. In larger practices, these may be compiled department by department. Work that is beyond the competence of the practice, where mistakes are more likely to happen, should be declined and, if possible, referred elsewhere.

Where work is accepted into the practice even though it has a higher risk profile than the norm, there should be special procedures to ensure that particular care is taken with it. One example is a matter that might seem to be quite straightforward, but where the potential loss in the event of a negligence claim would be at the upper end of the firm's maximum liability cover and might even exceed it. These risks should be known about from the start and be carefully managed throughout.

Assessment note: The awareness and documentation of risks to a practice will be the most significant aspect of the assessment. The list of risks and those responsible for any aspects must be available to the assessor. Practices should prove staff awareness of, ease of access to, and monitoring of, their risk lists.

6.7 Practices will analyse at least annually all risk assessment data generated within the practice. This must include:

(a) any indemnity claims;
(b) an analysis of client complaints trends;
(c) data generated by file reviews;
(d) the identification of remedial action.

It is important that the practice learns from its experience and continues to look to improve its quality and risk profile where possible. There needs to be an annual documented review, therefore, of all risk assessment data; this review could be conducted in conjunction with the quality review.

The format of the review is for each practice to determine for itself. It may be presented as an item at a regular strategic meeting or be independent from it. Steps should be taken to share the findings with all personnel within the practice and to act upon any issues that require remedial action.

> **Assessment note:** Assessors will need any supporting documentation relating to the risk review. Information on how the review is helping risk management develop in the practice will also be needed.

6.8 Operational risk will be considered and recorded in all matters before, during and after the processing of instructions. Before the matter is undertaken the adviser must:

(a) consider if a new client and/or matter should be accepted by the practice, in accordance with 8.2 below;
(b) assess the risk profile of all new instructions and notify the risk manager in accordance with procedures under 6.6 of any unusual or high risk considerations in order that appropriate action may be taken.

During the retainer the fee earner must:

(c) consider any change to the risk profile of the matter from the client's point of view and report and advise on such circumstances without delay, informing the risk manager if appropriate;
(d) inform the client in all cases where an adverse costs order is made against the practice in relation to the matter in question.

At the end of the matter the fee earner must:

(e) undertake a concluding risk assessment by considering if the client's objectives have been achieved and if the client could fairly complain or make a claim for damages in relation to the service provided;
(f) notify the risk manager of all such circumstances in accordance with documented procedures.

The essence of 6.8 is that risk needs to be considered and recorded before, during and after the work is performed for the client. The risk assessment must be recorded at the outset and at the end of each matter. During the matter, however, the risk assessment should only be recorded if the risk level has changed from the initial level.

An initial risk assessment should be based on the instructions received and must be recorded. Special risk will then need to be referred to the risk manager via a procedure established for doing so. This could either be a risk notice or a section in the matter opening form highlighting 'high' or 'unusual' risk associated with the instructions or the client or an entry in the risk register.

During the retainer the ongoing risk profile should be considered. It is only necessary to record the risk during the matter if it has changed from the initial risk category. If the risk to the client or the firm changes materially – for example, third parties are joined in litigation, materially adding to costs risks, or counsel's opinion is obtained casting doubt on advice already provided to the client – the client will need to be informed and consulted without delay. Adverse costs orders need to be reported immediately as they will usually have to be paid forthwith.

At the end of the matter the fee earner should consider whether the client could fairly claim or complain about the service provided. This is not as simple as looking at whether the transaction or litigation succeeded or not, but it is necessary to consider whether the client could feel that they were not as effectively represented as they might reasonably have expected. In such circumstances there will need to be a procedure for a report to be made to the risk manager. All such reports could be addressed initially to a departmental supervisor, such as the head of department.

> **Assessment note:** Details, particularly documents, of any operational risk must be provided to the Lexcel assessor and should clearly state which part of the system they relate to. The assessor will seek evidence of compliance through interviews with personnel. In addition, assessors will check that matter files contain evidence that the risks have been considered and recorded at appropriate intervals.

7   CLIENT CARE

7.1   Practices will have a documented policy for client care.

Every practice must consider the key issues that will ensure the effective delivery of its services and record its commitment in this regard in a client care policy. This policy may well overlap with, or be part of, the quality policy required by 1.3 above. It will be for each practice to determine its approach to the style and format of documentation and, in particular, whether it forms part of a more general policy document or is produced separately. Given the extensive overlaps between related management concerns, the aspects of the client care policy might be incorporated into one 'risk management' policy in many practices.

Assessment note: Assessors will seek evidence that the issues are addressed effectively by the practice, whatever the style of the documentation. These issues should include:

- responsibility for client care;
- general approach of the firm;
- actions that will be taken to test and improve client care;
- specific procedures as required by the other provisions of this section.

7.2   Practices will have processes to ensure compliance with Rule 2 of the Solicitors' Code of Conduct 2007.

The full text of Rule 2 (Client relations) of the Solicitors' Code of Conduct 2007 and its accompanying guidelines can be viewed at **www.rules.sra.org.uk**.

Rule 2 is a wide ranging set of provisions dealing with the retainer received from the client and the accompanying terms of business. It replaced the former Practice Rule 15 and its accompanying Costs Information and Client Care Code and various provisions from the *Guide to Professional Conduct* on 1 July 2007.

The main provisions can be summarised as follows.

Acceptance of instructions (subrule 2.01)

The practice is generally free to accept or decline instructions as long as it does not make such decisions on grounds that are discriminatory, but must not act where illegality or unprofessional conduct would be involved, or where it is believed that the client is acting under duress or undue influence.

Instructions must be declined where the practice lacks the resources or competence to deal with them.

The practice may only cease acting 'for good reason and on reasonable notice' (subrule 2.01(2)).

Client retainer

Subrule 2.02 puts more emphasis than before on the client retainer, as opposed to the terms of business including costs information. This is likely to be welcomed by insurers, in particular. This rule makes clearer the importance of working out what the practice will do for the client and then checking with them that they share the same understanding of the situation. Be aware in particular of the need to note the client's 'objectives' – not necessarily the same as their instructions. On this point also see 8.4 below.

Name and status

Receptionists and secretaries should not describe advisers as 'solicitors' unless they are qualified and need to be 'advised accordingly'.

Where there is a transfer of a matter handler or any other 'material alteration to the composition of the firm' (guidance note 20 to Rule 2), the client must be informed.

Costs information

The main provisions on the supply of costs information are now found in subrule 2.03(1) of the Solicitors' Code of Conduct 2007. Please refer to the Solicitors Regulation Authority website at **www.sra.org.uk.**

In relation to the supply of initial costs information, it remains the case that in most situations the provision of hourly rates without reference to the potential total time that may be incurred on the matter will not amount to the 'best information possible on the likely overall cost of a matter'. Hourly rates would not usually be quoted to clients where these do not form the basis on which fees will be calculated, such as in fixed fee work or domestic conveyancing work that will be charged on an estimate basis. Generally the hourly rates will need to be set out where they do apply, but they should be accompanied by some additional information, such as an estimate, an agreed costs ceiling or the date of a costs review.

The difficulties of providing an estimate in certain situations are recognised by the rule and this will mean that a file where no estimate has been provided to the client will not necessarily be non-compliant with Lexcel – see guidance note 36 to Rule 2 which provides that:

> It is often impossible to tell at the outset what the overall cost will be. Subrule 2.03 allows for this and requires that you provide the client with as much information as possible at the start and that you keep the client updated. If a precise figure cannot be given at the outset, you should explain the reason to the client and agree a ceiling figure or review dates.

It is important that the availability of other sources of funding is considered, particularly in litigation matters. Subrule 2.03(2)–(4) provides further information on such considerations.

The former provisions excused the full information not going out in two situations: where there was work of a 'repetitive nature' for regular clients and where it was professionally inappropriate. The new provisions talk more generally about long-standing clients and add cases of one-off advice.

The guidance requires that 'any likely payments' that the client will have to make must be set out: 'Where possible, you should give details of the probable cost and if this is not possible you should agree with the client to review these expenses and the need for them nearer the time ...' (guidance note 40 to Rule 2).

It should also be noted that in relation to the provision of ongoing costs information the former requirement for six monthly costs updates is removed and is replaced by a general requirement in subrule 2.03(1) to give the client the best possible information on the costs as appropriate as the matter progresses. Legal aid firms should note, however, that the six monthly costs update requirement remains part of the SQM notwithstanding the changes to the main professional rules (see SQM F2.3).

Subrule 2.03(5) provides that any information on the cost of the matter must be 'clear and confirmed in writing', but this is subject to the 'slip rule' at subrule 2.03(7). It should be noted that the duty to consider the cost-effectiveness of any 'legal case' must always be considered under subrule 2.03(6).

There is no need to set out the full complaints procedure at the outset and the Law Society's Practice Standards Unit discourages the practice of doing so.

Assessment note: Lexcel specifically invokes this rule as part of the standard and Lexcel assessments do monitor compliance with its provisions. Lexcel 7.2 does not paraphrase the requirements of Rule 2 and it will be necessary for practices and their advisers to consult the full text of the rule and its accompanying guidance. It should be noted in particular that many of the provisions do not apply to in-house departments, especially where the service is provided to the employer, not to members of the public or linked but independently funded organisations. See guidance note 29 to Rule 2 which recognises that 'much of 2.03 will be inappropriate if you are acting for your employer'.

7.3 **Practices must have a record of any standing terms of business with regular clients. The practice must be able to produce such terms in relation to the issues covered by this section.**

This provision is supplemental to the client relations rule and recognises the problems of managing client relationships with regular clients for whom the full terms of business are often inappropriate. Practices must be aware of the terms of business that pertain to each matter that is dealt with for regular clients.

> **Assessment note:** Practices will have to provide all records relating to terms of business with regular clients. If such documents are strictly confidential, practices must provide other evidence to prove compliance, such as a template document used in the production of such agreements.

7.4   Practices will operate a written complaints handling procedure that ensures compliance with Rule 2 of the Solicitors' Code of Conduct 2007 and in addition:

   (a) defines what the practice regards as a complaint and sets out how to identify and respond to complaints;
   (b) records and reports centrally all complaints received from clients;
   (c) identifies the cause of any problem of which the client has complained offering any appropriate redress, and correcting any unsatisfactory procedures;
   (d) practices will conduct reviews at least annually of complaints data and trends, such review(s) forming part of the review of risk.

The main requirements in relation to client problems and complaints are that:

- the client should be advised how and to whom they should raise any problems with the service received;
- practices need to operate a complaints handling process; and
- a written complaints handling procedure must be available on request.

Practices should be discouraged from setting out the full complaints procedure in initial correspondence.

The provisions for complaints handling must be 'fair and effective' (guidance note 49 to Rule 2). There is a provision (subrule 2.05(3)) prohibiting firms from charging for the time involved in resolving or defending complaints. Practices will need to determine how they will define what a 'complaint' is. A wide definition of 'any expression of client dissatisfaction, however it is expressed' will result in more numerous instances of having to report to the practice's system. An unduly restrictive definition – for example, that it has to be in writing – may not be regarded as adequate by the SRA or the Legal Complaints Service. The practice must satisfy the assessor that its approach is appropriate for its client base.

Reports to the central system could be pro forma or by e-mail or another format. The complaints handler need not be the risk manager of the practice but often the roles will be undertaken by the same person.

It may be more difficult for sole practitioners to provide clients with an opportunity to express dissatisfaction to someone who is not actually involved with the matter. If there is another solicitor or senior member of staff, he or she may respond to any complaint in relation to the principal. In some areas, and where there is no risk of conflicts of interests, sole practitioners may decide to act as complaints officers for each other's firms. In addition, some local law societies operate an independent informal mediation service between their members and clients.

The annual review of complaints data should form part of a review of the business plan and annual risk review. As with all annual reviews, the annual complaints review should receive attention from senior management.

Assessment note: Practices will have to provide proof of their written complaints handling procedure to assessors. This should cover how the practice identifies, records, reports and responds to complaints. Assessors will also look for evidence of the regularity with which such reviews are completed.

7.5   Practices will have a process to monitor client satisfaction.

It is necessary to test client satisfaction with the services within each 12-month period. There must be adequate data on which the practice can assess the effectiveness of the delivery of its services. Practices should choose the most appropriate method to monitor client feedback based on the types of work they undertake. For some practices this may involve conducting a client survey or having review meetings with clients.

The practice should specify how and when clients will be requested to provide feedback and the methodology it will use to analyse it. It is good practice to document the findings and outcome. Any client feedback data must be added to the review of risk assessment data under 6.7 above.

Assessment note: Assessors should be satisfied that the practice monitors client feedback. As this requirement is for a process, however, assessors can accept interview evidence if no documentation is available or is confidential.

8   FILE AND CASE MANAGEMENT

8.1   **Practices will document how client enquiries in relation to possible instructions are handled, with particular regard to:**

(a) telephone enquiries;
(b) clients who enquire in person in the reception area, including confidentiality;
(c) enquiries by correspondence and e-mail.

Practices should consider how they intend to acquire new clients when designing the documentation required in 8.1. A private practice that attracts work from the public will probably need more elaborate arrangements than the in-house department where work is transferred by e-mails from colleague departments, or firms where most of their work is from established commercial organisations.

Many firms let themselves down at the first enquiry stage by having no clear arrangements for handling enquiries about possible instructions. It is particularly important to plan how enquiries will be handled in areas such as domestic conveyancing, where telephone quotations are an important source of work for most firms.

Similar considerations apply to clients who enquire in person in the reception areas. When seeking information about the potential client's enquiry, it is nevertheless important to ensure that confidentiality is respected.

In relation to enquiries by correspondence or e-mail, practices might establish a minimum response time, in which case this will be taken into account by assessors. There might also be a 'general enquiries' file that all such messages are stored in. Many conveyancing departments keep notes of all enquiries in order to monitor success rates from quotations provided.

> **Assessment note:** The details of any documentation relating to this requirement should be evidenced to the Lexcel assessor. This includes any specific directions given to the recipient and whether or not the practice achieves such stipulations.

8.2   **Practices will document how decisions will be made as to whether to accept new instructions from existing clients or instructions from clients who have not instructed the practice before.**

In most firms greater attention will be paid to the acceptance of new clients than new instructions from existing clients. Where there is any policy of declining work – for example, in relation to the financial viability of the work or past experience with that client – this must be documented. Practices may not decline to act for reasons that are discriminatory, as discussed in 1.4 above.

Assessors will accept that in-house practices may not be able to decline instructions, but the rule on conflicts of interests does recognise that employed solicitors should not compromise their position and must decline work where there is a problem, even if this means therefore losing their job. The reasons why a practice might decline work should be set out in the office manual and could include:

- work is not of a specialisation that the practice undertakes;
- work would not be sufficiently profitable or meet the practice's strategy;
- work could be of a type that the practice does not wish to be associated with;
- conflict of interests, professional or commercial;
- past record of unsatisfactory experience with this client;
- an individual or department is operating at capacity.

Practices will need to consider who can decide if and when work should be declined, whether from existing or new clients, and document if and how this will be communicated to the potential or existing client.

> **Assessment note:** Practices will need to provide assessors with documentary evidence of any documents produced in line with 8.2. Alternatively, assessors may interview key personnel to ascertain compliance.

8.3   Practices will document their arrangements to ensure that conflicts of interests are identified and acted upon in an appropriate manner.

The current rule on conflicts of interests is intended to be deregulatory in nature – a solicitor will not be in breach if they continue to observe the former and more familiar rules. The new rules therefore permit solicitors to act in more situations than would previously have been possible.

There are three forms of conflict:

(a) where the interests of two or more clients conflict;
(b) where the interests of the adviser and the client conflict;
(c) where the duty of the solicitor to an existing or former client to keep their information confidential would conflict with the duty to a subsequent client to reveal all material information to them.

This latter situation is now dealt with as a confidentiality issue under Rule 4 of the Solicitors' Code of Conduct 2007 and not a conflict of interests issue under Rule 3.

The standard requires that there should be arrangements in place for monitoring the issue. In some departments conflicts of interests will rarely arise, e.g. the practice offers a service in immigration law and would never act for the relevant government department. It follows that very different procedures might be in place for different departments within the same practice.

Conflicts of interests are remote in in-house practice since the department will, in effect, represent one client only. The possibility of conflict can arise, however – for example, personal conflicts are possible.

Although conflict most obviously arises as an issue at the outset of a matter, it could develop at any stage. Fee earners need to be alert to the dangers of conflicts developing once work has started on the matter.

Practices may choose to extend arrangements on conflicts of interests to include commercial considerations. This is most likely with larger commercial practices where a particular client may seek an exclusivity agreement (that the firm will not represent other businesses in that sector).

> **Assessment note:** Practices will need to provide their assessor with the documentation relating to how they deal with conflicts of interests. The assessor will ensure that the process is in effective operation and will gather evidence during interviews with personnel and file reviews.

8.4   At the outset of the matter the fee earner will:

  (a) establish as full an understanding as possible of the client's requirements and objectives (where incomplete, this must be supplemented subsequently);
  (b) provide a clear explanation of the issues raised and the advice given;
  (c) explain what the fee earner will do and in what timescale;
  (d) establish the method of funding, including the availability or suitability of insurance, trade union benefits, conditional or contingency fee arrangements, or costs insurance products;
  (e) consider whether the intended action would be merited on a cost-benefit analysis and whether, in public funding cases, the guidance in the funding code would be satisfied.

The issues covered in (a)–(e) above must be confirmed to the client, ordinarily in writing, unless it would be appropriate not to do so. In all cases, a note of these issues must appear on the matter file.

The importance of a clear start to the matter file should be readily apparent. Likewise, a clear note at the start of the matter file setting out all pertinent details and the instructions received should always be a priority. The fee earner must note not only the instructions but also the client's objectives. All too often there is no clear note of the first meeting or conversation. Confusion, errors and embarrassment can result from this. This issue is now given greater prominence in the Solicitors' Code of Conduct 2007 at subrule 2.02 which highlights the need for the client's objectives to be identified and for the client to be given a clear explanation of the issues involved.

If a contemporaneous letter or e-mail to the client confirms all issues that would have been covered in the first meeting or communication, it could be accepted as an adequate note of the meeting. The date and time of any meeting must be referred to, however, and this is best achieved through an attendance note. The availability of computer time records might also be taken into account.

It will not always be possible to confirm all details with confidence at the outset (e.g. timescale), in which case the advice might be in outline and confirmed as soon as it becomes clearer. In certain matters it may never be realistic to establish a timescale, in which case this provision would clearly be inappropriate.

On 8.4(d) and (e), along with the final provision in relation to written confirmation of such terms, see 7 above (Client care).

Some practices may operate general files in relation to some instructions. For example, in-house practices may have general files in which they record enquiries from instructing departments. Similarly, in private practice, telephone only duty solicitor attendances in crime are usually filed together by date rather than by opening an individual matter file.

In-house practices may comply with the requirements of this section by way of a document which is distributed to client departments. Such a document may also cover other procedures, e.g. charges (see 7.2–7.3), complaints (see 7.4), and document and deed storage arrangements (see 8.8(b) and 8.10(d)). Any exceptions to this overall agreement must be confirmed in writing to the client department.

Assessment note: Evidence of fee earners' documentation will be required as evidence of the extent and clarity of the communication with clients. The assessor will expect to see the evidence within a random selection of matter files. Where in-house practices record instructions from other departments, assessors will expect to see criteria which set out when a matter-specific file should be opened.

8.5 **Practices will ensure that the strategy for the matter is always apparent on the matter file and that in complex cases a project plan is developed.**

All matters must have a clear strategy which will be apparent for the matter. However, in complex matters a separate project plan is required. In this case, the practice must make the decision about whether or not a matter is complex and requires a separate project plan.

Assessment note: The assessor will seek interview evidence to understand the decision-making process and documentary evidence on the matter file to confirm that the strategy of the matter is clear, regardless of the complexity.

8.6 **Practices will have documented procedures to ensure that matters are progressed in an appropriate manner. In particular:**

   (a) key information must be recorded on the file;
   (b) key dates must be defined and recorded on the file and in a back-up system;
   (c) there must be a process to monitor key dates;
   (d) a timely response is made to telephone calls and correspondence from the client and others;
   (e) continuing information on cost is provided;
   (f) clients are informed in writing if the person with conduct of their matter changes, or there is a change of person to whom any problem with service should be addressed.

Section 8.6 requires practices to ensure that matters are progressed effectively. All too often matters 'drift' when the initial work has been done. Delay remains one of the principal causes of complaint by clients to the Legal Complaints Service.

Whether 'key information' is shown on the file will depend on any particular arrangements in place for the practice. It has become increasingly common to have a file summary sheet, which could be combined with a progress check in various areas of work, but this would probably be too basic for very substantial files running to numerous lever arch files. On the other hand, a very straightforward matter with few documents, attendance notes or correspondence, may not need a schedule or file summary sheet. The standard for this section is that the file (with any accompanying data records which form part of the practice's filing system) should tell the story of what is going on in that matter. Very often this will be achieved through systematic noting of all actions and conversations in relation to that matter by way of attendance notes.

A key date should be seen as any date, which, if missed, could give rise to a claim against or a loss by the practice. There are key dates in all areas of legal work: it is for every practice to determine its list of relevant key dates. All key dates must be noted on the file (which could include data records where these form part of the filing arrangements in question). They will often be highlighted in any file summary sheet, but do not necessarily need to be so. However, where they are not, they must still be readily apparent to anyone reading the file or accessing the data record.

The back-up system for key dates is increasingly likely to be a computer-based system, but the fee earner's personal diary may be accepted if it does not leave the practice's premises. Where a hard copy diary is used for this purpose, a departmental or team diary would generally be seen as being preferable. Practices must define how key dates will be monitored to avoid missing them.

There is now a suggestion in the professional rules to the effect that clients must be advised of any significant changes in relation to the handling of their matter – see the Solicitors' Code of Conduct 2007, guidance note 20 to Rule 2 which provides that:

> All clients affected by a material alteration to the composition of the firm must be informed personally. Where the person having conduct of a matter leaves a firm, the client in question must be informed, preferably in advance, and told the name and status of the person who is to take over their matter.

Solicitors must provide their clients with the 'best possible' information on costs as a matter progresses. These updates should take place when 'appropriate'.

Assessment note: In assessing whether sufficient information has been given on the progress of matters and a timely response has been made to telephone calls or correspondence, the assessor will take into account any instructions or preferences that the client has expressed in this regard (8.6(c)–(e)). Where a firm stipulates response times (e.g. all telephone calls from clients to be returned within 24 hours) they will be assessed on this basis. The assessor will seek evidence of compliance both through checks on the matter files and interviews with personnel.

8.7   Practices will document procedures for the giving, monitoring and discharge of undertakings.

The Solicitors' Code of Conduct 2007, subrule 5.01(1)(f) requires arrangements to be in place for the control of undertakings. These are now defined and regulated by subrule 10.05 which sets out the circumstances where a solicitor must honour an undertaking. Failure to honour an undertaking on the face of it is professional misconduct. This could be dealt with at a disciplinary tribunal and is enforceable by the courts through their inherent jurisdiction.

Given the potential damage that could be suffered, practices will wish to consider when and how undertakings should be provided. Common arrangements will be to distinguish routine and non-routine undertakings and apply different safeguards to them. Conveyancing departments are likely to specify who can provide routine undertakings on exchange and completion of contracts. Consideration should be given to the procedure for authorising undertakings required by a court as practicalities may require special arrangements.

There is no requirement for a central register of undertakings, though some practices find this helpful and it is considered good practice.

Assessment note: Any documentation outlining a practice's procedure for giving, monitoring or discharging undertakings should be provided to the Lexcel assessor. Where this causes concerns regarding confidentiality, assessors can accept interview evidence if no documentation is available. The assessor will check for compliance against the documented procedure.

8.8   Practices will have a documented procedure to:

(a) list open and closed matters, identify all matters for a single client and linked files where relevant and all files for particular funders;

(b) ensure that they are able to identify and trace any documents, files, deeds, wills or any other items relating to a matter;

(c) safeguard the confidentiality of matter files and all other client information;

(d) ensure that the status of the matter and the action taken can be easily checked by other members of the practice;

(e) ensure that documents are stored on the matter file(s) in an orderly way.

Most practices will be able to identify the funders of matters (e.g. the Legal Services Commission, named trade unions or legal expense insurers) through a computer coding system.

Conveyancing departments should be able to link sale and purchase files for the same client in linked transactions.

As a general rule all papers relating to a matter should be capable of being traced by being on the file. When a file is contained in a number of folders or lever arch files, there should be some method by which they can be shown to belong to the same matter. This could be by use of the client/matter reference number and an indication on each part, e.g. '1 of 2'; '2 of 2', etc. or 'Correspondence from 01.01.03 to 09.09.03' or by listing on a schedule, kept in a prominent part of the file. Where there are ancillary papers or other records (e.g. X-rays or medical records in clinical negligence work) they should be linked to the file in question by tagging or use of the client/matter numbering system.

Consideration should be given to all the circumstances where safeguarding the confidentiality of the client could be at risk (e.g. files being worked on during a train journey, files left in unattended cars, etc.). Where clients are seen in the reception area there should be arrangements for consultations, even if very short, to be conducted out of earshot of other clients or visitors in the reception area.

The state of matter files is an important consideration under this section. Showing key information on a file summary sheet or colour-coding of notes of meetings, reviews or letters to the client are helpful options. Where computer case management systems are used, the assessor will need to check the protocols for naming and storing documents and for making regular backups.

> **Assessment note:** Assessors will judge the tidiness of files under 8.8(e). In order to comply with this requirement, attendance notes need to be filed in date order, and papers need to be secured within the file. Attendance notes in cardboard folders should be secured on 'treasury tags' or other fastenings. More substantial documents may be placed together in file pockets, plastic wallets or similar.

8.9   Practices will have a documented procedure for using barristers, expert witnesses and other external advisers who are involved in the delivery of legal services, which will include provision for the following:

   (a) use of clear selection criteria;
   (b) where appropriate, consultation with the client in relation to selection, and proper advice to the client on choice of advocate or other professional;
   (c) clients to be advised of the name and status of the person being instructed, how long he or she might take to respond, and where disbursements are to be paid by the client, the cost involved;
   (d) maintenance of records (centrally, by department or office) on barristers and experts used, including evidence of assessment against the criteria;
   (e) evaluation of performance, for the information of other members of the practice;
   (f) giving clear instructions;
   (g) checking of opinions and reports received to ensure they adequately provide the information sought (and, in litigation matters, comply with the rules of court and any court orders);
   (h) payment of fees.

Where outsiders to the practice are involved in the service provided, checks should be in place to ensure that the practice's commitment to quality is still assured.

It is necessary for the practice to maintain lists of counsel and other experts used. This may be one list for the practice as a whole or it could be devolved to the departments or teams within the practice to maintain their own lists.

Lists must never be closed: it should always be possible to add newcomers. The list will be a useful first point of contact; where counsel or an expert are used for the first time, checks should be made as to their suitability, and a note made on file of why they have been instructed. When appropriate, consideration should be given as to whether to include that provider on the approved list.

Many practices might be interested to maintain a non-approved list. The combination of the rights of the data subject and the law of defamation mean that this should be very carefully controlled. However, such a list can avoid counsel or an expert being instructed subsequently, when he or she has already failed to meet the practice's quality standards.

There will need to be procedures for how instructions are provided and checked. The client's consent to the instruction of an outsider would usually be needed, not least so that they can express any preference and understand the implications for the fees that they will or may have to pay.

Procedures for paying fees are likely to differ depending on the way cases are funded.

Assessment note: Practices must provide documentation to support the procedure of selection, retention and assessment of external experts. Assessors can interview staff to ensure they have the appropriate access to the expert and any non-expert lists. Should client confidentiality be an issue for a practice, assessors can use the interview evidence to support compliance with 8.9.

8.10 **Practices will have documented procedures to ensure that, at the end of the matter, the practice:**

(a) reports to the client on the outcome and explains any further action that the client is required to take in the matter and what (if anything) the practice will do;
(b) accounts to the client for any outstanding money;
(c) returns to the client any original documents or other property belonging to the client if required (save for items that are by agreement to be stored by the practice);
(d) if appropriate, advises the client about arrangements for storage and retrieval of papers and other items retained (insofar as this has not already been dealt with, for example in terms of business) and any charges to be made in this regard;
(e) advises the client whether they should review the matter in future and, if so, when and why;
(f) archives and destroys files in an appropriate manner.

It is essential that matters are closed effectively. In most firms a reminder and checklist are provided for the issues covered in this section either on the file summary or in an archiving instruction sheet.

Those with conduct of cases should also remember to conduct a final risk assessment to consider if there are circumstances that should be reported to the practice's risk manager. If a sole principal is the person responsible for risk management, a note of any such circumstances should still be made in relation to his or her own files as this information contributes to the annual review of risk (see also 6.7). In private practice, noting issues of concern at the end of a matter might necessitate a report to the firm's insurers.

Neither the Law Society nor the SRA advise on any particular period for the retention of files before they are destroyed, but practices should note that the Money Laundering Regulations require certain records to be kept for at least five years. The Legal Services Commission stipulates as a term of its criminal and civil contracts that files must be retained for six years after closure.

When files are being archived or destroyed, practices should give consideration to the confidentiality, data protection and information security issues which are dealt with in 4A.

Assessment note: Practices must provide documentation of their procedure and examples of the documents and checks carried out. Staff whose role or responsibilities include this area may be interviewed by the Lexcel assessor in order to analyse the effective implementation and development of procedures. Archived files may provide evidence that files are closed appropriately.

APPENDIX A

Table of policies and plans required by Lexcel

The requirements below require you to:

(a) name the person responsible for the policy or plan
(b) conduct an annual review.

Key words	Lexcel requirement	
Risk management	1.2	Practices will have a risk management policy, which must include: (a) strategic risk; (b) operational risk; (c) regulatory risk.
Quality	1.3	Practices will have a quality policy, which must include: (a) the role that the quality system plays in the overall strategy of the practice; (b) a process for personnel to suggest improvements to the quality system.
Equality and diversity	1.4	Practices will have a policy on the avoidance of discrimination and the promotion of equality and diversity, to include: (a) employment and partnership, recruitment and selection, training and conditions of service and promotions within the practice; (b) the delivery of service; (c) the instruction of counsel and experts in all professional dealings.
Money laundering	1.5	Practices will have a policy to ensure compliance with anti-money laundering legislation. The policy must include: (a) the appointment of a Nominated Officer usually referred to as a Money Laundering Reporting Officer (MLRO);

Key words	Lexcel requirement
	(b) a process for making disclosures within the practice and by the MLRO to the authorities; (c) identification checking; (d) training of personnel; (e) the proper maintenance of records.
Health and safety	1.7 Practices will have a policy in relation to the health and safety of all personnel and visitors to the practice.
Community and social responsibility	1.8 Practices should have a policy in relation to community and social responsibility.
Business continuity	2.4 Practices will have a business continuity plan, which must include: (a) an evaluation of potential threats and the likelihood of their impact; (b) ways to reduce, avoid and transfer the risk; (c) processes for testing and checking the plan.
ICT	4A.1 Practices will have an information communication technology (ICT) plan, including: (a) the application of all ICT facilities within the practice; (b) the role of ICT in facilitating services for clients.
Data protection	4A.2 Practices will have a policy in relation to data protection compliance issues, which must include: (a) ensuring registration with the Information Commissioner; (b) training of personnel.
Information management	4A.3 Practices will have an information management policy, including: (a) relevant information assets of both the practice and clients; (b) the risks to these assets, their likelihood and their impact; (c) procedures for the protection and security of the assets; (d) a process for training personnel.

Key words	Lexcel requirement
E-mail	4A.4 Practices must have an e-mail policy, including: (a) the scope of permitted and prohibited use; (b) any procedures for monitoring personnel using e-mail; (c) procedures for proper management and security; (d) procedures for its proper storage and destruction.
Website management	4A.5 If the practice has a website, the practice must have a website management policy, including: (a) a process for document approval and publishing; (b) the scope of permitted and prohibited use; (c) procedures for the proper management of its security and contents.
Internet access	4A.6 If personnel in the practice have internet access the practice must have an internet access policy, including: (a) the scope of permitted and prohibited use; (b) any procedures for monitoring personnel accessing the internet.
Recruitment and training	5.1 Practices will have a plan for: (a) the recruitment of personnel, including likely recruitment needs; (b) the training and development of personnel. 5.5 Practices must have a training and development policy and will: (a) ensure that appropriate training is provided to personnel within the practice in accordance with its policy; (b) ensure that all supervisors and managers receive appropriate training; (c) have a process to evaluate training.
Client care	7.1 Practices will have a documented policy for client care.

APPENDIX B

Table of information management policies

Practices must ensure they comply with relevant legal and regulatory provisions in relation to all the below policies ensure that all personnel receive appropriate training to understand the policies.

Key words	Lexcel requirement
Data protection	4A.2 Practices will have a policy in relation to data protection compliance issues, which must include: (a) ensuring registration with the Information Commissioner; (b) training of personnel.
Information management	4A.3 Practices will have an information management policy, including: (a) relevant information assets of both the practice and clients; (b) the risks to these assets, their likelihood and their impact; (c) procedures for the protection and security of the assets; (d) a process for training personnel.
E-mail	4A.4 Practices must have an e-mail policy, including: (a) the scope of permitted and prohibited use; (b) any procedures for monitoring personnel using e-mail; (c) procedures for proper management and security; (d) procedures for its proper storage and destruction.
Website management	4A.5 If the practice has a website, the practice must have a website management policy, including: (a) a process for document approval and publishing; (b) the scope of permitted and prohibited use; (c) procedures for the proper management of its security and contents.

Key words	Lexcel requirement
Internet access	4A.6 If personnel in the practice have internet access the practice must have an internet access policy, including: (a) the scope of permitted and prohibited use; (b) any procedures for monitoring personnel accessing the internet.

Index